Welcome to The London Baby Directory: 10th edition

It is fascinating to see how much the British entrepren has flourished amongst parents over the last ten years. Directories have witnessed seed ideas become businesses, and for many, the advent of parenthood bri determination and confidence to try new things.

We continue to be the best source for all those essential goods and services you will need in bringing up your baby as well as being a local grapevine of the latest news.

Don't forget to add **www.babydirectory.com** to your list of favourites, which includes the **Encyclopedia of Pregnancy** and our guide to **Children's Health**. We also have a monthly e-newsletter which keeps you informed about new product launches, special offers and giveaways - so don't forget to register.

Clare, Georgia 5yrs and Max 3yrs

There is no doubt that London is a great place to raise a young family. There is plenty to see and do, great baby and toddler activities, good-quality shopping, and loving nursery schools catering for even the busiest of working mums. If we have left anything out, which you think deserves a slot, then please don't hesitate to email me at editor@babydirectory.com.

Whether you are pregnant, a very new parent or planning your life with a toddler - we hope you will use this guide to make life that much easier! And remember if you are moving out of London we have six regional publications and three in the pipeline covering the whole of the UK.

Clare Flawn-Thomas

Clare Flawn-Thomas
Editor

Edited, designed and published by
The Baby Directory Limited

Tel **+44 (0)20 8678 9000**

Fax **+44 (0)20 8671 1919**

Editor	Clare Flawn-Thomas
Deputy Editor	Sue Carpenter
Researchers	Lally Holme
	Kirsty Holme
	Saima Hasnain
Sales Manager	Patricia Bellotti
Online sales	Geeta Chamdal
Design, Photogrphy & Production	Christopher Burke
Printers	Polestar Wheatons Ltd

All Images © The Baby Directory except: page 185 © Natural History Museum; page 1, page 15, page 151, page 175, page 201, page 199 © Chris Burke

ISBN: 1-903288-19-3

contents

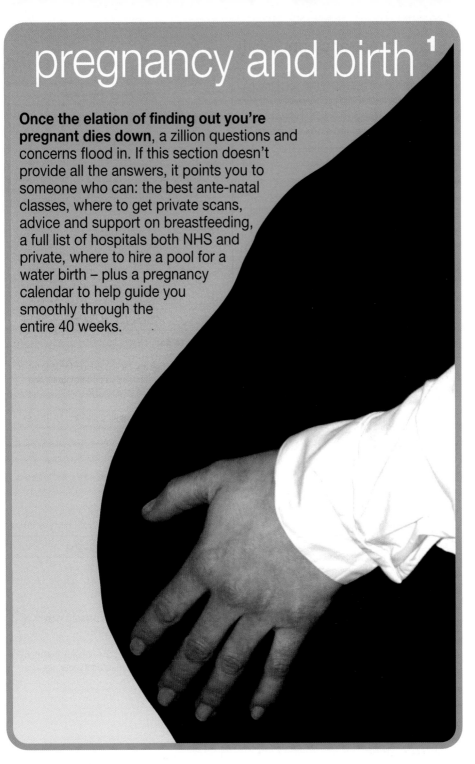

Once the elation of finding out you're pregnant dies down, a zillion questions and concerns flood in. If this section doesn't provide all the answers, it points you to someone who can: the best ante-natal classes, where to get private scans, advice and support on breastfeeding, a full list of hospitals both NHS and private, where to hire a pool for a water birth – plus a pregnancy calendar to help guide you smoothly through the entire 40 weeks.

Your pregnancy calendar

You can follow the suggestions for each month and also make your own notes in the relevant spaces.

Weeks 1-4

Things to do:

- Start taking a daily amount of folic acid (400mg).

- Avoid smoking and taking any drugs or medication.

Notes:

Weeks 5-9

Things to do:

- Get in touch with local hospitals and see what facilities they have, or research home birth.

- Keep a note of everything you read in pregnancy books and magazines.

- Consider complementary therapies to keep morning sickness under control (see aromatherapy, pg 10 and reflexology, pg 17).

- Start looking for pregnancy exercise classes (see pg 12, yoga, pg 17).

Notes:

Weeks 10-14

Things to do:

- You will be offered a 12-week scan - the first time you see your baby.

- Consider booking a maternity nurse or doula - popular ones get booked very quickly so contact agencies now for a list of candidates (see pg 49).

Notes:

Weeks 15-19

Things to do:

- If your clothes are feeling uncomfortable, start ordering the maternity wear catalogues and visiting the stores (see pg 34).

- Book ante-natal/parenting classes as they get booked up (see pg 4).

Notes:

Weeks 20-24

Things to do:

- 20 week fetal anomaly scan.

- 22 weeks: book yourself a personalised baby shopping service (see pg 37)

- Think about decorating the nursery (see murals, pg 35 and nursery furniture/interiors, pg 37).

Notes:

Weeks 25-29

Things to do:

- If you would like one last trip abroad, now's the time to go. Some airlines won't let you fly after 28 weeks. Also check that your travel insurance covers pregnancy. Most will provide cover if you return by week 32.

- Think about whether you'll be returning to work, and make arrangements with your employer. You can take maternity leave from week 29.

- If you are thinking of returning to work, visit and register with your local nurseries - popular ones can have up to 1-year waiting lists (see pg 53-110).

Notes:

Weeks 30-34

Things to do:

- Order some of the larger items you will need when your baby arrives (such as prams, cots and car seats), as they can take 6 weeks to order (see cribs and cots, pg 28 and prams and pushchairs, pg 51).

- Treat yourself to a pregnancy massage (see pg 14).

- Consider body painting, life casting and pregnancy photography (see pg 5).

Notes:

Weeks 35-39

Things to do:

- Sort out all the things you need if you are having a home birth (see waterbirth pool hire, pg 8).

- Organise TENS hire (pg 7).

- Prepare your list of friends and family for sending birth announcement cards (see pg 21).

- Order your stem cell collection kit (see pg 7).

Notes:

Weeks 40-42

Things to do:

- Stock your larder and freezer and get online with home delivery supermarkets (see pg 30).

- Don't get too fed up if your baby arrives after the estimated date. Use the time to relax, see friends and generally organise yourself.

Notes:

ante- and post-natal classes

Congratulations! You are pregnant. So what do you do first? Most women do a home pregnancy tet to confirm that they are pregnant, and then book an appointment with their GP or local health centre. This confirms your pregnancy "officially", giving you an idea of your due date and setting up an appointment with a midwife at your local ante-natal clinic for the first consultation and scans. You do, however, have the option to choose the style of your ante-natal care as well as where to have the baby (hospital: private or NHS, home birth, midwife-led, obstetrician or your GP). The norm is for midwives to provide all your ante-natal care, labour and post-natal check-ups from your local hospital. But there is great choice now, and you may wish to do something different for each pregnancy.

We have selected London's top ante-natal teachers and courses which help prepare you for labour, birth and life with a new baby. They also provide opportunities to meet other mums-to-be who live near you and have a similar due date. Important to book early as these classes are extremely popular

National Health Service (NHS) Classes

If you have chosen a hospital birth you will be offered NHS ante-natal classes at the hospital or at a midwife-led clinic. The classes are not very flexible in terms of when you can join or when they are held, and classes are large. Or you can just go on a hospital tour to see where you need to come in when in labour.

National Childbirth Trust   0870 444 8707

www.nctpregnancyandbabycare.com

The teachers have been trained by the NCT and the classes tend to be informal and are generally held in the teacher's home. There are couples courses, women-only courses, 8-week courses and weekend courses. The courses include relaxation and practising different positions for labour as well as information on pain relief, life with a new baby and post-natal care. There are often only 5-7 couples per course so you have a chance to get to know other people with a similar due date. NCT classes cost about £70+ per course depending on where you live. If you would like to attend but cannot afford it then the NCT will happily accept a contribution. They are popular so we recommend that you book early.

OUTSIDE LONDON
The Baby Gurus   01786 826 550

www.thebabygurus.com

Luxury ante-natal weekends held in 4 and 5 star hotels in Scotland.

Choices Ante-natal Classes   0800 977 4225
www.choicesantenatal.co.uk
Ante-natal classes held monthly in the Cotswolds.

Active Birth Centre   020 7281 6760
25 Bickerton Road, London, N19 5JT
www.activebirth.com
Active Birth classes are centred around gentle yoga from your 12th week of pregnancy to help strengthen your body for birth and life with a new baby.   Below are the Active Birth Teachers in London.

- **Kathleen Beegan**   020 8769 3613
South West and South East London

- **Jill Benjoya Miller**   020 8445 1159
North Finchley

- **Alice Charlwood**   020 7281 6760
North London

- **Arlene Dunkley-Wood**   020 8923 6452
East London

- **Annabel Hargrave**   020 8287 5411
Wimbledon

- **Lesley-Anne Kerr**   07871 528 309
SW1 and SW11

- **Julie Krausz**   020 8459 2903
North West (NW6, NW10, W9, W10) and South (SW11). Julie has run active birth and yoga classes for the last 15yrs. Her birth preparation workshops are for couples preparing for labour and birth.

- **Lynn Murphy**   020 7281 6760
North London

- **Val Orrow**   020 8789 8885
Putney, SW15

- **Ella Van Meelis**   020 8567 1599
West London, W13

NORTH LONDON

Karen Arkle   0115 963 4599
Registered midwife and hypnotherapist. Hypnotherapy for birth, helping you towards a positive birth experience. One-to-one or small group sessions available. Also birth and parenting preparation sessions. Classes take place at the Hospital of St John & Elizabeth, St John's Wood, NW8.

Trish Ferguson   020 7354 5228
56 Morton Road, N1 3BE

You and Your Baby   07736 258 267
Julie Whitehead is a registered midwife, nurse and lactation consultant. She runs active birth classes at weekends at Zita West's Devonshire Street clinic, and at Yoga Base, Liverpool Road in Islington for couples. This includes a breastfeeding talk - including how to breastfeed twins and life with twins.

Yvonne Moore Birth Preparation   020 7794 2056
Ante-natal yoga classes in North London.

EAST LONDON

Bridget Baker   020 7249 3224
Childbirth preparation classes - group or individual sessions.

Jeyarani Gentle Birth Programme   020 8530 1146
34 Cleveland Road, South Woodford, E18 2AL
www.jeyarani.com
Founded by Dr Gowri Motha in 1987, The Gentle Birth Programme prepares you for a natural delivery by teaching you how to get "birth fit". The emphasis of the programme is to make you physically fit and supple, and have a positive and confident frame of mind to manage your own labour. Fortunately, due to Dr Motha's classes being so oversubscribed, you can purchase her month-by-month guide as well as other complementary products from her website.

SOUTH LONDON

Annabel Hargrave   020 8287 5411
www.yogabirth.org
Ante-natal yoga for pregnancy, birth preparation workshops and post-natal classes in SW18 and SW19.

Heather Guerrini   020 7352 0245
30 Redesdale Street, SW3 4BJ

Kathleen Beegan   020 8769 3613
41 Stanthorpe Road, SW16 2DZ

Mama-Rhythms   020 8879 7081
Wimbledon, SW19

Sue Lewis   020 8946 8561
65 Vineyard Hill Road, London, SW19 7JL
Small classes in preparation for birth and refresher courses
for existing mothers.

Verona Hall   020 8637 0768
www.veronahall.co.uk
Currently run over a five-week period; topics include active
birth, coping strategies for labour, post-natal care of mum
and baby. The classes are held in Dulwich, SE24.

WEST LONDON

Insights for Life   020 8746 5267
(As 2 Become 3)
www.as2become3.org
A one-day course for pregnant couples expecting their first
child. The course runs on a Saturday once a month and
helps to equip parents-to-be for the exciting journey ahead so
that they can meet the challenges of parenthood together.

Christine Hill Associates   020 8994 4349
Strand End, 78 Grove Park Road, London, W4 3QA
A well-established team who run top flight ante- and post-
natal classes.

HypnoBirthing®   07766 963 228
www.hypnobirthing.me.uk
Suzanne Austen is a qualified HypnoBirthing® Practitioner
with the HypnoBirthing® Instititute of America. Her ante-natal
classes help mothers achieve a natural, fear-free and drug-
free birthing experience. Classes are run in and around
London regularly. Check out Suzanne's website for more
details.

Lolly Stirk & Rose Ryan   020 8674 6997
St John's Church, Ladbroke Grove, W11 2NN

Lynda Leach   01707 660 318
Ante-natal classes designed for couples (although women
may attend on their own). Courses last for 5 weeks and are
held from 6.30pm to 8.30pm on Thursday evenings in
Notting Hill, W11. All classes are led by Lynda, who is a
practising midwife and lactation consultant. Classes have an
informal atmosphere and are interactive; they do not focus
solely on information-giving and they are designed to help
prospective parents develop coping strategies for labour and
the transition to parenthood. Bookings at approximately 20
weeks gestation. Also available are one-to-one sessions
(including refresher) in client's home.

New Baby Company   020 7751 1152
8 Souldern Road, London, W14 0JE
www.newbabycompany.com
Professional, practical, personal advice and help during
pregnancy (see ad left).

Stacia Smales Hill   020 7385 7417
Weekly ante-natal courses and weekend intensive courses
held in Fulham.

The Portland Hospital   **020 7390 8061**
234 Great Portland Street, London, W1N 6AH
www.theportlandhospital.com
1-2-1 classes and group courses available in central London.

The Zita West Clinic   **020 7580 2169**
43 Devonshire Street, London, W1G 7AL
www.zitawest.com
One-to-one ante-natal birth and parenting workshops for
couples plus HypnoBirthing®, breastfeeding and twins
classes.

ante-natal tests and scans

The following are private ante-natal testing services
which offer a range of scans and blood tests not
necessarily available to you on the NHS without
referral. Alternatively you may wish to have a 3D or
4D scan and preserve images of your baby for
prosperity

The Portland Hospital   **020 7390 8032**
234 Great Portland Street, London, W1N 6AH
www.theportlandhospital.com
Full range of ante-natal scanning services, consultations and
fetal medicine tests. Includes 3D and 4D scanning services.

Apeekaboo Imaging   **0870 493 1427**
9 Gunnery Terrace, Royal Arsenal, Woolwich, SE18
www.apeekabooimaging.co.uk
Midwife-led ultrasound company specialising in 3D and 4D
bonding scans. Here within a stylish clinic they can offer you
a personal one-to-one service. Opening hours from 9.30am-
5pm 7 days a week, with no extra cost for Saturday or
Sunday appointments. Scans are performed by either a
specialist midwife or senior obstetric sonographer. The team
is highly experienced and is fully qualified in ultrasound
scanning. Check the website for other branch openings.

Baby Premier - London   **0845 345 7262**
2nd Floor, 101 Harley Street, London, W1G 6AH
www.babypremier.co.uk
Baby Premier is not just a 4D studio - it is an accredited
ultrasound service which offers a full range of obstetric and
gynaecological ultrasound examinations to both self-funding and
privately insured patients. You are provided with a 4D bonding
scan showing detailed moving images of your unborn child.
Photographs and a video of your baby are provided on DVD and
CD to enable the printing of pictures. Clinics accredited by
BUPA, AXA, PPA and other private medical insurers.

body painting & belly casting

Carolyn Cowan   **020 7701 3845**
www.mooncycles.co.uk
Portraits with a fusion of photography and body painting.

Everlasting Castings   **0870 020 3593**
www.everlastingcastings.co.uk
An easy-to-use deluxe belly casting kit to enable pregnant
mums to capture their unique shape in plaster .

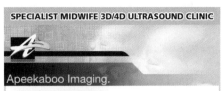
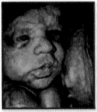

breastfeeding

If you are trying to breastfeed and find it difficult (or your baby finds it difficult), then it is best to turn to people who really know how to help. The following breastfeeding counsellors can either come to your home or help you over the telephone and have considerable experience in sorting out problems or alleviating anxieties. The organisations also offer support and advice.

Assoc. of Breastfeeding   **020 7813 1481**
Mothers
A charity offering a network of local breastfeeding counsellors around the country.

Jane's Breastfeeding Resources
www.breastfeeding.co.uk
Website with many useful articles, FAQs, help and support for breastfeeding mothers.

La Leche League   **020 7242 1278**
www.laleche.org.uk
Information and support including those in special situations eg multiple births, premature babies, cleft or soft palate.

London Breastfeeding Practice 07947 741 415
Invaluable support and advice, in home consultations, highly experienced breastfeeding specialists, kind and caring

manner. Call Geraldine Miskin on 07947 741 415 or Ann Dobson on 07980 017 607.

National Childbirth Trust   **0870 444 8708**
www.nctpregnancyandbabycare.com
The Trust provides trained counsellors who are available via their breastfeeding helpline (8am – 10pm). Also help for mothers and babies with special situations eg, multiple birth, feeding a toddler and newborn at the same time, feeding after breast surgery.

Regents Midwifery Practice   **07906 166 949**
Experienced midwife provides breastfeeding workshops and home consultations for breastfeeding problems.

Vicki Scott - Baby Confidence   **07960 611 987**
www.babyconfidence.co.uk
Experienced midwife offering up-to-date practical help and advice. Also troubleshooting and baby routines.

home births

For a home birth we recommend an independent midwife. Their big strength is that they are very positive about the whole home birth experience, and can reassure mothers who want to deliver at home rather than in a hospital. During your ante-natal care you will be visited by your midwife at home, who in some cases can provide complementary therapies throughout your pregnancy and birth. They will also continue to provide support and visits post-natally to ensure that you are getting on well with your new baby. For further information visit www.homebirth.org.uk or ring the Regents Midwifery Practice who are a members of the independent midwives association

Regents Midwifery Practice   **07906 166 949**
www.midwivesinpartnership.com
Independent midwifes providing the very best in one-to-one midwifery care at home or in hospital.

hospitals: private maternity

St John & St Elizabeth   **020 7286 5126**
Grove End Road, London, NW8
www.hje.org.uk

St Mary's Lindo Wing   **020 7886 1465**
South Wharf Road, London, W2

Sir Stanley Clayton Ward   **020 8383 3569**
Queen Charlotte's Hospital

The Birth Centre   **020 7820 6661**
37 Coverton Road, Tooting, London, SW17
www.birthcentre.com
Give birth at home, in hospital or in their purpose-designed.

The Kensington Wing   **020 8746 8616**
Chelsea & Westminster Hospital, Fulham Road, SW10

The Lansdell Maternity Suite   020 7188 3457
St Thomas's Hospital, 6th Floor, North Wing, SE1
The Lansdell Suite offers access to consultant obstetricians and private ante-natal scans alongside private midwife-led care for pregnancy, labour and birth, using the facilities of one of the UK's top teaching hospitals.There is breastfeeding support given as and when necessary and continuous post-natal care.

The Portland Hospital   020 7390 8269
205-209 Great Portland Street, W1
www.theportlandhospital.com
Consultant and midwife led maternity care with a specialist, private children's hospital and other women's health services on an in-patient or out-patient basis.

hospitals: NHS maternity

(In case of emergency call 999 or NHS Direct on 0845 46 47)

N18
North Middlesex Hospital   020 8887 2000
Sterling Way, Edmonton

N19
Whittington Hospital   020 7272 3070
Highgate Hill, Archway

NW3
Royal Free Hospital   020 7794 0500
Pond Street, Hampstead

NW10
Central Middlesex Hospital   020 8965 5733
Acton Lane, Park Royal

E1
Royal London Hospital   020 7377 7000
Whitechapel

E9
Homerton Hospital   020 8510 5555
Homerton Row, Hackney

E11
Whipps Cross Hospital   020 8539 5522
Whipps Cross Road

E13
Newham General Hospital   020 7476 4000
Glen Road, Plaistow

SE1
St Thomas's Hospital   020 7188 7188
Lambeth Palace Road

SE5
King's College Hospital   020 7737 4000
Denmark Hill, Camberwell

SE10
Queen Elizabeth Hospital   020 8836 6000
Vanbrugh Hill

SE13
Lewisham University Hospital   020 8333 3000
Lewisham High Street

SW10
Chelsea & Westminster Hospital   020 8846 7903
369 Fulham Road

SW15
Queen Mary's University Hospital   020 8789 6611
Roehampton Lane

SW17
St George's Hospital   020 8672 1255
Blackshaw Road

W1
Middlesex Hospital   020 7636 8333
Mortimer Street

W2
St Mary's Hospital   020 7886 6666
Praed Street, Paddington

W12
Queen Charlotte's Hospital   020 8383 1000
Du Cane Road

WC1
Elizabeth Garrett Anderson   020 7387 9300
Elizabeth Garrett Anderson, Huntley Street

Hospital for Sick Children   020 7405 9200
Great Ormond Street

midwives

Midwivesonline.com   01274 427 132
This is a website service providing advice and support to new parents and families in every aspect of pregnancy and parenting.

Regents Midwifery Practice   07906 166 949
www.midwivesinpartnership.com
Independent midwifes providing the very best in one-to-one midwifery care at home or in hospital throughout London.

pregnancy essentials

Pregna-Pillo   0870 460 5482
Can't find a comfortable way to lie with your bump? Here's a pillow that's designed to cup your tummy to support you and your baby's weight, relieving back, pelvic and abdominal pain. The Pregna-Pillo will alleviate any twisting of the spine or strain on your back or abdominal muscles. Its specially contoured shape cups around your bump to support both you and baby.

www.babydirectory.com

stem cells

For the treatment of some terminal childhood illnesses you can have your baby's cord blood collected at birth and stored for any necessary medical treatments in the future. With a monthly payment schedule to cover the costs, what price would you put on a potentially life-saving opportunity? The collection of cord blood is from the placenta and umbilical cord and is totally painless. Depending on the policy in your NHS hospital, it is not possible for midwives or obstetricians to collect the cord blood on your behalf. However, you are provided with a pack and instructions as set out by the companies below or you can ask an independent midwife

Cells Limited   **0845 226 0844**
www.cellslimited.com
Store your baby's cord blood stem cells with us for greater peace of mind. ISO 17025 accredited lab. Strictly complying with EU tissues and cells directive. Please call the number above or visit the website for more information.

Future Health Technologies   **0870 874 0400**
www.futurehealth.com
Safe, painless and non-invasive cord blood collection process.

Smart Cells   **020 7436 9966**
www.smartcells.com
Cord blood collection and storage.

TENS hire

Pain relief without drugs. An effective form of pain relief in labour, the TENS machine (Transcutaneous Electrical Nerve Stimulation) consists of four electrodes taped to your back which give a tingling sensation as a current passes through

Ameda Egnell   **01823 336 362**
www.ameda.demon.co.uk
4 week Tens hire £25 inc p&p plus free extension and cancellation within notice period.

Babycare TENS   **020 8532 9595**
www.babycaretens.com
This model comes with a boost button for use in early labour and between contractions. The Lady Tens can be hired for £22 for 30 days' hire. There is then a one-week extension (free of charge) if you baby hasn't arrived, with futher weeks charged at £5.

MamaTENS   **0845 230 4647**
81 East Street, Epsom, Surrey, KT17 1DT
www.mama-tens.info
Easy to use drug-free pain relief durng labour, allowing you to stay in control and keep mobile.

waterbirth pool hire

If planning a hospital delivery, check with your local hospital for their facilities and policies on water birth (see hospitals: NHS and hospitals, private). For useful information visit www.waterbirth.org

Aqua Birth Pool Hire   **01202 518 152**
122 the Grove, Moordown, Bournemouth, BH9
Cheapest pool hire prices in the UK.

Good Birth Company   **0800 035 0514**
www.thegoodbirth.co.uk
Affordable birth pool hire and Medela breast pumps.

Gentle Water Birthing Pools   **01273 474 927**
50 North Way, Lewes, BN7 1DJ
www.gentlewater.co.uk
New, CE marked, heated, filtered birthing pools available.

Splashdown Water Birth Services **0845 612 3405**
www.waterbirth.co.uk
All shapes supplied as well as inflatables. Waterbirth workshops also run for mums-to-be and couples.

MIDWIVESONLINE.COM

Ask A Midwife

about

your pregnancy, birth
and newborn baby

health and wellbeing

Good health is not just about a lack of illness, but a sense of positive wellness – something overworked and stressed mums and mums-to-be can find elusive. Here we list practitioners of a variety of therapies to help you relax before, during and after labour, to deal with common ailments in both mothers and babies, and to help you regain your shape and vitality after the birth. You'll find everything from acupuncture to yoga, as well as complementary health centres, health clubs and details of professional bodies such as the International Federation of Aromatherapists, which can provide a list of therapists in your area. And if you're worried about immunisations or need tips on first aid, read on.

acupuncture

(see also complementary health)

Recommended for morning sickness, tiredness and bleeding during pregnancy. In children sometimes used for recurrent colds, poor appetite and hay fever

British Acupuncture Council   020 8735 0400
63 Jeddo Road, W12
www.acupuncture.org.uk
Members (MBAcC) have all completed a 3yr training course and are bound by the BAcC code of conduct. The website lists practitioners by postcode.

British Medical   01925 730 727
Acupuncture Society
Royal London Homeopathic Hospital
Greenwell Street, W1W 5EP
www.medical-acupuncture.co.uk
Central London clinic and also a list of London GPs and doctors who have completed the 3yr diploma.

NORTH LONDON

Alison Courtney MBAcC   07790 264 515
Mackenzie Road Practice, 125 Mackenzie Road, N7
  Meredith &   020 8444 1007
Wainwright Churchill
49 Woodland Gardens, N10 3UE
Specialising in pregnancy, children and also infertility/recurrent miscarriage.

Fertility Support Company   020 8621 0798
www.fertilitysupportcompany.co.uk
An holistic approach to male and female fertility; from IVF preparation to having a Doula at the birth. Treatment approach utilises acupuncture, herbal medicine, nutrition and mind/body therapy to treat the underlying causes of fertility, strengthen the body to increase sperm count, improve the success rate of IVF/IUI and support mothers through pregnancy, labour and recovery. Also provide a range of acupressure and herbal treatments for newborns and young children. Clinics in Muswell Hill, Hendon, Highgate and Harrow.

Sarah Moon MBAcC   020 8969 1506
30 Linden Avenue, NW10 5RE

Anne Lewthwaite MBAcC   020 7267 9995
Courthope Road, NW3 2LE

EAST LONDON

Alison Courtney MBAcC   07790 264 515
Clockwork Pharmacy, 398-400 Mare Street, E8
Holistic House, Broadway Mt   020 7275 8434

SOUTH LONDON

Traditional Acupuncture Clinic   020 7928 8333
75 Roupell Street, SE1 8SS
www.acupuncturecentre.org.uk

Southfields Clinic   020 8874 4125
41 Southfields Road, SW18 1QW

Shooters Hill Clinic   020 8854 2734
145 Eglinton Hill, London, SE18 3DU

WEST LONDON
Alternative Therapy Clinic   020 7487 5873
140 Harley Street, W1G 7LB
www.brightpractice.com

The Ladbroke Rooms   020 8960 0846
8 Telford Road, W10 5SH
www.theladbrokerooms.com

Liu Clinic   020 8993 2549
13 Gunnersbury Avenue, W5 3XD
www.liuclinic.co.uk

Chiswick Acupuncture Clinic   020 8747 4816
251 Acton Lane, W5 5DG

The Zita West Clinic   020 7580 2169
43 Devonshire Street, London, W1G 7AL
www.zitawest.com
Complementary therapies, advice and support for fertility and pregnancy, plus IVF support programme.

aromatherapy

(see also complementary health and massage)

In pregnancy often used to relieve tiredness, nausea, fluid retention as well as pain and anxiety during labour. For baby the oils can be used for gentle massage or in the bath

ISPA   01455 637 987
www.the-ispa.org
International Society of Professional Aromatherapists. List of local practitioners available online or by request.

Lisa Barnwell   020 7751 4170
Me & My Baby Therapy Rooms & Clinic
236d Fulham Road, SW10
www.meandmybabyclinic.co.uk
Signature ante- and post-natal treatment combining aromatherapy and reflexology. Personal blends for conception, pregnancy, labour and the post-natal period. Gift vouchers available.

Micheline Arcier   020 7235 3545
7 William Street, SW1

RETAIL
Earth Mother   020 8442 1704
59 Muswell Avenue, N10

Neal's Yard Remedies
68 Chalk Farm Road, NW1   020 7284 2039
32 Blackheath Village, SE3   020 8318 6655
15 Neal's Yard, WC2   020 7379 7222

9 Elgin Crescent, W11	**020 7727 3998**
6 Northcote Road, SW11	**020 7223 7141**
15 King's Street, Richmond, TW9	**020 8948 9248**

www.nealsyardremedies.com

Verde

15 Flask Walk, NW3	**020 7431 3314**
75 Northcote Road, SW11	**020 7924 4379**

www.verde.co.uk
Chamomile Baby Balm, Bizzy Kids Bathtime Oil and more.

MAIL ORDER
Absolute Aromas   **01420 549 991**
www.absolute-aromas.co.uk

A. Nelson & Co   **020 7495 2404**
www.nelsonbach.com

Jurlique   **0870 770 0980**
www.jurlique.com.au
Organic essential oils also available as water sprays, massage & bath oils.

Mama Mio   **020 7287 3028**
www.mamamio.com
Developed by three mums, with thirteen children between them, who have put together a range of pregnancy salvation products - Tummy Rub, Boob Tube and a massage oil. Great smells.

Tisserand   **01273 325 666**
www.tisserand.com

Verde   **0870 603 9186**
www.verde.co.uk
Mother and baby range. 16 products including Extra Rich Stretch Mark Oil, Chamomile Baby Body Balm, Bizzy Kids Bathtime Soother, Lice Repel Lotion. Organic and pure plant preparations.

chemists, late opening

Not only do these chemists stay open late for medication such as Calpol and Children's Nurofen, they are also well stocked with nappies, bottles and a range of baby foods

NW6
Bliss Chemists   **020 7624 8000**
50-56 Willesden Lane, NW6
9am-midnight.

NW11
Warman Free Pharmacy   **020 8455 4351**
45 Golders Green Road, NW11
8.30am-midnight.

SE24
Fourway Pharmacy   **020 7924 9344**
12 Half Moon Lane, Herne Hill, SE24
9am–7pm.

SW5
Zafash Pharmacy 020 7373 3506
233-235 Old Brompton Road, SW5
24hr, 365 days a year.

W1
Bliss Chemists 020 7723 6116
5-6 Marble Arch, W1
9am-midnight.

complementary health

These centres and therapists offer a range of complementary treatments for pregnant women, babies and young children. Treatments include acupuncture, hypnotherapy, osteopathy, cranial osteopathy, reflexology, massage, homeopathy, reiki and counselling

Natural Mother 0709 202 2020
www.naturalmother.co.uk
A specialist service bringing natural therapies and treatments to your home. No travel, no stress. London wide.

NORTH LONDON

Chatsworth Clinic 020 8451 4754
4 Chatsworth Road, NW2 4BN
www.ihms.co.uk

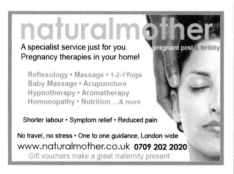

natural**mother**
pregnant post & fertility
A specialist service just for you.
Pregnancy therapies in your home!

Reflexology • Massage • 1-2-1 Yoga
Baby Massage • Acupuncture
Hypnotherapy • Aromatherapy
Homoeopathy • Nutrition ...& more

Shorter labour • Symptom relief • Reduced pain

No travel, no stress • One to one guidance, London wide
www.naturalmother.co.uk 0709 202 2020
Gift vouchers make a great maternity present

Me & my **Baby**
Therapy Rooms & Clinic
Dedicated to wellbeing before, during and after your pregnancy

The **specialists** in caring for **you** and **your baby**

236d Fulham Road
opposite
Chelsea & Westminster Hospital

T: 020 7751 4170

Open 7 days

www.meandmybabyclinic.co.uk

Health Centre 020 7249 2990
154 Stoke Newington Church Street, N16 0JU

The C.H.A.I.M Centre 020 8452 0900
10a Station Parade, Willesden Green, NW2 4NH
www.chaimcentre.com
This is a well-established therapy centre offering a wide range of natural treatments for fertility, pregnancy, mother and baby. Treatments include acupuncture, reflexology, homeopathy, cranial osteopathy/craniosacral therapy, reflexology, pregnancy massage, hypnotherapy, ante-natal yoga, mum and baby yoga and baby massage courses.

Muswell Healing Arts 020 8365 3545
169 Avenue Mews, N10 3NN

Viveka 020 7483 0099
27a Queen's Terrace, NW8 6EA

Women and Health 020 7482 2786
4 Carol Street, NW1

SOUTH LONDON

Me & My Baby 020 7751 4170
Therapy Rooms & Clinic
236d Fulham Road, SW10
www.meandmybabyclinic.co.uk
Treatment rooms offering birth preparation classes, acupuncture, aromatherapy, breastfeeding support, massage, reflexology, hypnotherapy and hpynobirthing, homeopathy, councelling, yoga and pilates. At home service. Gift vouchers. Treatments for men also available.

Awareness in Pregnancy 020 8856 8797
16 Balderton Street, SE3 0NE

Clapham Common Clinic 020 7627 8890
151/3 Clapham High Street, SW4 7SS

The Vale Practice 020 8299 9798
64 Grove Vale, SE22 8DT
www.thevalepractice.co.uk

Family Natural Health Centre 020 8693 5515
106 Lordship Lane, East Dulwich, SE22 8HF

The Karuna Healing Centre 020 8699 4046
103 Dartmouth Road, Forest Hill, SE23

Living Centre Clinic 020 8946 2331
32 Durham Road, Raynes Park, SW20 0TW

Health Care Centre 020 8659 5001
48 Newlands Park, Sydenham, SE26 5NE

Putney Natural Therapy Clinic 020 8789 2548
11 Montserrat Road, SW15 2LD

The Vitality Centre 020 8871 4677
Alexander House, 155 Merton Road, SW18 5EQ

Natural Health Centre 020 7720 8817
7a Clapham Common Southside, SW4

Westover House 020 8877 1877
18 Earlsfield Road, SW18 3DW
www.westoverhouse.com

WEST LONDON
BushMaster 020 8749 3792
Natural Health Practice
204 Uxbridge Road, W12 7JD

Complementary Care 0870 241 4025
19 Gloucester Place, W1

Craven Clinic 020 8563 8133
54 Cambridge Grove, W6 0LA

Equilibrium 020 8742 7701
150 Chiswick High Road, W4 1PR

The Hale Clinic 020 7631 0156
7 Park Crescent, Harley Street, W1B 1PF

Life Centre 020 7221 4602
15 Edge Street, W8 7PN

Holli Rubin
www.hollirubin.com
29 Basuto Road, SW6 020 7736 7557
137 Harley St, W1 020 7725 0528
Fulham Osteopathic Practice, SW6 020 7384 1851
Holli specialises in fertility, pregnancy and parenthood. Holli's
approachable and non-judgmental manner enables you to
open up and comfortably talk about all the common feelings
that arise during these times.

The Portland Hospital 020 7390 8061
234 Great Portland Street, W1W 5QT
www.theportlandhospital.com
Treatments include Bowen therapy, massage, reflexology and
osteopathy.

The Zita West Clinic 020 7580 2169
43 Devonshire Street, London, W1G 7AL
www.zitawest.com
Complementary therapies, advice and support for fertility and
pregnancy, plus IVF support programme.

exercise pre-and post-natal

These classes have programmes specifically
designed to help mothers regain their shape after
pregnancy. Exercise during pregnancy can help you
improve posture, maintain circulation to prevent
varicose veins, control your weight gain and
improve your stamina and energy levels

Chrysalis Fitness 020 8877 9553
www.chrysalisfitness.co.uk
Exercise classes and personal training for mothers and
mothers-to-be in South West London.

Judy Difiore 020 8931 2085
Specialist ante-natal and post-natal fitness consultant, pilates
instructor and remedial massage therapist. Classes and
personal training sessions available together with postural re-
alignment through massage - great for post-natal recovery.
North West London area.

London Academy of 0870 442 3231
Personal Fitness
www.lapf.co.uk
London's top motivational instructors. Complete ante- and
post-natal programmes incl. yoga, pilates etc.

Live Well Fitness 07917 605 520
www.livewellfitness.co.uk
Covering Herts and London, Phil Pledger is a fully qualified
personal trainer with many years experience. Qualified in both
NABBA and YMCA (LifetimeHF) which includes ante- and
post-natal fitness.

MUM2B Pre and Post Natal 07814 004 501
Lifestyle programme
Your health is the best gift you could give to your baby. Pre- and
post-natal health and fitness specialists. Home and gym-based
personal training and health screening. Free consultations.

Newborn Fitness 07736 463 981
www.newbornfitness.co.uk
Don't be worried about your baby weight. These highly
qualified and fully insured personal trainers and nutritional
advisors will help you get back in shape quickly, safey and
effectively.

Pushy Mothers 020 7267 6578
www.pushymothers.com
Buggy workouts for mummies who want to be yummy! Safe,
specific and effective one-hour workouts. Visit the website to
find your nearest instructor or call 07989 831 256 or 07973
800 219.

Revolution Health 07958 464 770
kappleson@hotmail.co.uk
Pre- and post-natal Pilates, personal training and a Pushy
Mother classes (NW2 & NW6). Fully qualified with Pilates
Foundation UK and fully insured. Approachable and
encouraging (North, North-West and Central London only.)

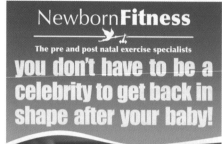

Wonder Women Fitness — 07989 831 256
www.wonderwomen.co.uk
Pre-natal and post-natal specific personal training from Rachel Berg. Tailor-made workouts in the comfort of your own home. Visit the website to find out more.

first aid and safety

These courses offer practical tuition and peace of mind for parents and carers wanting to know the principal causes of accidents and how to prevent and treat them, including resuscitation and general first aid (burns, breaks and poisoning)

First Aid for Kids — 020 7854 2861
www.firstaidforkids.com
First Aid for Kids is a complete CD-ROM that gives comprehensive first aid advice, tuition, reference and guidance to any parent or child carer, so that you can deal quickly, confidently and effectively with many childhood emergencies. A percentage of sales goes to Great Ormond Street and the King's College Hospital Silver Lining Appeal.

Marie Askin First Aid — 020 7603 8103
Small classes for parents held in your own home. Registered nurse with 10yrs first aid experience.

The Parent Company — 020 7935 9635
www.theparentcompany.co.uk
Learn how to respond confidently in an emergency involving your child or someone else's with this leading provider of first aid training for parents and carers.

R.E.D.I First Aid & Safety — 020 7610 0710
www.redi-training. co.uk
Our qualified nurses teach you to look after a sick or injured child; we come to your home at a time most convenient to you: mornings, afternoons, evenings or weekends. We offer practical advice and teach you quick and easy assessments for common illnesses and injuries. The sessions cover a number of common complaints including the non-breathing/choking child, head injuries, burns, allergies and meningitis.

Safe & Sound — 020 8449 8722
www.safe-and-sound.uk.net
Safe & Sound trainers are all experienced medical professionals dedicated to promoting high quality paediatric first aid training.first aid training.

Tinies Paediatric First Aid course — 020 7384 0322
www.tinieschildcare.co.uk
Unit 14 Block A, 126-128 New Kings Road, SW6
Certified course for parents focused upon baby and child resuscitation. Learn enough to save your child's life.

Verona Hall Independent   **020 8637 0768**
Midwife
www.veronahall.co.uk
A workshop covering topics such as how to tell if your child is unwell, dealing with a choking baby, resuscitation. A chance to practise on mannequins. Also find out about non-pharmacological agents to be used in first aid.

health clubs: private

Harbour Club
Watermeadow Lane, SW6 2RR   **020 7371 7700**
1 Alfred Road, W2   **020 7751 9443**
Excellent sports and heath clubs. Children's activities from 7 mths to 12 yrs with programmes designed to develop children's physical and motor skills, including agility, balance, flexibility and co-ordination. Classes include tumbling, music, gymnastics, karate, football, dance yoga, swimming and tennis.

David Lloyd Leisure
www.daivdlloydleisure.co.uk
This is the UK's largest provider of specialist junior tennis centres. In addition they offer swimming programmes, and additional children's activities such as music groups, mini-gym and dance classes. They also have crèche facilities. Branches are: Finchley, Fulham, Hounslow, Kensington and Kingston.

Hogarth Health Club   **020 8995 4600**
1a Airedale Avenue, London, W4 2NW
www.myhogarth.co.uk
Popular health club with an excellent crèche and full range of children's activities including Art-e-Fact, Crazy Cooking, Ballet, Tumble Bugs and Symphony Corner.

Holmes Place   **020 7562 2100**
www.holmesplace.com
Branches at: Bank, Barbican, Broadgate, Canary Riverside, Chelsea, Clapham, Crouch End, Crickelwood, Ealing, Fulham, Hammersmith, Kensington, Kingston, Marylebone, Mayfair, Mill Hill, Moorgate, Notting Hill, Oxford Stret, Putney, Regent's Park, South Wimbledon, Strand, Streatham, Tower Bridge, Wood Green.

tennis | swimming | restaurant | classes | spa | beauty | fitness
crèche | children's activities

London's finest tennis, health and fitness Clubs

HARBOUR CLUB - CHELSEA
WATERMEADOW LANE, LONDON, SW6 2RR T +44 (0)20 7371 7700

HARBOUR CLUB - NOTTING HILL
1 ALFRED ROAD, LONDON, W2 5EU T +44 (0)20 7266 9300

www.harbourclub.com

JAGS Sports Club 020 8299 4286
144 East Dulwich Grove, London, SE22 8TE
www.jagssportsclub.co.uk
Part of James Allen's Girls School, but during the holidays
and out of school hours offers private members excellent
facilities for families and children.

Lingfield Health Club 020 7483 6800
81 Belsize Park Gardens, London, NW3 4NJ

Manor Health & Leisure Club 020 8883 0500
140 Fortis Green, London, N10 3EF

Roehampton Club 020 8480 4200
Roehampton Lane, London, SW15 5LR
www.roehamptonclub.co.uk

Sunstone Health and Leisure Club 020 7923 1991
16 Northwold Road, Stoke Newington, London, N16
www.sunstonewomen.com
Women-only health club.

The Laboratory Spa 020 8201 5500
Hall Lane, London, NW4 4TJ
www.labspa.co.uk

Virgin Spas 0845 130 4747
www.virginactive.co.uk
Branches are: Islington, Merton Abbey, Stockley Park,
Wandsworth, West London. These gyms have swimming pools,
sauna and steam rooms, spas, crèches, hair and beauty salons.

homeopathy

Homeopathy is a very safe, gentle and effective
form of treatment. Because homeopathic remedies
gently stimulate the body's natural tendency to heal
itself, and are natural, non-addictive and do not
have side effects, they are ideal for use during
pregnancy, labour and for any problems that may
arise for mum or baby after the birth. Used during
pregnancy to treat conditions such as nausea,
heartburn, thrush, cramps and emotional distress
during labour. In children used for building up
overall health and immunity to common colds.

British Homeopathic Association 0870 444 3950
15 Clerkenwell Close, EC1R 0AA
www.trusthomeopathy.org
On this website you can read about how homeopathic
treatment works as well as access a directory of
homeopathically qualified doctors, nurses, dentists and
pharmacists.

Homeopathic Medical Association 01474 560 336
www.the-hma.org
This association also provides a list of fully qualified, fully
insured and rigorously vetted homeopaths. Visit their website
or call for a list.

Society of Homeopaths   0845 450 6611
www.homeopathy-soh.org
This association has a register of licensed members who have completed at least 3 years' training. They can provide this as a hard copy or if you visit their website there is a link to 'find a homeopath' by county. They also provide a number of useful booklets, including one on pregnancy and childcare.

Weleda   0115 944 8200
www.weleda.co.uk
Homeopathic remedies can be purchased mail order or online via the Weleda website. There is also a remedy finder for a variety of conditions. For children you should ask for the "soft tablets" which dissolve very quickly on the tongue.

Charles Harry Pharmacy   020 8286 4943
366 Richmond Road, Twickenham, London, TW1
Kay Gale offers homeopathic treatment for children at this South West London clinic.

NORTH LONDON

Becker Homeopathy   07976 391 498
in NW11
gabyjbecker@hotmail.com
Gaby Becker, BA (Hons), LCPH, MARH, has a solid background and an excellent track record. Babies, children and pregnant women are all treated usually with quick results. Nits, molluscum, excema, IBS, thrush, ADHD etc plus vaccine antedotes to help combat any ill effects without compromising protection. Gaby is also a qualified reflexologist - excellent for detoxing/relaxation, suitable in pregnancy.

Homeopathy Allergy Centre   020 7483 1640
15 Westbourne Road, N7

SOUTH LONDON

Acute Homeopathic Clinic   020 8877 1877
at Westover House, 18 Earlsfield Rd, SW18 3DW
www.westoverhouse.com

Dr Charles Innes   020 7589 6414
The Health Partnership, 12a Thurloe St, SW7 2ST

Liz Whitehead   020 8488 2027
2 Desensons Road, SE21 7DN

Olga Lawrence Jones   020 7737 1294
10 Stockwell Park Crescent, SW8 0DE

The Vale Practice   020 8299 9798
64 Grove Vale, SE22 8DT

Fulham Osteopathic Practice   020 7384 1851
769 Fulham Road, London, SW6 5HA
All age groups treated, child-friendly, easy parking, ground floor.

WEST LONDON
Royal London   020 7837 8833
Homeopathic Hospital, Great Ormond Street, WC1

Homeopathic Children's Clinic   020 8741 9264
Brackenbury Natural Health Centre,
30 Brackenbury Road, W6 0BA

Dr Max Deacon   020 7602 1006
63 Rowan Road, W6 7DT

hypnotherapy

HypnoBirthing®   07766 963 228
Box 347, 22 Notting Hill Gate, London, W11 3JE
www.hypnobirthing.me.uk
Suzanne Austen is a qualified HypnoBirthing® Practitioner with the HypnoBirthing® Instititute of America. Her ante-natal classes help mothers achieve a natural, fear-free and drug-free birthing experience. Classes are run in and around London regularly. Check out Suzanne's website for more details.

Hypnobirthing Teacher   020 8743 4995
and Doula: Sarah Johnson
www.sarahjohnson.co.uk
Many women want a natural birth without drugs or interventions - but worry about how they will handle pain. Sarah Johnson, who is a doula and mother of four, brings her hands-on knowledge of hypnobirthing and local hospitals to the task of preparing her clients for any turn their birthing takes. Based in West London, Sarah offers private classes in a couple's own home over several weeks.

Karen Arkle   0115 963 4599
Registered midwife and hypnotherapist. Hypnotherapy for pregnancy, birth, women's health issues, phobias and habit breaking. Classes take place at the Hospital of St John & Elizabeth, St John's Wood, NW8

Natal Hypnotherapy   01428 712 615
www.natalhypnotherapy.co.uk
The UK's leading provider of Hypnosis CDs for pregnancy and birth. The CDs teach safe, easy-to-use techniques, including effective breathing, relaxation and pain management.

The Hypnoclinic   0845 108 0419
3 Stowe Crescent, E17 5EG
www.hypnoclinic.net
This is an easy-to-follow birth preparation course offered over a weekend or two Saturdays in both North West and South London. Check out the website for some great testimonials.

Yvonne Drysdale: 020 8743 4205
Confidence Matters
10 Harley Street, London, W1G 9PF
www.themindmatters.co.uk
Introducing Easy Birth courses for pregnant women. The courses are designed to empower mothers, teach them relaxation techniques, give them a sense of control over events, teach them pain management and help them overcome anxiety and fear.

immunisation

Children's Immunisation Centre   0870 161 0009
69 Harley Street, London, W1
www.childrensimmunisation.com
A clinic offering private immunisations.

Direct Health 2000   0870 2000 999
6-7 Grove Market Place, Court Yard, Eltham,
London, SE9 5PU
www.dh2.co.uk
Private but affordable healthcare centre offering single
vaccinations and BCG/Heaf testing. Also walk-in GP service.

JABS   020 8442 0105
www.jabs.org.uk
This is the support group for "vaccine-damaged" children.
Also provides details of local doctors who give single
vaccinations for measles, mumps and rubella.

NHS Immunisation Information
www.immunisation.nhs.uk
Information for parents who have concerns about childhood
vaccinations. Also visit www.mmrthefacts.nhs.uk where you
can order free leaflets online.

The Portland Hospital   020 7390 8312
234 Great Portland Street, W1W 5QT
www.theportlandhospital.com
Private vaccinations service (single MMR vaccination not available).

Vaccinations - Yes or No?   0870 720 0067
www.vaccinations-yesorno.co.uk
A must-have, unbiased book for parents facing the dilemma
of MMR and the other childhood vaccinations.

Immunisation checklist		Source: NHS
Age	Protects against	How it is given
2 mths	polio	by mouth
	meningitis C	1 injection
	Hib haemophilus influenza B DPT - diphtheria, pertussis (whooping cough) and tetanus	1 injection
3 mths	same as for 2 months	
4 mths	same as for 2 months	
12-15 mths	MMR	1 injection
3-5yrs	polio	by mouth
	DTaP - diphtheria, tetanus & accellular pertussis	1 injection
	MMR	1 injection
10-14yrs	BCG - tuberculosis	skin test then injection if needed
13-18yrs	Tb-tetanus and diphtheria	1 injection
	polio	by mouth

infertility

CHILD - National Infertility   01424 732 361
Support Network
Charterhouse, 43 St Leonards Road, Bexhill on
Sea, TN39 3WA
www.infertilitynetworkuk.com

Human Fertilisation and   020 7291 8200
Embryology Authority
21 Bloomsbury Street, London, WC1B 3HF
www.hfea.gov.uk

The Fertility Support Company 020 8621 0798
www.fertilitysupportcompany.co.uk
A holistic approach to male and female fertility; from IVF
preparation to having a doula at the birth. Treatment approach
utilises acupuncture, herbal medicine, nutrition and mind/body
therapy to treat the underlying causes of fertility, strengthen the
body to increase sperm count, improve the success rate of
IVF/IUI and support mothers through pregnancy, labour and
recovery. Also provide a range of acupressure and herbal
treatments for newborns and young children. Clinics in
Muswell Hill, Hendon, Highgate and Harrow.

Karen Arkle   0115 963 4599
Registered midwife and hypnotherapist. Hypnotherapy and
positive visualisation to support your chances of success.
Classes take place at the Hospital of St John & Elizabeth, St
John's Wood, NW8.

Natural Mother   0709 202 2020
www.naturalmother.co.uk
Specialised therapies to help you conceive. Treatments at home. No travel, no stress. London wide.

The Zita West Clinic   020 7580 2169
43 Devonshire Street, London, W1G 7AL
www.zitawest.com
Complementary therapies, advice and support for fertility and pregnancy, plus IVF support programme.

massage

Massage during pregnancy is a luxury everyone should treat themselves to. Easing tension and boosting energy levels are some of the benefits. Newborns and babies, who are too young to play, benefit mentally and physically from regular massage. It is both a communicative experience for parents and can settle a baby prior to sleep. With some tuition you can learn to use more complex strokes as your baby grows. These practitioners hold local classes or come to your home

Amber White Baby Massage   07799 077 205
Small groups in North London with experienced teacher. Private groups by arrangement.

Baby Massage with   020 7639 2397
Clare Mundy
www.blissfulbaby.co.uk
Classes and home visits. Author of "The A-Z of Baby Massage" (published by Dinedor Books).

Baby Massage with   07815 786 641
Bhavini Dattani
www.simplymassages.co.uk
Learn the gentle art of Baby Massage with a Certified Instructor at home. Small groups by arrangement. Also Body Massage, Indian Head Massage, Reflexology and Reiki treatments available..

Catherine Owens   07976 803 886
Edwardes Square, W8
'The finest pregnancy and post-natal massage therapist in London' Harpers & Queen 2002.

Natural Mother   0709 202 2020
www.naturalmother.co.uk
Expert pregnancy, post-natal and baby massage at home. Also aromatherapy, reflexology and fertility treatments. No travel, no stress. London wide.

Nurturer   0141 337 3328
www.nurturer.co.uk
Khutso Dunbar has outlets and groups of therapists nationwide who offer a range of services including; ante-natal massage, baby massage, ante- and post-natal yoga, pedicure, manicure, facials and personal trainers.

The Portland Hospital   020 7390 8061
234 Great Portland Street, W1W 5QT
www.theportlandhospital.com
Ante- and post-natal massage for mothers. Baby massage technique taught as part of post-natal mother and baby workshops.

Verona Hall: 020 8637 0768
Independent Midwife
Four-week classes in Dulwich for babies from 6 wks. Learn the art of baby massage and the benefits for you and your baby.

medical advice

NHS Direct   0845 46 47
The 24hr NHS helpline is extremely useful and comforting when you are concerned about your child's health. Initially your details are taken and then within a short period of time a trained nurse will call back and help you decide what further action should be taken. The number, although short, is correct.

Direct Health 2000   0870 2000 999
6-7 Grove Market Place, Court Yard, SE9 5PU
Private doctor service provided Mon-Fri. Price £45.

Doctorcall   07000 372255
16 Wimpole Street, W1
24hr call out service. Price around £85 for central London depending on postcode. Private clinic Mon-Fri.

Doctors Direct   020 7751 9701
73 –77 Britannia Road, SW6 2JR
24hr call out service. Price around £90 during week out of hours, depending on postcode. Private clinic Mon-Fri.

Minor Injuries Treatment Centre   020 8355 3002
Queen Mary's Hospital, Roehampton Lane

The Gynae Centre   020 7935 7525
93 Harley Street, W1N 1DF
Private gynaecological clinic. Price £80; no referrals required.

SOS Doctors Direct   020 7751 9701
24hr doctor call out service. Price around £80 depending on time and postcode.

Westover House   020 8877 1877
18 Earlsfield Road, SW18 3DW
www.westoverhouse.com
Private general practice with visiting consultant specialist and in-house complementary therapists.

The Portland Hospital　　　**020 7390 8312**
234 Great Portland Street, W1W 5QT
www.theportlandhospital.com
Private appointments for children with specialist consultant paediatricians. Urgent referral appointments available.

nutrition

British Dietetic Association　　　**0121 200 8080**
www.bda.uk.com

The Zita West Clinic　　　**020 7580 2169**
43 Devonshire Street, London, W1G 7AL
www.zitawest.com
Complementary therapies, advice and support for fertility and pregnancy, plus IVF support programme.

The Centre for Nutritional　　　**0845 128 5048**
Medicine Ltd
www.nutritionalmedicine.co.uk
A medically supported nutrition service with an expertise in pregnancy.

Find My Nutritionist
www.findmynutritionist.co.uk
Website helping you to locate a specialist nutritionist either for particular medical needs, or just locally.

obstetricians & gynaecologists

Mr Paul Armstrong　　　**020 7580 5754**
Portland Hospital, 209 Great Portland Street, W1
Armstrong is a consultant at the Portland Hospital advising mothers who have lost a baby or have had complicated pregnancies.

Miss Shohred Beski　　　**020 7272 5752**
St Barts, Whitechapel, E1 1BB
Heading up the high-risk obstetric clinic at St Barts, Beski deals regularly with high-risk pregnancies and deliveries. She has been a consultant obstetrician and gynaecologist at Barts and the London NHS Trust for over 5 years, as well as seeing private patients at the Portland, the London Independent Hospital and the Clementine Churchill Hospital. She has a specialist interest in acupuncture.

Professor Phillip Bennett　　　**020 7594 2141**
Queens Charlotte's Hospital, Du Cane Road, W12
Consultant obstetrician at Queen Charlotte's, Bennett provides ante-natal care as well as delivering. He specialises in recurrent miscarriages as well as normal deliveries, favouring waterbirths.

Mr Colin Davies　　　**020 7616 7753**
The London Clinic, 149 Harley Street, W1
A young consultant obstetrician and gynaecologist at the Royal London, Davies specialises in infertility due to polycystic ovaries and endometriosis. He consults privately at the London Clinic and at the Portland.

Dr Keith Robert Duncan　　　**020 8846 7902**
Chelsea & Westminster, 365 Fulham Road, SW10
Duncan is a consultant obstetrican and fetal medicine specialist and also the Service Director of the Kensington Wing at the Chelsea & Westminster Hospital. His speciality is multiple pregnancies and he delivers at the Chelsea & Westminster and also the Portland.

Ms Friedericke Eben　　　**020 7390 8089**
Consulting Rooms, 212-214 Great Portland St, W1
Over the last 15yrs, Eben has been a consultant obstetrician and gynaecologist at the Portland Hospital dealing with high-risk pregnancies and particularly women with fibroids which may affect fertility. She consults private on Wednesday at the Consulting Rooms in W1, but delivers at the Portland.

Ms Katrina Erskine   020 7390 8079
Consulting Rooms, 212-214 Great Portland St, W1
Consultant obstetrician and gynaecologist at the Homerton, Erskine deal with high-risk pregnancies (diabetes or other medical problems) and those with abnormal smears. She consults privately on Thursdays at the Consulting Rooms.

Mr Alan Farthing   020 7487 4394
106 Harley Street, W1G 7JE
Highly recommended general gynaecologist and fellow of the Royal College of Obstetricians and Gynaecologist. Farthing specialises in laparoscopic surgery and oncology, as well as polycystic ovaries and other fertility problems. He takes private consultations in Harley Street, as well as practising at St Mary's Paddington and Hammersmith.

Mr Malcolm Gillard   020 7486 2856
First-Floor Suite, 1 Devonshire Place, W1
Famous for his A-list celebrity clientele, including Victoria Beckham, Gillard delivers at the Portland hospital. His speciality as a high-risk obsterican and general gynaecologist allows mothers to stay with him through pregnancy and after.

Mr Kevin Francis Harrington   020 7387 0022
Hospital of St John & Elizabeth, NW8
Highly regarded consultant specialising in endometriosis as well as maternal and fetal medicine, Harrington delivers at the Portland, the Hospital of St John and Elizabeth as well as seeing private clients at the London Clinic.

Mr Thomas Ind   020 7201 2666
The Sloane Street Clinic, 51 Sloane Street, SW1
Ind is a senior gynaecologist and was awarded a sub-specialty accreditation in gynaecological oncology. His special interests are, abnormal smears, pelvic pain, endometriosis and cancer surgery.

Mr Mark Johnson   020 8846 7892
Highly regarded by parents from both the Chelsea and Westminster as well as the Portland, Johnson practised as a GP for over 10 years before becoming a consultant obstetrician.

Miss Amma Kyei-Mensah   020 8341 3422
Woolaston House, 25 Southwood Lane, Highgate, London, N6 5ED
www.woolastonhouse.com
A mother of two, Kyei-Mensah gives pre-pregnancy consultations and counselling for those with potential high-risk pregnancies or fertility problems. She has been a consultant obstetrician and gynaecologist at the Whittington for 15yrs, as well as delivering privately at the Portland and St John & Elizabeth. She's also interested in nutritional and homeopathic medicine and yoga.

Mr Karl Murphy   020 7886 1692
Lindo Wing, St Mary's Hospital, W2
Murphy is a senior consultant at St Mary's Lindo wing, and is a foetal-maternal specialist seeing mothers right from the start of their pregnancy, delivering at St Mary's Lindo Wing and for six weeks post-nally.

Mr T G Teoh   020 7224 4460
96 Harley Street, W1G 7HY
If you are considering an elective caesarian then Teoh is your man. He delivers at the Kensington Wing, Chelsea & Westminster, as well as St Mary's Lindo Wing and the Portland. He has a specialist interest in high risk obstetrics and foetal medicine, and is considered to be the leading consultant at the Ultrasound Diagnostic clinic in Harley Street for amniocentesis, nuchal and diagnostic scans.

Mr Guy Thorpe-Beeston   020 7224 4460
96 Harley Street, W1
Delivering at St Mary's Lindo Wing, the Portland as well as the Chelsea & Westminster, Thorpe-Beeston has a specialist interest in high-risk pregnancies where the mother has additional medical complications such as high-blood pressure.

Mr Charles Wright   01895 279 446
Hillingdon Hospital, Pield Heath Road, UB8 3NN
Wright is a senior consultant obstetrician at the Hillingdon Hospital, as well as a general gynaecologist. He sees private patients at St Mary's Lindo Wing, the Portland Hospital as well as the private consulting rooms at the Hillingdon. His specialist areas of interest are high risk obstetrics such as pre-eclampsia as well as oncology.

Ms Yoon   020 7730 2383
The Lister Hospital, Chelsea Bridge Road, SW1
Jeannie Yoon is a Consultant Obstetrician and Gynaecologist. Her NHS practice is at The Homerton Hospital. She trained at St Thomas' Hospital and has worked in major teaching hospitals - including St Thomas', Queen Charlotte's, Chelsea and Westminster and the John Radcliffe Hospital in Oxford – all of which are tertiary referral centres for high-risk pregnancies and specialist gynaecological services. In addition her specialist interests are with polycystic ovarian disease, menstrual disorders, PMT, problems of the menopause and contraception, with excellent knowledge of abnormal smears and colposcopy,

osteopathy & cranial osteopathy

Osteopathy is a hands-on therapy that combines soft-tissue massage and manipulation and spine-cracking. Osteopathic treatment may relieve back pain in pregnancy and aid recovery post-natally. In babies, cranial osteopathy has been used for sleeplessness, colic, sticky eye, teething and earache

Battersea Osteopathic   020 7738 9199
Practice
2b Ashness Road, Webbs Road entrance, SW11 6RY

Belsize Osteopathic Practice   020 7317 8118
47 Belsize Square, London, NW3 4HN
Dave Gibson BSc (Hons) Ost, MED is a registered osteopath, cranial osteopath and naturopath.

British College of   020 7435 7830
Naturopathy and Osteopathy
6 Netherhall Gardens, Hampstead, NW3 5RR

British Osteopathic Council   020 7357 665
www.osteopathy.org.uk

Docklands Children's   020 7536 0004
Osteopathic Clinic
8b Lanterns Court, Millharbour, E14 9TU

Fulham Osteopathic Practice 020 7384 1851
769 Fulham Road, SW6 5HA
All age groups treated, child-friendly, easy parking, ground floor.

Grania Stewart-Smith   020 7286 2615
31 Grove End Road, NW8 (opposite St. John & Elizabeth Hospital)
Treatment of pregnant women.

Kane and Ross Clinics
9 Upper Wimpole Street,   020 7486 9588
London, W1G 6LJ
28 Knightsbridge Court,   020 7235 8300
London, SW1X 9LJ
www.kaneandrossclinics.co.uk
Structural and cranial osteopaths in the West End and Knightsbridge.

Martien Jonkers   07748 938 299
BSc (Ost) Hons, DO, Dip/Ot
Neals Yard, 9 Elgin Crescent, W11   020 7727 3998

Maxine Hamilton   020 7730 7928
Stubber, BSc Ost (Hons)
Wilbraham Place Practice, 9a Wilbraham Place, (off Sloane Square), SW1X 9AE

Nik Casse   020 8542 4455
Albany Clinic, 277 The Broadway, 1st floor, Wimbledon, SW19

Osteopathic Centre for Children   020 7486 6160
109 Harley Street, W1N 1DG

Westover House   020 8877 1877
18 Earlsfield Road, SW18 3DW
Structural and cranial osteopathy. Specialising in pregnancy and children.

The College Practice   020 7267 6445
60 Highgate Road, NW5 1PA

The Hale Clinic   020 7631 0156
7 Park Crescent, W1N 3HE

The Maris Practice   020 8891 3400
13 Baylis Mews, Amyand Park Road, Twickenham, TW1 3HQ
A team of osteopaths and homeopaths experienced in the treatment of children and babies.

The Vale Practice   020 8299 9798
64 Grove Vale, East Dulwich, SE22 8DT

Tideswell Road Clinic   020 8788 5761
7 Tideswell Road, Putney, SW15 6LJ

Total Care   07748 938 299
30 Fortis Green, East Finchley, N2 9EL
For colic, sleep disturbance, constant crying, neuro-developmental problems, etc.

West London Osteopaths   020 8749 0581
65 Vespan Road, W12 9QG

physiotherapists

Kiki's Children's Clinic   020 7207 4234
133 Thurleigh Road, SW12 8TX
www.kikisclinic.com
Physiotherapy and occupational therapy for babies and children using neuro-developmental therapy and play to stimulate movement and the ability to learn.

Physio for All   020 7228 2141
The Battersea Practice, 40 Webbs Road
www.physio4all.com
Back pain, sports injuries, incontinence, cranio-sacral therapy, chest infection.

Physio for All   020 7351 9918
The Chelsea Practice, 186 Fulham Road
www.physio4all.com
Back pain, sports injuries, pelvic floor and incontinence problems.

Physio for All   020 7591 1910
The South Ken. Practice, 21 Thurloe Place, SW7
www.physio4all.com
Back pain, sports injuries, pelvic floor and incontinence problems, chest infections.

The Chartered Society   020 7306 6666
of Physiotherapists
14 Bedford Row, WC1R 4ED
Contact for details of qualified physios in your area.

The Portland Hospital   020 7390 8061
234 Great Portland Street, W1W5QT
www.theportlandhospital.com
Physiotherapy and complementary healthcare for pregnancy including treatment for back pain. Rehabilitative physiotherapy also available for children following medical referral.

pyschologists

Child Psychotherapy Trust   020 7284 1355
Star House, 104-108 Grafton Road, NW5 4BD
www.childpsychotherapytrust.org.uk

Counselling for Children   07957 586 656
139 Lillie Road, London, SW6 7SX

Joyce Vonderweidt, PhD   020 7589 7614
24 Donne Place, London, SW3 2NH

Holli Rubin   020 7725 0528
www.Hollirubin.com
Psychotherapist specialising in pregnancy and motherhood. She can help you to reflect on issues such as body image, mood swings, difficult birth, coping with a newborn and changes in your relationships - ensuring that the transition to motherhood is a rewarding and fulfilling experience.

reflexology

Reflexology has been around for thousands of years, but the modern form was established in the early 20th century when a system of massage through reflex points on the feet, hands and head was developed and used to relieve tension and treat illness in the corresponding zones of the body. In pregnancy reflexology can alleviate morning sickness, constipation and rid the body of excess catarrh and stubborn colds. Post-natally, the therapy is said to boost energy levels and increase breastmilk supplies

British Reflexology Association   01886 821 207
Monks Orchard, Whitbourne, WR6 5RB

Andrea Allardyce BA, MIFR, ITEC   020 8995 5037
4a Oxford Road North, W4 4DN

Feet First   07956 684 455
Louise Sanders specialises in reflexology and holistic massage during pregancy and post-natally.

Denise Cameron   07769 656 008
Home visits in South and West London-Denise offers pre- and post-natal reflexology to restore the body's vital energy (SW10, SW3, SW7, W8, W11, SW11, SW12).

Natural Mother 0709 202 2020
www.naturalmother.co.uk
Expert treatments during pregnancy and post-natally, with
baby massage and aromatherapy at home. No travel, no
stress. London wide.

The Healing Company 07958 396 956
32 Heathfield Road, Wandsworth, SW18 2ZZ
www.thehealingcompany.com
Treatments for stress, pregnancy, baby colic.

The Ladbroke Rooms 020 8960 0846
8 Telford Road, W10 5SH
www.theladbrokerooms.com
Treating the whole body via the feet.

The Portland Hospital 020 7390 8061
234 Great Portland Street, W1W5QT
www.theportlandhospital.com

yoga

Yoga classes are particularly recommended during
pregnancy as they are less energetic, but build and
maintain strength as your body changes shape.
Recommended from 12 weeks (see also antenatal
teachers for ante-natal and yoga classes)

Anna Lempriere 07971 290 464
Kundalini yoga teacher runs classes for women in
Dulwich,with a faithful clientele. Babies welcome.

Annabel Hargrave 020 8287 5411
www.yogabirth.org
Ante-natal yoga for pregnancy, birth prepartion workshops
and post-natal classes in SW18 and SW19.

Iyengar Yoga Institute 020 7624 3080
223a Randolph Avenue, London, W9 1NL
www.iyi.org.uk
Ante-natal yoga classes and yoga for children (7yrs+) with
highly qualified teachers in beautiful fully-equipped purpose-
built studios. "I can't recommend these classes highly
enough" readers comments.

Julie Krausz 020 8459 2903
Ante-natal yoga classes held at Queens Park, NW6 on
Wednesday evenings and Thursday mornings, and in
Battersea on Monday afternoons and evenings; and post-
natal yoga classes held on Thursdays afternoons in NW6
(with monthly baby massage).

Kundalini Yoga in South London 020 7701 3845
www.southernlightyoga.co.uk
Carolyn Cowan runs excellent yoga classes at her studio in
Camberwell, specialising in empowering women and for
pregnant women from 12-42 weeks. A powerful, energising
form of yoga involving special breathing, as well as some
chanting and meditation. Her DVDs are available from
www.devotion.org.uk.

Natasha Rhoden Baby 020 8291 1325
Yoga and Massage
Baby yoga and massage at LA Fitness in Sydenham, SE26
on Thursdays, for newborns and crawlers. Bookings taken for
6-week courses but spaces available for drop-in. Toddler
yoga classes also available.

Me & My Baby 020 7751 4170
Therapy Rooms & Clinic
236d Fulham Road, SW10
www.meandmybabyclinic.co.uk
Wide selection of daytime, evening and week-end classes of
pregnancy yoga with Active Birth, Birthing from Within and
YogaBirth teachers. Kundalini yoga, mummy & baby post-
natal yoga, physiotherapy post-natal Pilates and Method
Putkisto. Relaxed, small classes. One-to-one appointments
available.

The Grove Health Centre 020 7221 2266
182-184 Kensington Church Street, W8 4DP

Pilates with Zoe 07780 614 265
www.pilateswithzoe.com
Pilates teacher for all ages, concentrating on improving
posture, toning the body and focussing the mind.

Relax Kids 020 8208 8303
www.relaxkids.com
Relaxation courses, books and CDs.

The Portland Hospital 020 7390 8061
234 Great Portland Street, W1W 5QT
www.theportlandhospital.com
Yoga and Pilates classes especially for pregnant ladies.
Post-natal exercise classes also available.

Starchild Yoga 01628 482 109
Starchild Yoga is yoga for children aged 3-8yrs. Classes are
held weekly 4.00-4.45pm in Swiss Cottage Community
Centre, 19 Winchester Road, London, NW3. Booking is
essential.

Special Yoga Centre 020 8933 5475
Tay Building, 2a Wrentham Avenue, NW10 3HA
www.specialyoga.org.uk

The Life Centre 020 7221 4602
15 Edge Street, W8
www.thelifecentre.com

Tanya Goodman Prenatal Yoga 0207 592 9706 or
07977 070 187
Birthlight pregnancy yoga classes in central London on
Thursday evenings. Refreshments served after class. Please
contact Tanya before attending after 12 weeks into
pregnancy.

Triyoga 020 7483 3344
Erskine Road, Primrose Hill, NW3
www.triyoga.co.uk
Pregnancy yoga, Mummy & Me, baby massage and post-
natal yoga classes are held weekly at this excellent yoga
centre.

Whyoga 020 8874 3858
170a Garratt Lane, SW18 4DA
www.whyoga.com
Inspirational yoga retreats and children's yoga parties.

YogaBugs 020 8772 1800
www.yogabugs.com
Classes developed by yoga teacher Nell Lindsell for children
aged 2½ to 7yrs, available at locations throughout London.
For those who don't have a local class you could consider
the Yogabugs video. The benefits of yoga for flexibility,
strength, concentration and relaxation, but Yogabugs
transforms the postures into mime adventures and creative
stories, which further benefit children's confidence and
imagination.

Yoga for Pregnancy 020 8287 5411
Annabel Hargrave
www.yogabirth.org
Gentle exercises, using breathing and relaxation techniques in
preparation for labour.

Yoga For Pregnancy 07989 233 719.
Rachel Usher
Rachel Usher is a pregnancy yoga therapist. She offers
private tuition or small group classes in SW10.

Yoga Junction 020 7263 3113
The Whittington Park Community Centre,
Yerbury Road, N19 4RS

Yogabananas 020 8874 3858
170A Garratt Lane, SW18 4DA
www.yogabananas.com

Yogahome 020 7249 2425
11 Allen Road, N16 8SB

Yoga Therapy Centre 020 7419 7195
60 Great Ormond Street, WC1N 3HR
www.yogatherapy.org
Pregnancy yoga, baby and children's yoga classes are offered
at this therapy centre. Fot the babies' classes from newborn-
10mths there was a waiting list - so do register early.

Yoga Vision 020 7354 2450
www.yogavision.co.uk
Rena Nicholaou runs weekly ante-natal classes (from the 12th
week of your pregnancy) at Yoga Base in 225 Liverpool
Road, N1. Rena is a member of Birthlight which is
specifically adapted yoga for pregnancy. She also teaches
mother and baby yoga at Highbury Round House, 71
Ronald's Road, N5 (weekly classes). Children's yoga classes
are also run from 6yrs+ at the North London Buddhist Centre,
72 Holloway Road, N7.

Yvonne Moore Birth Preparation 020 7794 2056
South Hill Park, NW3
Ante-natal yoga-based exercise classes in North London.

shopping

Your favourite pastime is about to skyrocket to new levels. That burgeoning bump will require a new wardrobe for a start. Next, you'll be stockpiling bottles, breast pumps, sterilising units, nappies and lotions and potions, not to mention the baby carrier, the buggy, the car seat, the cot and the new linen. Then comes the fun bit – dear little outfits for babies, toddlers and tweenies, as well as dressing-up gear, swimwear and toys. Not sure where to find all this? Here we guide you to the best shops, mail-order catalogues and websites in the country. Plus you'll find creative ways to announce baby's arrival to the world, as well as sources of pretty presents and a stash of portrait artists and photographers to capture you and your offspring for posterity.

shopping: essential items

✓ Items	Buy from...	Borrow from...	Gift from...

For the nursery

- ☐ cot and mattress
- ☐ moses basket/crib
- ☐ linen (sheets, blankets, etc)
- ☐ changing mat/table
- ☐ wardrobe
- ☐ chest of drawers
- ☐ playmat

Clothing

- ☐ 6 cotton sleepsuits
- ☐ 3 sleeping bags
- ☐ 4 cotton vests
- ☐ 1-2 two-piece outfits
- ☐ 2-4 cardigans
- ☐ 4-6 pairs socks/bootees
- ☐ 1 pair gloves/mittens (for winter)
- ☐ 1 snowsuit (for winter)
- ☐ muslin cloths/ bibs
- ☐ 1 hat

Essential supplies

- ☐ disposable or washable nappies
- ☐ baby wipes, cotton wool
- ☐ nappy bags
- ☐ barrier cream, Vaseline
- ☐ breast pump
- ☐ bottles
- ☐ sterilizer

For travelling

- ☐ pram/pushchair
- ☐ rain cover and Buggysnuggle
- ☐ car seat
- ☐ baby carrier/sling
- ☐ travel and changing bag
- ☐ travel cot

baby accessories

These suppliers have designed unique and stylish products that offer something practical with a great sense of style

Babylist   **020 7371 5145**
The Broomhouse, 50 Sulivan Road, SW6 3DX
www.babylist.com
You might be wondering how much baby 'stuff' is really all that necessary. If so, then you need to book an appointment with Babylist, the longest running nursery advisory service in London. They will take you through their list of essentials, as well as the nice-to-haves in the comfort of their SW6 showroom. This is not an exclusive, A-list celebrities-only service (although they have had quite a few), but a thoroughly sensible way of tailoring your needs with the amazing range of products on offer.

Babyworld   **01491 821 877**
www.babyworld.co.uk
Online store with a unique range of high-quality, innovative accessories, delivered within 2 working days.

Hippychick art/eater suit   **01278 434 440**
www.hippychick.com
All-in-one protective bib for painting and eating sessions. Less mess, less stress!

Jacob's Adder   **0800 093 2458**
www.jacobsadder.co.uk
The Jacob's Adder bracelet has a simple design and allows you to count the number of kicks you feel during the day during pregnancy, remember whether you fed from the left or right during breastfeeding or for counting 10 sets of pelvic floor exercises.

Prince Lionheart   **0870 766 5197**
www.princelionheart.com
Established for over 30 years, Prince Lionheart has a range of innovative, high qulaity products designed to help you enjoy you new life with baby - from Slumber Bears and bebe PODS to Wipes, Warmers, Seatsavers and dishwasheer baskets. Don't miss their range of squidgy foam furniture guards to keep your little one safe in the home. Call for your local stockist or to request a catalogue.

ZPM   **020 8288 1091**
www.zpm.com
Funky range of bibs, bags, aprons, sponge bags and changin mats.

baby equipment hire

Chelsea Baby Hire   **020 8789 9673**
www.chelseababyhire.com
A personal and reliable service offering top brand equipment for long and short-term hire. Call 07802 846 742.

Lilliput   **020 7720 5554**
255-259 Queenstown Rd, SW8
www.lilliput.com

Little Stars   020 8621 4378/020 8537 0980
www.littlestars.co.uk
Breastpumps to Buggies, Cots to Car Seats, Sterilisers to Swings. Hire it - don't buy it! Nationwide delivery. Call 020 8537 0980 or 020 8621 4378 for free brochure.

birth announcements

Announce It!   **020 8286 4044**
www.announceit.co.uk
Your beautiful baby, our gorgeous range of birth announcements mailed within 3 days.

Flutterby   **020 7751 3172**
www.flutterbycards.com
Birth announcements and holiday photocards, personalised stationery for mother and child, baby shower invitations, lithography and letterpress specialist.

Happyhands   **020 8671 2020**
www.happyhands.co.uk
Your baby's hand and foot prints on cards. Ingenious ink-free kit provided.

Heard the News?   **01285 869 674**
www.haveyouheardthenews.com
Beautiful personalised announcements, co-ordinating thank-you cards, invitations and keepsake boxes. Hand-made by Ellen in 5-7 days. Personal and reliable service.

HeavenSent Creations   **01732 453 654**
www.heavensentcreations.co.uk
Your baby's birth is one of your life's most precious events. Share your joyful news with family and friends with a personalised keepsake. Choose from many designs including christening invitations too. Fast delivery.

Heritage Personalised Stationery 01256 861 738
www.heritage-stationery.com
Top-quality, traditional hand-finished birth announcement and christening stationery, delivered in hours.

Hyperbubba   **07932 447 752**
www.hyperbubba.com
Calling all trendy babies! Stylish, personalised and colourful birth announcement cards, printed on high-quality, gloss-laminated paper. Top quality and cutting-edge designs.

Special Announcements   **07752 508 360**
www.specialannouncements.co.uk
Personalised photo birth announcement cards. Choose from a range of elegant designs and have your chosen picture incorporated to show of that special moment in style to all of your family and friends.

Stork Post   **07092 347 074**
www.storkpost.co.uk
Birth and christening cards for modern papas and mamas. Proudly announce your new arrival with your own special message and a photograph in a card sourced from Europe's finest card houses ensuring quality and individuality.

annôunce it!

for birth announcements,
wedding invitations, christenings,
parties, moving house, anything…

We offer a wide range of beautiful cards and gifts personalised with your own message, including ribbons or photographs if required and a free proof.

Come and browse or have a chat at our shop
99 Station Road Hampton TW12 020 8286 4044

To see our new designs for 2006 and to order on-line visit our web site **www.announceit.co.uk**

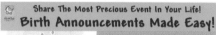

bookshops for children

All these bookshops are either specialist children's bookshops or those who have a specialist children's department. They also hold regular story-telling sessions, as well as visits and signings with popular children's authors.

NORTH

Angel Bookshop   020 7226 2904
102 Islington High Street, N1

Muswell Hill Bookshop   020 8444 7588
72 Fortis Green Road, N10

Children's Bookshop   020 8444 5500
29 Fortis Green Road, N10

Stoke Newington Bookshop   020 7249 2808
159 Stoke Newington High Street, N16

NORTH WEST

Primrose Hill Bookshop   020 7586 2022
134 Regents Park Road, NW1

Daunt Books
193 Haverstock Hill, NW3   020 7794 4006
83-84 Marylebone High St   020 7224 2295
51 South End Road, NW3   020 7224 2295

Karnac Books   020 7431 1075
118 Finchley Road, NW3

Owl Bookshop   020 7485 7793
211 Kentish Town Road, NW5

West End Lane Books   020 7431 3770
277 West End Lane, West Hampstead, NW6

Kilburn Bookshop   020 7328 7071
8 Kilburn Bridge, Kilburn High Road, NW6

Willesden Bookshop   020 8451 7000
Willesden Green Library Centre, 95 The High Road

Bookworm   020 8201 9811
1177 Finchley Road, NW11

EAST

Eastside Books   020 7247 0216
178 Whitechapel Road, E1

Centerprise Bookshop   020 7254 9632
136-138 Kingsland High Street, E8

Newham Bookshop   020 8552 9993
745-747 Barking Road, E13

Hammicks   020 8521 3669
259 High Street, E17

SOUTH EAST

Arcade Bookshop   020 8850 7803
3-4 The Arcade, Eltham, SE9

Bookseller Crow on the Hill   020 8771 8831
50 Weston Street, Crystal Palace, SE19

The Bookshop   020 8693 2808
Dulwich Village
1d Calton Avenue, SE21

Dulwich Books   020 8670 1920
6 Croxted Road, West Dulwich, SE21

Kirkdale Bookshop   020 8778 4701
272 Kirkdale, Sydenham, SE26

Tales on Moon Lane   020 7274 5759
25 Half Moon Lane, SE24
www.talesonmoonlane.co.uk
This is a charming, award-winning children's bookshop with weekly storytelling sessions and regular events with children's authors during the holidays and half-terms. They sell books for all ages, from toddlers to teenagers. As well as all the classics, such as Narnia and Beatrix Potter, we also sell books by modern authors such as JK Rowling and Philip Pullman. You can even take a seat on their sofa while you browse through the collection.

SOUTH WEST

Harrods   020 7225 5721
Children's Book Department
4th floor, Harrods, Knightsbridge, SW1

Daisy & Tom   020 7352 5000
181 King's Road, SW3
www.daisyandtom.com
Excellent range of children's picture books taking up half the ground floor of this large Chelsea store.

Young Book Trust   020 8516 2977
Book House, 45 East Hill, SW18 2QZ
www.booktrusted.com

Nomad Books   020 7736 4000
781 Fulham Road, SW6

The French Bookshop   020 7584 2840
28 Bute Street, SW7

Pan Bookshop   020 7373 4997
160 Fulham Road, SW10

Bolingbroke Bookshop   020 7223 9344
147 Northcote Road, SW11

My Back Pages   020 8675 9346
8-10 Balham Station, SW12

Beaumonts   020 8741 0786
60 Church Road, Barnes, SW13

INSPIRING A LIFE LONG LOVE OF READING

TALES ON MOON LANE
THE CHILDREN'S BOOKSHOP

Let your children lead the way

The first book free on presentation of The London Baby Directory (restrictions apply)
25 Half Moon lane, London, SE24 9JU   T: **0207 274 5759**   **www.talesonmoonlane.co.uk**

Bookstop	**020 7228 9079**
375 Upper Richmond Road West, East Sheen, SW14	
Ottakar's	**020 8780 2401**
6-6a Exchange Centre, Putney, SW15	
Beckett's Bookshop	**020 8672 4413**
6 Bellevue Road, SW17	
Golden Treasury	**020 8333 0167**
29 Replingham Road, Southfields, SW18	
Langton's Bookshop	**020 8892 3800**
44-45 Church Street, Twickenham, TW1	
Kew Bookshop	**020 8940 0030**
1-2 Station Approach, Kew, Richmond, TW9	

WEST
Bookcase	**020 8742 3919**
268 Chiswick High Road, W4	
Pitshanger Bookshop	**020 8991 8131**
Pitshanger Lane, W5	
Children's Book Company	**020 8567 4324**
11 The Green, W5	
Children's Book Centre	**020 7937 7497**
237 Kensington High Street, W8	

bottles

The following companies manufacture a wide range of bottles and feeding accessories, including anti-colic teats. They are generally widely available through supermarkets, chemists and nursery goods stores

Steri-bottle   **0500 979 899**
www.steribottle.com
The only pre-sterilised, ready-to-use, disposable bottle. Perfect for holidays, days out or when you're extra busy. Ideal for breast or formula milk.

Avent   **0800 289 064**
www.avent.com
This bottle, which is widely available in the UK, has a silicone teat and a broad design which encourages baby to latch on to the bottle with a wide open mouth, allowing suckling during bottle feeding. Your baby uses this same latching and suckling when breastfeeding, so combining breast and bottle feeding is possible.

MAM   **020 8943 8880**
www.mamuk.com
The wide-necked ULTIvent bottle has been designed to counteract the effects of colic. The base of the bottle can also be unscrewed for easier cleaning.

breast pumps

Breast pumps allow you to express and store milk, which can then be bottle-fed to your baby. You can either select a hand-operated model or an electric/battery model. The manual models are quieter, lighter and easier to travel with – but can be slow and tiring (on the hand). Electronic pumps are faster and generally more effective

Ameda Lactaline   **01823 336 362**
www.ameda.demon.co.uk
This double pump runs on mains, battery or in the car. User-friendly and efficient although quite bulky to carry around. It is hygienic, and offers variable suction to accommodate different needs. This is £75.95 to hire but there is a selection of other Ameda models available to hire from £19.95 for 30 days including next day delivery and collection.

Avent Isis Breast Pump   **0800 289 064**
www.aventbaby.com
The ISIS pump naturally imitates the way your baby breastfeeds. Inside the funnel of the pump is a soft silicone cover with five petal sections. As you pump, the petals flex in and out, gently massaging the area around the nipple and stimulating the let-down reflex. Easy to use and quiet. Price £25-£30.

Chicco UK   **01623 750 870**
www.chicco.com
The Chicco adjustable breast pump is an uncomplicated manual pump with silicone breast shield and lever action. They also have a battery-operated model and a syringe breast pump, which ensures a gentle, adjustable suction of excess milk.

Medela   **0161 776 0400**
www.medela.co.uk
Medela manufacture a range of manual, battery and electric breast pumps. They also have a small travel set which can be used effectively for mums who go back to work but want to continue feeding breast milk full time; and a set of pumps if you are breastfeeding twins. They can also be hired.

NUK   **0845 300 2467**
www.nuk.de
NUK make a manual and battery-operated model. This manual model has adjustable strength, swivel handle for left- or right-handed mothers, plus a soft silicone cushion which massages as you express.

The First Years   **0800 526 829**
www.thefirstyears.com
This pump offers adjustable hand-positioning options to maximize comfort while pumping. Available from many leading nursery retailers.

Whittlestone Expresser   **01538 386 650**
www.whittlestone.co.uk
The Whittlestone Expresser uses gentle pulsation to stimulate the let-down of your breast milk, and then expresses your breastmilk.

car safety

In June it became law that children under 4' 5" need to be secured in an appropriate car or booster seat. For car seat fitting, seat belt adjusting or fixing ISOFIX anchorages, Autosafe actually come to you for a very modest fee (within M25)

Autosafe   **020 7372 3141**
www.auto-safe.co.uk
Seat belt fitting specialist and makers of the new seat belt height adjuster for children aged 4-12yrs combining comfort and safety

Babies R Us   **0845 786 9778**
www.babiesrus.co.uk

Halfords   **0845 7626 625**
www.halfords.com
If you purchase a car seat from Halfords their specially trained staff will ensure that it is correctly fitted in your car. Without your receipt they will charge £9.99.

www.babydirectory.com

carriers and slings

In the early days a comfortable baby sling is an essential. There are two types to look into; the fabric slings which have become very fashionable and can be used to carry both babies and toddlers; as well as the more structured carriers which are more comfortable for long periods. Best thing is to try them on to see which suits your own physique and weight of your baby

Babyhut   01273 245 864
www.babyhut.net
Experts in cotton baby slings and baby hammocks.

Baby Bjorn   0870 120 0543
www.babybjorn.com
The Baby Carrier Active, suitable from 0-18mths has a unique lumbar support panel sewn into the back to give a better fitting and more comfortable weight distribution.

Baba Slings   0845 2222 468
www.babaslings.com
The Baba Sling is a new and original sling-style carrier with a unique buckle and adjustment system makes it super-quick and easy to use. It allows you to carry a baby in 7 different positions and can be used for newborn babies up to children of 30 months. Made from 100% cotton with various padded zones.

Babyworld   01491 821 877
www.babyworld.co.uk
Online retailer of carriers and accessories including Bushbaby, Wilkinet, Hippychick and Tomy. Orders delivered within 2 working days.

Better Baby Sling   01923 444 442
www.betterbabysling.co.uk
'Wonderfully easy to put on and very comfortable' *The Independent*

Bill Amberg   020 7727 3560
www.billamberg.com
Leather and sheepskin baby carrier. Very luxurious and soft for the baby.

Hippychick Child Hip Seat   01278 434 440
www.hippychick.com
If you carry your child around on your hip you may end up with a twisted spine. Enter the Hipseat, a back-supporting belt with a shelf for the child to sit on, which supports their weight and allows your back to stay straight. From 6mths-3yrs. £34.96.

castings: hands & feet

Most mothers regret that they never got round to taking their baby's hand or foot prints, or struggled with a tube of paint. These companies offer a range of styles (casts, prints and imprints) to suit all budgets

Everlasting Castings   **0870 020 3593**
www.everlastingcastings.co.uk
Never want to forget how huge your pregnant belly was or
how tiny your baby's hands and feet were? Everlasting
Castings specialise in belly and baby casting kits to suit all
budgets. Full torso and fruit bowl belly casts in glass also
available.

Happyhands   **020 8671 2020**
www.happyhands.co.uk
Your baby's hand and footprints on ceramics. Ink-free kit
provided for taking prints at home.

Imprints
www.imprints.org
Imprints offer a professional hand and foot printing service
exclusively through John Lewis stores. Not casts, the original
clay impression is beautifully finished and framed in their own
workshop. Visit the website to book an appointment.

Lowestoft Porcelain   **01502 572 940**
www.lowestoftporcelain.com
First produced over 200 years ago these ceramic birth tablets
are hand-painted by the skilled craftsmen of Lowestoft
Porcelain. Issued with a certificate of authenticity and
presented in a silk lined box they come with two suspension
holes for hanging on the crib or on the wall.

Sarah Page Sculpture   **020 731 8789**
www.sarahpagesculpture.co.uk
Immaculate and sensitive fine and applied castings from
babies' and children's hands and feet.

Small Steps
www.firstshoeframing.co.uk
Small steps is an online specialist framing service dedicated
to framing your little ones first shoes. Your shoes will be
collected and returned to your door, expertly framed.

Wrightson & Platt   **020 7639 9085**
www.wrightsonandplatt.com
Your baby's hands and feet in silver, bronze, glass and resin.
Children holding hands, complex family pieces too - all
professionally cast from life. Made for you by experienced,
trained artists. Luxury service, including home visit. Vouchers
available for the perfect gift.

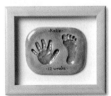
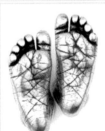

christening gifts

There is now such a plethora of items suitable for
godchildren, we have selected those companies
which we think offer the highest quality, originality
and personalised service at the right price. See also
gifts for newborns, and gifts, personalised (pg45)

Asprey & Garrard   020 7493 6767
167 New Bond Street, W1S 4AR
www.asprey-garrard.com
Cups, spoons, plates and yo-yos - engraved with
initials/name.

Babylist   020 7371 5145
www.babylist.com
The Babylist team have hand-selected a range of traditional
and contemporary christening gifts, which include luxuries
such as a Daniella Besso cashmere blanket. They can also
organise for gifts to be personalised as necessary.

Braybrook & Britten   020 8993 7334
www.braybrook.com
A large range of silver gifts for children from £30 upwards -
most can be personalised. 'Silversmiths by Post', they can
receive orders from anywhere in the UK.

Happyhands **020 8671 2020**
www.christening-presents.com
Gift box for hand and foot imprints on ceramic, packaged in a red box with white ribbon. Price £35.

Little Folk **01509 670 335**
www.littlefolk.co.uk
Meet the extra special Little Folk family, illustrated by designer Ruth Calladine. Beautiful personalised gifts for girls and boys. Choose your favourite from an exclusive range of delightful Little Folk characters and colours. They personalise your gift with your child's name, and on the framed prints include your own special message (see ad under "gifts").

Molly Brown London **0870 851 8818**
www.mollybrownlondon.co.uk
Charming Jelly Bean and Dolly Mixture enamel and silver necklaces and bracelets.

Photallic **01895 851 434**
www.photallic.com
The ultimate personalised gift - they can engrave your baby's photo into gold- and silver-plated pendants and keyrings, toothboxes, curlboxes, business card holders - treasured memories made into beautiful keepsakes.

The Little Picture Gallery **020 8998 9880**
www.thelittlepicturegallery.com
Delightful range of watercolour prints for children featuring a range of farm animals, trains & boats as well as those that can be personalised.

christening gowns

If you are starting from scratch and don't have a family heirloom christening gown, then a trip to Christening Gowns is well worth a visit. Otherwise there are a few expert retailers in London who stock a small selection alongside other children's clothes

Christening Gowns **01536 515 401**
www.christeningoutfits.co.uk
Over 500 gowns, dresses and romper suits in stock. Accessories including personalised bibs. Mail order throughout the UK.

Little Darlings **01604 846 655**
www.littledarlings.co.uk
Visit the website to view their full christening and fashion ranges.

Patrizia Wigan Designs **020 7823 7080**
19 Walton Street, SW3 2HX
www.patriziawigan.com
Refined gifts, babywear, christening, bridesmaid and pageboy outfits.

clothing shops: fashion

If your once-favourite pastime has diminished now that you can't browse at leisure without kids in tow, many brands have good catalogue and online purchasing routes

JoJo Maman Bébé **020 8731 8961**
3 Ashbourne Parade, 1259 Finchley Road, NW11
68 Northcote Road, SW11 **020 7228 0322**
80 Turnham Green Terrace, W4 **020 8994 0379**
30 The Exchange, Putney, SW15 **020 8780 5165**
www.jojomamanbebe.co.uk
A great range of French-inspired baby clothing as well as toys and gifts, maternity wear and nursery goods.

NORTH LONDON

American Collections **020 8806 0702**
41 Oldhill Street, N16 6LR

So Precious
childrenswear boutique
0207 354 1141
www.sopreciousuk.com

Early Clothing 020 8444 9309
79-85 Fortis Green Road, Muswell Hill, N10 3HP

Kiddie Chic 020 8880 1500
19 Amhurst Parade, Stamford Hill, N16 5AA

Igloo Kids 020 7354 7300
300 Upper Street, N1 2TU

Mini Kin 020 8341 6898
22, Broadway Parade, London, N8 9DE

So Precious 020 7354 1141
67 Highbury Park, N5 1UA
www.sopreciousuk.com
The boutique with its creative and cosy atmosphere allows parents to peruse exclusive ranges for their precious ones at their doorstep. Catering to both boys and girls from 0-6 years there is a mix of classic, contemporary and international brands sourced from Italy, France, Belgium and Britain. The range also includes christening and Holy Communion wear (up to age 9), shoes, gifts, baby essentials and accessories. Mention the Baby Directory for a 15% discount (not applicable for sale items).

Thoe Tho 020 8442 0419
55 Fortis Green Road, Muswell Hill, N10 3HP

Trendys 020 7837 9070
72 Chapel Market, N1 9ER

Za Trendy Kids 020 8365 8382
Wood Green Shopping City, High Road, N22 6YQ

NORTH WEST LONDON

Adam & Eve Children's Boutique 020 8455 8645
5 The Market Place, Hampstead Garden Suburb, NW11 6LB

Charly's 020 7723 6811
71 Church Street, NW8 8EU

Daphne & Mum 020 8458 7095
7 Belmont Parade, 838 Finchley Road, NW11 6XP

Dynasty 020 8731 8521
1-2 Russel Parade, Golders Green Road

Humla 020 7794 8449
13 Flask Walk, NW3 1HJ

Look Who's Walking 020 7433 3855
78 Heath Street, Hampstead Village, NW3 1DN

Purple Heart 020 7328 2830
13a College Parade, Salusbury Road, NW6 6RN

Tartan Turtle 020 8959 9938
52 The Broadway, Mill Hill, NW7 3LH

Tiddlywinks 020 7722 3033
23 St Johns Wood High Street, NW8 7NH

Trotters 020 8202 1888
Brent Cross Shopping Centre, NW4 3FP

EAST LONDON

Bambini 020 7474 3591
317 Barking Road, E13 8EE

Chi 020 8510 9000
251 Graham Road, E8 1PE

Kool Kids 020 7247 2878
9-11 New Goulston Street, E1 7QD

Jakss 020 8981 2233
469 Roman Road, E3 5LX

Tiddlywinks 020 8981 7000
414 Roman Road, E3 5LU

SOUTH EAST LONDON

Bunny London 020 7928 6269
Unit 1, 22 Oxo Tower Wharf, Bargehouse Street, SE1 9PH

Peppermint for Kids 020 7703 9638
321-323 Walworth Road, SE17 2TG

Biff 020 8299 0911
43 Dulwich Village, SE21 7BN

SOUTH WEST LONDON

Agnes b 020 7225 3477
111 Fulham Road, SW3 6OL

Baby Dior 020 7823 2039
6 Harriet Street, SW1X 9JW

Barney's 020 8944 2915
6 Church Road, SW19 5DL

Bonpoint 020 7235 1441
35b Sloane Street, SW1X 9LP

Bug Circus 020 8741 4244
153 Church Road, SW13 9HR

Caramel Baby 020 7589 7001
291 Brompton Road, SW3

Children's Kingdom 020 8682 2233
209 Upper Tooting Road, SW19

Daisy & Tom 020 7352 5000
181 King's Road, SW3 5EB
www.daisyandtom.com
Great range of baby and children's clothes, including good quality basics and designer labels, party and christening gowns, shoes and boots. Located on the top floor of this Chelsea store along with a puppet show to keep the children captivated whilst you shop.

Greater Tomorrow 020 7737 5276
80 Atlantic Road, SW9 8PX

Gucci 020 7235 6707
17-18 Sloane Street, SW1X 9NE

Iana
Putney Exch, Putney High St, SW15 020 8789 2022
186 King's Road, SW3 5XP 020 7352 0060

Kanga-roo 020 7384 4518
359 Fulham Palace Road, SW6

Kent & Carey
154 Wandsworth Bridge Rd, SW6 020 7736 5554
30 Bellevue Road, SW17 020 8682 2282

Lizzies 020 7738 2973
143 Northcote Road, SW11 6PX

Membery's 020 8876 2910
1 Church Road, SW13 9HE

Marie-Chantal 020 7838 1111
148 Walton Street, SW3 2JJ

Oilily 020 7823 2505
9 Sloane Street, SW1X 9LE

Pollyanna 020 7731 0673
811 Fulham Road, SW6 5HG

Patrizia Wigan Designs 020 7823 7080
19 Walton Street, SW3 2HX

Semmalina 020 7730 9333
225 Ebury Street, SW1

Tomboy Kids 020 7223 8030
176 Northcote Road, Battersea, SW11

Young England 020 7259 9003
47 Elizabeth Street, SW1

WEST & CENTRAL LONDON
Baby e 020 8840 8197
20 The Green, Ealing, W5 5DA
www.babye.co.uk
Designer boutique specialising in baby and childrenswear from Dior and Kenzo and many more.

Come see us at the boutique, or to arrange an appointment please contact our personal stylist
31 Connaught Street, Hyde Park, London, W2 2AY
020 7402 7109   www.chrysaliss.co.uk

Bill Amberg Shop 020 7727 3560
10 Chepstow Road, W2 5BD

Bon Bleu
16 Hammersmith Mall, W6 020 8834 7205
Kendal Court, Kendal Avenue, W3 020 8992 5611

Bonpoint
17 Victoria Grove, W8 020 7584 5131
38 Old Bond Street, W1 020 7495 1680
197 Westbourne Grove, W11 020 7792 2515

Natural Mat Company 020 7985 0474
99 Talbot Road, W11 2AT
www.naturalmat.com
Funky t-shirts and jumpers, cotton sleeping bags and PJs and soft cashmere baby range.

Burberry 020 7839 5222
21-23 New Bond Street, W1S 2RE

The Cross 020 7727 6760
141 Portland Road, W11 4LR

Chrysaliss 020 7402 7109
31 Connaught Street, Hyde Park, W2 2AY
www.chrysaliss.co.uk
Exquisite boutique with a calm, creative atmosphere and an interactive children's play area, keeping little ones thoroughly entertained whilst you browse in peace. International range including the Chrysaliss own brand 0-8yrs.

Catimini
52 South Molton Street, W1Y 1HF   020 7629 8099
3 Paradise Road, TW9   020 8541 4635
38 High Street, Kingston   020 8541 4635
75 Upper Thames Walk, Bluewater   01322 624 765

Darch & Duff   020 8840 0100
68 Northfield Avenue, W13

Jou Jou & Lucy   020 7289 0866
32 Clifton Road, W9 1ST

Mamas & Papas   0870 830 7700
256-258 Regent Street, W1B 3AF
www.mamasandpapas.co.uk
Fashion is the most popular department at Regent Street as all the collections are extremely fashion focused. The attention to detail that Mamas & Papas are renowned for is reflect in the quality and fit of each seasonal range, whether that be our city capsule collection for the working mum-to-be, the occasional wear with delicate detail and fabrics or the casual wear of separates and designer fit jeans.

Pearlfisher   020 7603 8666
12 Addison Avenue, W11 4QR

Paul Smith for Children   020 7727 3553
122 Kensington Park Road, W11 2EP

Rachel Riley   020 7935 7007
82 Marylebone High Street, W1U 4QW

Ralph Lauren   020 7535 4888
143 New Bond Street, W1

Tartine et Chocolat   020 7629 7233
66 South Molton Street, W1Y 1HH

Their Nibs   020 7221 4263
214 Kensington Park Road, W11 1NR

Tots   020 8995 0520
39 Turnham Green Terrace, W4 1RG

Tournicoti   020 7229 3022
52 Lonsdale Road, W11 2DE

Trotters   020 7937 9373
127 Kensington High Street, W8 6LE

clothing: high street

BabyGap
223-245 Oxford Street, W1R 1AB   020 7734 3312
122 King's Road, SW3   020 7823 7272
1-7 Shaftesbury Avenue, W1   020 7437 0138
Kew Retail Park, TW9   020 8876 8684
Brent Cross, NW4   020 8203 9696
99-101 Kensington High Street, W8   020 7368 2900
22-26 Chiswick High Road, W4   020 8995 3255
www.gap.co.uk

French Connection Junior   020 7225 3302
140-144 Kings Road, SW3

Jigsaw Junior
126-127 New Bond Street, W1   020 7491 4484
190 Westbourne Grove, W11   020 7229 8654
97 Fulham Road, SW3   020 7823 8915

Petit Bateau
133 Northcote Road, SW11   020 7228 7233
73 Ledbury Road, W11   020 7243 6331
19 Hampstead High Street, NW3   020 7794 1731
106 King's Road, SW3   020 7838 0818
188 Chiswick High Road, W4   020 8987 0288
62 South Molton Street, W1   020 7491 4498
www.petit-bateau.fr

clothing: outdoor

Bushbaby   0161 474 7097
www.bush-baby.com

Hippychick Togz   01278 434 440
www.hippychick.com
The Togz range of outdoor clothing is 100% waterproof and made from Teflon-coated, breathable nylon fabric. A choice of dungarees, trousers, jackets and bootees, all in great colours. Machine washable with velcro leg and arm fastenings.

Little Trekkers   01484 868 321
www.littletrekkers.co.uk

Muddy Puddles   0870 420 4943
www.muddypuddles.com

Raindrops   01730 810 031
www.raindrops.co.uk

Welligogs   01785 662 277
www.welligogs.com

clothing: online/mail order

Aztec   020 8877 9954
www.aztecstore.com
Fun range of cotton knitwear and t-shirts with embroidered tractors, strawberries etc.

Mini Boden   0845 677 5000
www.boden.co.uk
Great range of everyday, practical clothing for babies and children - especially their "pull-ups" - which makes getting dressed such a simple task.

Children's Warehouse   020 8752 1166
www.childrens-warehouse.com
Fresh, fun and appealing range of everyday clothing for children. Also nightwear, swimwear and school uniforms.

Cheeky B   020 8398 5595
www.cheekyb.co.uk
Children's clothes from 2yrs+. We like their ballerina cardigan and chiffon skirts for girls and the bermuda shorts for boys.

Clothes 4 Boys   **01420 520 677**
www.clothes4boys.co.uk
Online store that specialises in boys' clothing.

Cyrillus   **020 7734 6660**
www.cyrillus.com
Classic French catalogue for babies and children.

Groe Baby   **01258 452 175**
www.groebaby.co.uk
Stimulate your baby's eyesight and brain development by
wearing the right kind of T-shirt - that is, one of Groe Baby's
new designs with geometric swirls and stripes in eye-
smarting black on white.

Mitty James   **020 8693 5018**
www.mittyjames.com
Luxuriously soft towelling beach and holiday wear.

Nappy Head   **01582 573 630**
www.nappyhead.co.uk
Funky slogan baby wear with captions such as "Wipe My
Butt Sucker" and "My Daddy Rocks" offering parents an
alternative to the mainstream.

Pink Bamboo   **020 8874 8660**
www.pinkbamboo.com
This collection has an oriental influence and features
gorgeous appliqué, embroidered details, traditional Chinese
fastenings and bead and sequin trims. Pyjamas, dresses,
cardigans – wonderfully unique.

Schmidt Natural Clothing   **0845 345 0498**
www.naturalclothing.co.uk
Organic fairtrade clothing, washable nappies and bedliners.
Babies', children's and adults' underwear, slippers and
nightwear in soft cotton, merino wool and silk. Biodynamic
lambskins and soft toys. Sensitive skin specialists.

So Pretty   **020 7224 1166**
www.sopretty.co.uk
Contemporary fabrics combined with traditional English
designs - including smocked dresses, Harris tweed coats and
bonnets, silk tartan party dresses and cosy cashmere
cardigans - the height of luxury.

The Baby Closet   **020 7924 4457**
www.thebabycloset.co.uk
Selection of quality but lesser known items which are hand-
wrapped and despatched within 24 hrs of placing the order.

Tiny-Labels   **01952 585 640**
www.tiny-labels.co.uk
You can now buy last season's designer clothes at a fraction
of their retail prices via Tiny Labels. With easy online
navigation and a great range of clothes for 0-7yrs - you'll
definitely find a beautiful bargain. Brands include Cacherel,
Catimini, Miniman, DKNY etc

White Rabbit Clothing   **020 8440 3227**
www.whiterabbitclothing.com
Long-sleeved baby suits with an attached t-shirt overlay,
giving twice the layers with half the hassle - and no ride-up.

cribs, cots & first beds

All the following offer high-quality cots, cot-bed and
first beds. For standard cots with adjustable bases
we recommend looking at "nursery goods stores"
and see standard models on display. For new
mattresses see below

Babylist   **020 7371 5145**
The Broomhouse, 50 Sulivan Road, SW6 3DX
www.babylist.com
Babylist offers one of the largest ranges of cotbeds, including
many high quality brands sourced from around the world.
They come in all sorts of designs, as well as hand-painted or
in solid beech, oak or cherry. And you have the luxury of
looking at them all from the comfort of their SW6 showroom.

Babyworld   **01491 821 877**
babyworld.co.uk
Huge range of quality cribs, cots, cradles, hammocks and
mattresses from Global, Amby, Leander, Lindam, BabyDan
and Kaloo. Order online for fast delivery.

Bump   **020 7249 7000**
www.bumpstuff.com
Traditional Swedish cot-beds and beds.

Fun Beds   **01428 607 878**
www.funbeds.co.uk
Thomas the Tank Engine beds. Colour brochure available.

Simon Horn   **020 7731 1279**
117-121 Wandsworth Bridge Road, London
www.simonhorn.com
Hand-made wooden cots which transform into a bed then
a sofa.

The Children's   **020 7737 7303**
Furniture Company
www.thechildrensfurniturecompany.com
Award-winning range of beautiful hardwood and painted
furniture - beds and bunks.

The Natural Mat Company   **020 7985 0474**
99 Talbot Road, London
www.naturalmat.com
Stylish cribs, cots, beds and the best natural mattresses.

MATTRESSES
The Natural Mat Company   **020 7985 0474**
99 Talbot Road, London
www.naturalmat.com
The best range of baby mattresses on offer in 100% natural
materials and 100% safe. Standard sizes available as well as
made-to-measure.

Hippychick Bed Protector   **01278 434 440**
www.hippychick.com
Two layers of brushed cotton, sandwiching a waterproof
polyurethane layer.

department stores

Department stores are useful places, especially when it's bucketing outside. And with the recent changes at Selfridges, and refurbishment at Peter Jones, they're good for a quick nappy trip, major purchase or just a fun day out

Harrods 020 7730 1234
87-135 Brompton Road, SW1
www.harrods.com
A trip to Harrods wouldn't be complete without a visit to the ice-cream parlour, but for shopping head for the 4th floor where you will find the top of the range in nursery furniture, furnishings, fashion, toys, collectables and a kids' hair-dressing salon. Pushchair access, nappy changing facilities and play area.

John Lewis
278-306 Oxford Street, W1   020 7629 7711
Peter Jones, SW1   020 7730 3434
Brent Cross   020 8202 6535
Shopping Centre, NW4
www.johnlewis.com
Famed for their school uniform departments, the John Lewis stores offer a practical range of clothing and shoes, nursery equipment and toiletries. They also offer a good range of car seats, pushchairs, cots and highchairs. Pushchair access, nappy changing facility, play area.

Selfridges 020 7629 7711
400 Oxford Street, W1A 1EX
www.selfridges.com
Head for the 3rd floor Kids Universe to see fashion clothing, shoes and toys. Pushchair access, nappy changing facilities.

dressing up

No nursery toybox would be complete without a few dressing up clothes to extend the imagination and explore role play. Many of these suppliers manufacture in the UK and therefore you can be assured of good-quality fabrics and well made accessories. Kits are also provided so when you are required to make something for the school play you won't be letting the side down

MAIL ORDER
Charlie Crow 01782 417 133
www.charliecrow.co.uk

Frilly Lily 01666 510 055
www.frillylily.co.uk

Hopscotch Dressing 01483 813 728
Up Clothes
www.hopscotchdressingup.co.uk
Shop online for high quality children's fancy dress costumes and hats delivered to your door.

food organic

Despite the expense, feeding your baby on organic baby food whether pre-prepared or by organising organic home delivery, you can be assured that the residual level of pesticides is minimised. Below you will find a selection of organic box schemes that deliver across London.

The Soil Association 0117 929 0661
www.soilassociation.org
The main UK body which supervises the standard for UK organic produce and promotes organic farming. Check here for verifying the authenticity of labelling.

Farm Around 01748 821 116
www.farmaround.co.uk
Farm Around specializes in the weekly home delivery of assorted selections of organic fruit and vegetables. They also have a useful selection of recipes to give you some seasonal inspiration.

Abel & Cole 0845 626 262
www.abel-cole.co.uk

Riverford Home Delivery 020 7738 5076
www.riverford.co.uk

Fresh Food Company 020 8749 8778
www.freshfood.co.uk

Bumble Bee 020 7607 1936
www.bumblebee.co.uk

Organic Delivery Company 020 7739 8181
www.organicdelivery.co.uk

ORGANIC BABY FOOD BRANDS
Baby Organix 0800 393 511
www.babyorganix.co.uk
Organic baby and toddler food.

Babylicious 020 8998 4189
www.babylicious.co.uk

Fresh Daisy Organic Babyfood 0870 240 7028
www.daisyfoods.com

Little Dish 020 7313 9845
www.littledish.co.uk
Fresh, healthy food for children aged 1-5yrs, just like you'd cook at home. Available on Ocado.com or at select Waitrose and Tesco stores nationwide.

Truuuly Scrumptious Organic 01761 239 300
Baby Food
www.bathorganicbabyfood.co.uk
Award-winning frozen organic baby and toddler food, just like homemade. For details of home delivery or a list of stockists see website or phone for details.

garden toys

With childhood being lost to hand-held gameboys and television, these companies encourage a return to good old-fashioned unsupervised fun. So if you're redeveloping your garden or house this year, why not allocate some of your budget towards imaginative and physical play

Great Little Trading Co   0870 860 6000
www.gltc.co.uk
Impressive range of activity toys and furniture for babies and children. Excellent catalogue of hundreds of items - many exclusive.

Loddon Valley Garden Toys   01256 473 546
www.lvgt.co.uk
Leading brands of garden play equipment for all your family, including swings, slides, climbing frames, wooden playsets, sandpits, trampolines and more.

gifts

Babylist   020 7371 5145
The Broomhouse, 50 Sulivan Road, SW6 3DX
www.babylist.com
Wonderful hand-embroidered range of clothing from Dimples, or Babylist's own range of smocked nighties. Babylist also offers a wish list service to clients who come in for full consultations, where clients can choose their own list of gifts which are made available to friends and family to purchase.

Bouquet Bouquet   01489 790 562
www.bouquetbouquet.co.uk
Beautiful bouquets of organic cotton baby clothes as well as gifts for babies and their parents. Organic and gorgeous!

Cuddle Pie Baby Gifts   020 8455 6991
www.cuddlepieretail.co.uk
www.cuddlepie.co.uk
Great selection of baby gifts made from the softest material, including unique height charts, soft toys, book ends etc. Stocked in Fortnum & Mason and other quality gift shops - or buy online. See their new range of kids' armchairs.

Especially Made for Me   0870 410 4173
www.especiallymadeforme.co.uk
Perfectly personalised gifts for any occasion; gift hampers, children's writing books and reward charts.

Natural Mat Company   020 7985 0474
99 Talbot Road, W11 2AT
www.naturalmat.com
Fun and colourful gifts for all occasions. Gift wrap service available in store.

Timecapsule Gifts   0113 274 9723
www.timecapsulegifts.co.uk
A unique newborn gift idea, it will capture all the happy memories from that special day and keep them alive forever!

For a brochure call 020 8871 1472 or buy online at www.bonne-nuit.co.uk

hairdressers

Angela Conway   01883 347 967
Home haircuts for adults and children in Clapham, Balham, Brixton, Dulwich and Wimbledon.

Cosmos   020 8995 9071
265 Chiswick High Road, W4 4PU

Daisy & Tom   020 7352 5000
181 King's Road, SW3 5EB

Hairloom   020 7736 5923
111 Munster Road, SW6 5EB
Children's haircuts for £6.95 during the week and £8.50 on Saturdays.

Harrods (Urban Retreat)   020 7730 1234
87-135 Brompton Road, SW1X 7XL
Children's haircuts for £20.

Headways   020 8995 9107
7 Chiswick Terrace, Acton Lane, W4 5LY

Hopes & Dreams   020 7833 9388
339-341 City Road, EC1V 1LJ
www.hopesanddreams.co.uk

Little Nippers   020 8293 4444
Plaza Arcade, 135 Vanbrugh Hill, Greenwich, SE10

Mini Kin   020 8341 6898
22 Broadway Parade, Crouch End, N8 9DE
Children's cuts from £10.95.

Patricia   020 8747 3045
Have your hair, your husband's hair and your children's hair cut at home by Patricia in W4.

The Little Trading Co   020 8742 3152
7 Bedford Corner, The Avenue, W4 1LD

Trotters
127 Kensington High St, W8   020 7937 9373
34 King's Road, SW3 4UD   020 7259 9620

Yummy Tots   020 8891 4678
6 Crown Road, St Margarets, TW1

linens and sleeping bags

Bonne Nuit   020 8871 1472
www.bonne-nuit.co.uk
Beautiful French baby sleeping bags, pyjamas and linen.

Comfort Blankets   020 8302 6510
www.comfortblankets.co.uk
Comfort blankets made from fleece and edged in satin, in a range of funky designs.

Hippychick   01278 434 440
www.hippychick.com
100% natural cotton fleece baby blankets in a wonderful array of colours.

Cuski International   0845 166 2906
www.cuski.co.uk
A natural cotton blanket comforter.

Damask   020 7731 3553
www.damask.co.uk
Luxury range of traditional nightwear – particularly their embroidered nighties which are available from Peter Jones.

Fig   020 7884 1312
www.figchildrensnightwear.co.uk
Children's classic nightwear from 12mths to teenagers.

Grobag   0870 606 0276
www.grobag.com

Libella Bedwear   0065 985 758 10
www.libellabedwear.com
Fine 100% cotton pyjamas for children and adults (matching sets available).

Natural Mat Company   020 7985 0474
99 Talbot Road, W11 2AT
Organic cotton sleeping bags and 2-part cotton combi sleeping bags. Pure cotton and flannelette sheets, duvet covers, pillow cases and mattress protectors. Colourful and stylish lambswool blankets and soft, unbleached cotton blankets. Soft lambskin fleeces for cots, prams, strollers and car seats. All 100% natural and ideal for your baby's delicate skin.

The White Company
0870 900 9555
www.thewhiteco.com
Classic range of white nursery linens, plaid blankets, PJs and accessories. Two shops in SW3 and one in W1.

The Nursery Company
020 8878 5167
www.nurserycompany.co.uk
Baby sleeping bags, covered coat hangers, quilts, bumpers, blankets and nightwear.

lotions and potions (natural)

If you are looking for something a little more special than the supermarket standards, all these suppliers offer an organic, additive- and SLS- free alternative

Barefoot Botanicals
0870 220 2273
www.barefootuk.com
Good-quality natural skincare including an SOS Skin Rescue Bath Oil with lavender, neroli and chamomile.

Bodywise (UK) Natracare
01179 823 492
www.natracare.com
Organic and natural baby toiletries and tampons.

E45 Junior
www.e45.com
Dermatologist- and paediatrician-approved. Developed for children with dry, sensitive skin or eczema. Available from all leading supermarkets and pharmacies.

Earth Friendly Baby
020 8424 8844
www.earthfriendlybaby.co.uk
This is a range of high-quality products that use natural plant-based ingredients with no artificial colouring or synthetic fragrances. Their range includes Lavender cleansing bar, Chamomile Shampoo, Calendular Daily Cream and Red Clover Nappy Cream. Available from Sainsburys, Green Baby and other health shops across the UK - or online at their own website.

Green Baby
020 7359 7037
www.greenbabyco.com
Natural baby toiletries and baby massage oils.

Green People
0870 240 1444
www.greenpeople.co.uk
Organic range of products developed for children with sensitive skins.

Little Miracles
020 7435 5555
www.littlemiracles.co.uk
A special range of flower remedies, developed by Serena Helene Smith over the last 12 years, to treat children's behavioural problems such as anxiety, lack of concentration or for the 'terrible twos' tantrums. With names such as Braveheart (for anxiety), Short Fuse (toddler tantrums) - and customer's testimonials - they are worth a closer look.

Neal's Yard Remedies
32 Blackheath Village, SE3 — 020 8318 6655
6 Northcote Road, SW11 — 020 7627 1949
15 Neal's Yard, Covent Garden — 020 7379 7222

9 Elgin Crescent, W11 — 020 7727 3998
Chelsea Farmers Market, SW3 — 020 7351 6380
68 Chalk Farm Road, NW1 — 020 7284 2039
Aromatherapy, homeopathy and herbal remedies plus a natural beauty range.

Smilechild
01242 269 635
www.smilechild.co.uk
Earth Friendly Baby, Badger, Faith in Nature brands offered as well as natural toothbrushes and sponges (includes natural lice products).

Verde
020 7720 1100
www.verde.co.uk
Mother and baby range. 16 products including Extra Rich Stretch Mark Oil, Chamomile Baby Body Balm, Bizzy Kids Bathtime Soother, Lice Repel Lotion.

maternity wear

RETAIL SHOPS
9 London
020 7352 7600
8 Hollywood Road, SW10 9HY

Blooming Marvellous
725 Fulham Road, SW6 3LE — 020 7371 0500
5 Bellevue Road, SW17 — 0845 458 7435
www.bloomingmarvellous.co.uk
This is one of the UK's favourite maternity brands that offers stylish and affordable maternity wear, both everyday essentials as well as evening and smart occasion pieces. They also have a fantastic catalogue with a great range of baby clothing and nursery products.

Blossom Mother & Child
020 7589 7500
164 Walton Street, SW3 2JL
www.blossommotherandchild.com
A new dimension in luxury maternity wear and lingerie. Includes own brand ready-to-wear, denim and lingerie as well as a mixture of non-maternity wear from established designers such as Matthew Williamson, Temperly, Issa and many others. Blossom also features its exclusive denim bar which includes the hottest designer jeans customised exclusively by Blossom for pregnancy.

Formes
28 Henrietta Street, WC2 8NA   **020 7240 4777**
313 Brompton Road, SW3 2DY   **020 7584 3337**
33 Brook Street, W1K 4HJ   **020 7493 2783**
66 Rosslyn Hill, Richford Street, NW3   **020 7431 7770**

Great Expectations   **020 7581 4886**
78 Fulham Road, SW3 6HH

JoJo Maman Bébé
3 Ashbourne Parade,   **020 8731 8961**
1259 Finchley Road, NW11
68 Northcote Road, SW11   **020 7228 0322**
80 Turnham Green Terrace, W4   **020 8994 0379**
30 The Exchange, Putney, SW15   **020 8780 5165**
www.jojomamanbebe.co.uk
A great brand for maternity wear, including 5 styles of
maternity jeans, their popular breastfeeding tops, occasion
and evening wear. They also stock nursery furniture,
essential nursery goods and a great range of French-inspired
baby clothing as well as toys and gifts.

La Conception   **020 7228 7498**
46 Webbs Road, SW11 6SF
www.laconception.com
Maternity wear that speaks for itself. Also children's wear
0-4yrs. Gifts for christenings, births and new mums.

Mamas & Papas   **0870 830 7700**
256-258 Regent Street, W1B 3AF
www.mamasandpapas.co.uk
Maternity Wear features everything a mum-to-be needs from
office to home, weekends to special occasions, sleeping to
swimming. Each collection interprets the seasonal trend on
catwalks and high street giving style and quality without
having to pay designer prices.

The Maternity Co.   **020 8995 4455**
42 Chiswick Lane, W4 2JQ
www.thematernityco.com
A refreshing look at maternity fashion! The search for
fashionable maternity wear stops here.

Mums 2 Be   **020 8332 6506**
3 Mortlake Terrace, Mortlake Road, Kew, TW9
157 Lower Richmond Road, SW15   **020 8789 0329**
119 Revelstoke Road, SW15   **020 8879 3467**
www.mums2be.co.uk
For all your fashion needs during pregnancy.

PUSH Maternity   **020 7359 2003**
9 Theberton Street, Islington, N1 0QY

Séraphine   **020 7937 3156**
28 Kensington Church Street, W8 2JQ
www.seraphine.com
Designer maternity wear and everything to set up your baby's
nursery, including layettes and nursery collections. Also
available by mail order and online tel 0870 609 2602.

maternity wear: online

9 Months and More   **01295 738 179**
www.9mandm.com
Offering a stylish collection of maternity and baby clothes (0-
24 months) that has been designed for you to look and feel
fantastic in, during and after pregnancy. Their online shop
offers everything from pre-natal products, elegantly designed
maternity wear, newborn essentials to beautiful outfits, gifts
and nursing wear for new mums.

Aphrodite Maternity Swimwear   **01202 311 289**
www.aphrodite-designs.com
Aphrodite specialises in producing comfortable swimwear
using innovative designs specially for pregnant women.

Arabella B   **020 7378 1688**
www.arabellaB.com
The Arabella B maternity collection has sexy, floaty styles to
show off your bump. Wholesale and retail (by private
appointment or online).

Blooming Marvellous   **020 8748 0025**
www.bloomingmarvellous.co.uk
A great range of maternity wear, nursery goods and toys
available from this well-known mail-order catalogue and
online store.

Brides n Bumps   **01252 377 725**
www.bridesnbumps.com
This website is not to be missed if you have your wedding
planned in the middle of your pregnancy. Made-to-measure
wedding dresses, bridesmaid dresses and evening gowns.
Based in Farnborough they take private appointments only.

Crave Maternity   **0870 240 547**
www.cravematernity.co.uk
Crave Maternity offers a stylish range of nearly 50 high-quality
complementary separates, from chic day wear to funky or
formal office styles and glamorous evening options.

Funky Mama   **020 7622 7564**
www.funkymama.co.uk
Contemporary range of maternity t-shirts with "Don't Push -
That's my Job" as well as other captions.

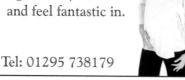

Isabella Oliver 0870 240 7612
www.IsabellaOliver.com
Isabella Oliver's collection for pregnant women who love clothes. Fabulous, flattering, sexy. Gift-wrapped at www.IsabellaOliver.com or 0870 240 7612.

Long Tall Sally 020 8649 9009
www.longtallsally.com
Maternity jeans for the long-legged. Secure online shopping.

Mamas & Papas 0870 830 7700
www.mamasandpapas.co.uk
Stylish collection of maternity clothes and maternity underwear (white, black and grey marl) as well as black hosiery.

Melba Clothing 020 8347 8811
www.melbaclothing.com
Fabulous, functional maternity wear for stylish mums-to-be.

The Maternity Co. 020 8995 4455
www.thematernityco.com
A refreshing look at maternity fashion. The search for fashionable maternity wear stops here.

Tiffany Rose Maternity 0870 420 8144
www.tiffanyrosematernity.com
For fun and glamorous maternity fashion.

maternity bra specialists

Body Comfort   020 8459 2910
www.maternitybras.co.uk
Mail-order company supplying a good range of maternity & nursing bras.

Bravado   020 7738 9121
www.bravadodesigns.com

Bravissimo
www.bravissimo.com
Offering lingerie for D-JJ cup sizes, swimwear and nursing bras. Also a mail-order catalogue.

Bresona   01624 670 380
www.9monthsplus.com
Bresona manufactures the largest selection of maternity/breast-feeding clothes on the internet and has a policy of manufacturing primarily in natural fibres.

Figleaves   0800 279 2557
www.figleaves.com
Possibly the best online and mail order catalogue for lingerie shopping. All brands, all sizes stocked and delivered.

Mothernature   0161 485 7359
www.mothernaturebras.co.uk
Comfortable pregnancy and breastfeeding bras.

magazines

Angels & Urchins   020 7603 13666
www.angelsandurchins.co.uk
London-based family lifestyle magazine published quarterly.

Baby & Toddler Gear   0870 262 6900
www.babyandtoddlergear.co.uk
Biannual specialising in in-depth product reviews, price comparisons and detailed fabric swatches.

Bumps & Babies (NCT)   0870 444 8707
www.nctpregnancyandbabycare.com
A free publication given out to new members of the NCT and at some ante-natal checks at 20 weeks.

Families Magazine   020 8696 9680
www.familiesmagazine.co.uk
Free monthly magazine covering London (South West, South East, East etc and the Thames Valley).

Junior Magazine   01858 438 874
www.juniormagazine.co.uk

Mother & Baby Magazine   01733 555 161
Bestselling monthly magazine with good advice, product reviews and reader experiences.

Parents Directory Publications   01243 527 605
Produced quarterly and distributed throughout London (editions are South West London, North West London and Central London).

"They really are the best maternity jeans around. They fit perfectly and are so, so comfortable."

Fashion editor, Marie Claire

The complete collection for nine months attitude.

Find it at www.seraphine.com

Brochure from 0870 609 2602

London store
28 Kensington Church St W8

Séraphine
maman et bébé

Practical Parenting   01444 475 675
From pregnancy to early childhood.

Pregnancy & Birth   020 7347 1800
www.pregnancyandbirth.co.uk

Prima Baby   01858 438 838
www.primababy.co.uk

Right Start   020 7878 2336
Produced in association with Tumble Tots for parents with
children aged 6mths-7yrs. Comes out 6 times a year.

murals

Cow Jumped Over the Moon   020 8883 0888
www.thecowjumpedoverthemoon.co.uk
Beautiful children's murals, paintings to order and hand-
painted furniture.

ELJ Design   07958 646 113
www.eljdesign.co.uk
Bespoke mural design and painting of old and new nursery
furniture.

Viv Howard   020 7737 4276
www.transformations.decor.org.uk
Hand-painted murals, furniture, paintings and paint effects.

Respisense™ is the **world's first** super-safe, perfectly portable infant breathing monitor with proactive response. The revolutionary invention is so small and light that it can be used **wherever baby may fall asleep**.

An audible **alarm** alerts the nearest caregiver when no breathing effort is detected for longer than 20 seconds. Also built-in is the unique **TummyTickle™ breathing stimulator** that gently rouses the baby to resume breathing before sounding the alarm, allowing an **instantaneous response** to unsafe periods of inactivity.

The **ingenious design** eliminates all cables, straps, glue and spent batteries that pose dangers to young explorers. Each unit is completely **maintenance free** and runs a self-test routine every time it is activated. The **Respisense™ Buzz** breathing effort monitor is recommended for babies up to six months old, to help guard against apnoea of prematurity, cot death and other life threatening events.

Telephone/Credit card sales 01252 658408

See more at **www.baby2bed.com**

monitors

A monitor is a must-have as soon as you decide to move the baby out of your own bedroom or would like the comfort of seeing and hearing your baby when you are not in the room. The sound and movement monitors are surprisingly inexpensive and good value for money

Bosie Boo   **01252 775 430**
www.bosieboo.com

Lindam   **08701 118 118**
www.lindam.co.uk

Philips Digital   **020 8781 8699**
www.philips.com/babycare

Respisense   **01252 658 408**
www.baby2bed.com
Respisense is the world's first super-safe, perfectly portable infant breathing effort monitor with proactive response. The award-winning and patented invention is so compact and light that it can be used wherever baby may fall asleep.

Tommee Tippee   **0500 979 899**
www.tommeetippee.com

Tomy   **02380 622 600**
www.tomy.co.uk

name tapes

Iron on, stick on and peel & press are all the rage. These suppliers still do the traditional embroidered name tapes as well as shoe stickers, bag tags and tapes that go on plastic (and in the dishwasher) so that you will no longer be left with six lids and only three beakers

Easy 2 Name   **01635 298 326**
www.easy2name.com
Suppliers of dishwasher-proof stickers and iron-on tapes. We like the white transfer nametapes which are perfect for dark-coloured socks.

nappies, cloth

There is now a huge range of cotton nappies available and many websites helping you select the most suitable design for your baby and lifestyle

WRAP   01983 401 959
www.nappyline.org.uk
The real nappy helpline, offering support and information to parents looking to use real nappies, as well as listing all the council-run incentive schemes (eg free starter packs, free laundry trials).

MANUFACTURERS
Bambino Mio   01604 883 777
www.bambino.co.uk
Cotton nappies which come in 3 different sizes, with a range of nappy covers, biodegradable liners and wipes, and swim nappies.

Cotton Bottoms   0500 979 899
www.cottonbottoms.co.uk
Easy-to-use, two-piece cotton nappy system.

Kushies   0870 120 2018
www.thebabycatalogue.com
All-in-one washable nappy made with 7 layers of cotton flannelette. It has an integrated waterproof layer so no need for wraps. Infant and toddler sizes with great outer wrap designs.

OneLife   01736 799 512
www.teamlollipop.co.uk
This OneLife cotton nappy is stylishly packaged and very similar to the Motherease brand.

Tots Bots   0141 550 1514
www.totsbots.com
Highly rated and award-winning shaped cotton nappies made from fluffy towelling with velcro fastenings and elasticated legs.

Yummies   01273 672 632
www.yummiesnappies.co.uk
Yummies makes cotton nappies and accessories. "An easy to put on pre-fold" is one mum's comment.

ADVICE & RETAILERS
The Buzzness   01280 841 262
www.thebuzzness.co.uk
Online retailer of a good range of washable nappies, wraps and natural baby products.

Green Baby Company   020 7226 9244
www.greenbaby.co.uk
Specialists in natural fibres, good for conscientious parents - offering a wide range of machine-washable cotton nappy styles as well as the traditional terries.

Little Green Earthlets   0870 162 4462
www.earthlets.co.uk
Specialising in eco-friendly baby products, including Moltex disposables and Motherease.

Nappies Online   01202 768 070
www.nappiesonline.co.uk
This site sells leading brands of washable nappies, plus offers lots of advice.

Naturally Nappies   0845 1664716
www.naturallynappies.com
They stock all major brands except those they don't consider up to scratch. You can try before you buy which is the key to getting the right fit for your baby.

Naturebotts   0845 226 2186
www.naturebotts.co.uk
An eco-friendly disposable nappy (Moltex Oko) that's kinder to baby and the environment. Via mail order; call for a free sample.

Plush Pants Cloth Nappies   01865 408 040
www.plushpants.com
Nappies, wraps, accessories, and treats for mum too. They also run a nappy trial scheme, hiring items for a week or two so that you can get used to using washable nappies and the ones you like most.

The Nappy Lady   0845 456 2441
www.thenappylady.co.uk
If you need advice before choosing your cotton nappy then the Nappy Lady has lots on offer including eco-disposables.

Twinkle Twinkle   0118 934 2120
www.twinkleontheweb.co.uk
Free advice on choosing washable nappies, and a huge range of nappies and supporting products in stock.

nappy laundry

Nappy Express   020 8361 4040
www.nappyexpress.co.uk

Number 1 for Nappies   07951 687 730
www.numberonefornappies.co.uk

nappies: disposable

Asda Baby
Price 12p per nappy. A good all-round nappy for value, fit and absorbancy (some say virtually leak-free), and the softest disposable on the market. But also half the price of the leading brands.

Huggies Newborn
Price 12p per nappy. The most absorbant nappy on the market, and with its stretchy waistband and curved leg elastic there are simply no leaks. The sizes cover Newborns, Active Babies 3mths+ and Toddlers 10mths+. They also do Little Swimmers swim nappies (essential).

Moltex OKO
Price 21p per nappy. Although more expensive than some other brands, if you buy them in bulk from suppliers such as Smilechild, you can significantly save on the pack cost.

Pampers Active Fit
www.pampers.com
Price 21p per nappy. Good shaped nappy with sticky
fastenings. The range includes New Baby, Active Fit and
Baby Dry. Good Easy Up Pants which have clever tear-away
sides for toddlers who won't lie down.

Safeway Baby Wriggler
www.safeway.co.uk
Price 9p per nappy (the cheapest on the market currently).
Not brilliant on absorbancy through the night – but great
through the day with active babies.

Tesco Unisex
Price 13p per nappy. Winning top marks for absoption from
Mumsnet reviewers - and particularly good for skinny babies
as they have a stretchy waistband, soft, elasticated legs but
at a better price than the rest.

Tushies
www.tushies.co.uk
Price 25p per nappy. An American range of gel-free
disposable nappies and alcohol-free wipes. They use a
cotton and non-chlorine bleached wood pulp so are highly
absorbant - but very expensive and shipped from the US - so
we're not totally convinced of their eco-friendly status.

nearly new

It is amazing how quickly your children will grow out of
both essential and everyday items. Depending on how
much space you have, or whether you are planning a
second baby, it is possible to claw back some of your
upfront investment at these nearly new shops

Boomerang   020 7610 5232
69 Blythe Road, W14 0HP
www.boomerang-online.co.uk

Merry Go Round   020 7737 6452
21 Half Moon Lane, SE24 9JU

Merry-Go-Round   020 8985 6308
22 Clarence Road, E5

Little Trading Company   020 8742 3152
7 Bedford Corner, The Avenue, W4 1LD

Pixies   020 8995 1568
14 Fauconberg Road, W4 3JY

Little Angel Xchange   020 8340 8003
249 Archway Road, N6
www.littleangelxchange.co.uk

Simply Outgrown   020 8801 0568
360 Lordship Lane, N17

The Rocking Horse   020 8542 4666
600 Kingston Road, SW20

Yummy Tots   020 8891 4678
6 Crown Road, St Margarets, TW1
www.yummytots.com

nursery furniture & interiors

INTERIORS

Baby Blinds   07836 770 880
www.babyblinds.com
Babyblinds.com is a one stop shopping experience for
parents and babies who like to sleep. They supply made to
measure bespoke Blackout blinds. Choose prints and
colours that stimulate your baby, and create a stylishly
comfortable and happy environment for her or him to relax
and sleep in. Their blind Styles range from Roller, Roman,
Pleated, Wood, Metal Venetian and Velux Skylights with
various baby safe options, such as cord and chain tidy
lengths, cleats, and electric controls. For a fully
comprehensive shopping experience visit
www.babyblinds.com.

Ecos Organic Paints   0845 345 7725
www.ecopaints.co.uk
When decorating your baby's room do consider using eco-
friendly paints, which are made from natural and organic
materials. Free from petrochemical solvents, pesticides, acrylics,
alkyds, vinyls or synthetic colours they reduce the carbon
emissions in your home by up to 30kg. They are easily tolerated
by allergy sufferers and any waste can simply be composted.

The Nesting Company   020 7371 2717
www.thenestingcompany.com
Interior design service creating and installing stylish and
contemporary nurseries that fit perfectly into your home.

RETAIL SHOPS

JoJo Maman Bébé
3 Ashbourne Parade,
1259 Finchley Road, NW11   020 8731 8961
68 Northcote Road, SW11   020 7228 0322
80 Turnham Green Terrace, W4   020 8994 0379
30 The Exchange, Putney, SW15   020 8780 5165
www.jojomamanbebe.co.uk
A great brand for nursery furniture, essential nursery goods, a
great range of French-inspired baby clothing as well as toys
and gifts.

NW3
Humla   020 7794 7877
13 Flask Walk, NW3

NW8
St John's Wood Interiors   020 7722 9204
27 St John's Wood High Street, NW8 7NH
A range of hand-painted nursery furniture including cots and
beds, toy chests etc.

Mark Wilkinson   020 7586 9579
41 St John's Wood High Street, NW8 7NJ

SW3
Daisy & Tom   020 7352 5000
181 King's Road, SW3
www.daisyandtom.com

Dragons of Walton Street 020 7589 3795
23 Walton Street, SW3 2HX
www.dragonsofwaltonstreet.com
Dragons offers a full interior design service alongside a unique range of hand-painted and hardwood furniture in both traditional and contemporary styles. They also display a large range of accessories and fabrics in this wonderful shop.

The Nursery Window 020 7581 3358
83 Walton Street, SW3 2HP
www.nurserywindow.co.uk
Exclusive accessories, fabrics, wallpapers, bedding and furniture in this great little shop. They also have a good selection of items to give as gifts.

SW6
Babylist 020 7371 5145
The Broomhouse, 50 Sulivan Road, SW6 3DX
www.babylist.com
Established over 10 years ago, the Babylist is a tailored service for parents wanting to find quality furniture for their children - without the hassle of traipsing around London at 6 months pregnant. Their furniture range includes all UK brands plus many more sourced all over the world. You need to book an appointment, but parents come from all over London to have their every need catered for.

Blue Lemon 020 7610 9464
160 Munster Road, SW6 5RA

Simon Horn 0207 736 1754
117-121 Wandsworth Bridge Road, SW6 2TP
www.simonhorn.com
Superb quality furniture for children that will last for generations. Their design enables you to use the furniture initially as a cot, then a bed. They also make co-ordinating wardrobes, chests etc in hardwoods.

SW8
Lilliput 020 7720 5554
255-259 Queenstown Road, SW8 3NP
www.lilliput.com
Great range of high-quality nursery furniture on display, including cribs, cots, beds, wardrobes, chests and changing units all laid out in room sets with co-ordinating linens, pillows and duvets.

SW15
Chic Shack 020 8785 7777
77 Lower Richmond Road, SW15 1ET
www.chicshack.net

W4
Red Studio 020 8994 7770
12a Spring Grove, W4 3NH

W8
Séraphine 0870 609 2602
28 Kensington Church Street, W8 4EP
www.seraphine.com
Nursery furniture, maternity wear and layette collections.

W11
Natural Mat Company 020 7985 0474
99 Talbot Road, W11
www.naturalmat.com
Stylish cribs, cots and beds and the very best natural mattresses.

MAIL ORDER & ONLINE
Aspace 01985 301 222
www.aspaceuk.com
A range of children's beds, wardrobes, chests of drawers, etc, with a few linen items and accessories.

Billie Bond Designs 01245 360 164
Warners Farm, Howe Street, CM3 1BL
www.billiebond.co.uk
Specialists in children's hand-painted toy boxes. Also offers personalised gifts such as hairbrushes, stools and door plaques.

The Children's 020 7737 7303
Furniture Company
www.thechildrensfurniturecompany.com
Beautiful hardwood and painted furniture - beds, bunks, chests, toyboxes, wardrobes, bookcases and much more.

lionwitchwardrobe 020 8318 2070
www.lionwitchwardrobe.co.uk
Hand-crafted contemporary furniture for style-conscious parents and their children.

nursery goods

NURSERY ADVISORY SERVICES

You can choose to shop without actually having to set foot on a pavement. All by appointment only

Babylist   **020 7371 5145**
The Broomhouse, 50 Sulivan Road, SW6 3DX
www.babylist.com
You can purchase all your nursery goods from Babylist, whether that's a cot, car seat, buggy or simply a babgro. And it's delivered directory to your home at a time convenient to you. You can try out many of the brands in their SW6 showroom and visit again when the baby is 6mths old to stock up on the next range of items required.

Baby Concierge   **020 8964 5500**
Studio 109, 300 Kensal Road, W10 5BE
www.babyconcierge.co.uk
One-to-one expert advice on what you do and don't need. High street prices. All major brands and many more exclusive ones. New London showroom open 10am-6pm Mon-Fri and by appointment weekends and evenings.

RETAIL

For Mothercare and John Lewis stores please see later.

NORTH LONDON

Green Baby Company   020 7226 4345
345 Upper Street, N1 0PD
www.greenbabyco.com
Baby equipment, linens, furniture, eco-friendly clothing,
reusable nappies and gifts.

Just Babies   020 7482 2500
38 & 46 Malden Road, Kentish Town, NW5
Enormous range of high-quality nursery goods from all
leading manufacturers (Silver Cross, Mamas & Papas,
Quinny, Stokke etc), as well as nursery furniture and bedding,
rocking horses, electric-powered toddler cars, wooden toys
and doll's houses.

Rub A Dub Dub   020 8342 9898
15 Park Road, Crouch End, N8 8TE
Linens, shoes, clothes and reusable nappies.

All Seasons Nursery Shop   020 8445 6314
654-656 High Road, Finchley, N12

Totland   020 8808 3466
4 Bruce Grove, N17
Baby equipment stockist including cots, prams, pushchairs
and general baby goods.

London Nursery Supplies   020 8889 3003
Hardy Passage, Berners Road, N22

Infantasia   020 8889 1494
103 Wood Green Shopping Centre, N22
www.infantasia.co.uk
Stockists of a wide range of baby equipment including cots,
pushchairs (and pushchair repairs).

NORTH WEST LONDON

Babies R Us   020 8209 0019
Tilling Road, NW2

Bush Babes   020 8203 2111
Fiveways Corner, Watford Way, NW7

Just Babies   020 7916 8762
38-46 Malden Road, Kentish Town, NW5

Mamas & Papas   0870 830 7700
Brent Cross Shopping Centre, Brent Park, Tilling Road, NW2

Yummy Kids   020 8201 8870
1-2 Russel Parade, Golders Green Road, NW11

EAST LONDON

Baby This n Baby That   020 8524 0009
26 Station Road, North Chingford, E4 7BE

Freedman at Salters   020 8472 2892
17-19 Barking Road, East Ham, E6

Kiddi Centre   020 8809 4251
147 Clapton Common, E5

London Prams   020 7720 5554
175-179 East India Dock Road, Poplar, E14

SOUTH EAST LONDON

Babies R Us   020 7732 7322
760 Old Kent Road, SE15

Goldilocks   020 7231 8550
214 Jamaica Road, SE16

Kindercare   020 7703 0488
207 Walworth Road, SE17

SOUTH WEST LONDON

Conran Shop   020 7589 7401
81 Fulham Road, SW3

Daisy & Tom   020 7349 5810
181-183 King's Road, SW3 5EB
www.daisyandtom.com
Daisy & Tom offers a good range of high-quality nursery furniture, and many other practical nursery goods via a personalised shopping service. This Chelsea store is a Mecca for discerning mums and dads - and there is a wonderful fairground carousel to keep children entertained.

Babylist   020 7371 5145
The Broomhouse, 50 Sulivan Road, SW6 3DX
www.babylist.com
By appointment only. You can buy all your nursery goods from the comfort of this Fulham showroom with a personal advisor helping you select only the things you need.

Lilliput   020 7720 5554
255-259 Queenstown Road, SW8
www.lilliput.com
Perfect for all South London mums as this store has the full range of nursery furniture laid out in room sets, as well as prams and pushchairs that you can try out. They also advise on car seats and how to install them correctly. Friendly staff and prices that compete with many online stores.

Greater Tomorrow   020 7737 5276
80 Atlantic Road, SW9

WEST & CENTRAL LONDON

Baby Boom 2000   01895 675 596

Green Baby   020 7792 8140
5 Elgin Crescent, W11 2JA
www.greenbaby.co.uk

Mamas & Papas   0870 830 7700
256-258 Regent Street, W1B 3AF
www.mamasandpapas.co.uk
Mamas & Papas creates the dream nursery look, whether that be something nostalgic and traditional or modern and linear. Each collection is carefully crafted in the best materials to guarantee that every piece offers a great investment for years to come. As each nursery set is made from solid wood, Mamas & Papas offer a Deliver & Build service that bring your dream nursery to your door, construct and position the pieces where and how you want them to be, then remove all packaging for recycling.

Natural Mat Company   020 7985 0474
99 Talbot Road, W11
www.naturalmat.com
An exclusive range of nursery furniture, linen and fine wool blankets, as well as natural clothing, toys and accessories.

Mamas & Papas   0870 830 7700
256-258 Regent Street, W1B 3AF
www.mamasandpapas.co.uk
Mamas & Papas nursery equipment ranges are always expanding to include chic reflections of contemporary interior design for their high chairs, incorporating the latest technology to educate or entertain baby and created with the plushest fabrics available to make baby comfortable and happy.

W J Daniel   020 8567 6789
132 138 Uxbridge Road, W13

Young Smarties   020 7723 6519
64 Edgware Road, W2 2EH

MOTHERCARE STORES

448 Holloway Road, N7	020 7607 0915
38-40 High Road, N22	020 8888 6920
Brent Cross Shopping Centre, NW4	020 8202 5377
115 High Street North, E6	020 8472 4948
33-34 The Mall, E15	020 8534 5714
146 High Street, SE9	020 8859 7957
41 Riverdale High Street, SE13	020 8852 2167
2 Aylesham Centre, SE15	020 7358 0093
Surrey Quays, SE16	020 7237 2025
62 Powis Street, SE18	020 8854 3540
316 North End Road, SW6	020 7381 6387
416 Brixton Road, SW9	020 7733 1494
71 St John's Road, SW11	020 7228 0391
14-16 High Street, SW17	020 8862 3947
461 Oxford Street, W1	020 7629 6621
1-8 The Broadway, W5	020 8579 6181
26 Kings Mall Shopping, W6	020 8741 0514
64 The Broadway, W13	020 8567 7067

www.mothercare.com

John Lewis
279-306 Oxford Street   **020 7629 7711**
Peter Jones, Sloane Square   **020 7730 3434**
Brent Cross Shopping Centre   **020 8202 6535**
www.johnlewis.com

nursery goods: online

Babyworld   **01491 821 877**
www.babyworld.co.uk
The UK's most efficient and well set-out online store, with customer reviews and articles to help you choose which are the most relevant products for your needs. Good delivery and stock levels. Full range of nursery furniture, prams, pushchairs, accessories etc.

Blooming Marvellous   **0845 458 7408**
www.bloomingmarvellous.co.uk
A well-established catalogue and online srvice providing a large range of everyday maternity basics, baby and children's clothing, as well as nursery goods, furniture, lots of really useful everyday items, accessories, toys and gifts.

e-niko   **01768 210 121**
www.e-niko.co.uk
Huge range of products including imaginative toys in unusual designs, childrens bedroom furniture, French designed bed linen and much more. Some of their best-sellers include the colourful baby toys such as the balloon music box and My Little House. Lots of new things being added all the time.

Great Little Trading Company   **0870 850 6000**
www.gltc.co.uk
Hundreds of practical products designed to make your life as a parent a great deal easier - catalogue and online.

Hippychick   **01278 434 440**
www.hippychick.com
Innovative range of baby goods and accessories from this much loved brand of children's products.

JoJo Maman Bébé   **0870 241 0560**
www.jojomamanbebe.co.uk
A great brand for maternity wear, including 5 styles of maternity jeans, their popular breastfeeding tops, occasion and evening wear. They also stock nursery furniture, essential nursery goods and a great range of French-inspired baby clothing as well as toys and gifts.

Prince Lionheart   **0870 766 5197**
www.princelionheart.com
Established for over 30 years, Prince Lionheart has a range of innovative, high quality products designed to help you enjoy you new life with baby - from Slumber Bears and bebe PODS to Wipes, Warmers, Seatsavers and dishwasheer baskets. Don't miss their range of squidgy foam furniture guards to keep your little one safe in the home. Call for your local stockist or to request a catalogue.

Online Baby Store
www.onlinebabystore.co.uk
Prams and pushchairs at rock-bottom prices.

Special Baby   **01502 501 673**
www.specialbaby.co.uk
We offer a beautiful range of baby nursery and storage baskets with quality blue, pink and cream cotton gingham lining. Also introducing the wonderful new Felicity Floral selection, all made with superb white or cream wicker to include storage sets, nursery units, laundry baskets, shoppers, ottomans, trunks and more.Treat someone special with our pamper products, bath bombs & cocoa butter treats and solve your wrapping problems with our Gift Wrap Kits.

Urchin 0870 112 6006
www.urchin.co.uk
They supply the best, brightest, most innovative, useful and good-looking products for 0-8yrs. Furniture, nursery goods, travel items, toys, kitchen and bathroom products - all delivered hassle-free. Free catalogue by phone or online.

photographers

Carolyn Cowan 020 7701 3845
www.mooncycles.co.uk
Ordinary people, extraordinary photographs.

Charles Teton 0778 660 5026
www.shootingangels.com
Child photographer.

Family Portraits 020 8693 3925
www.familyportraits.uk.com
Exceptional black and white hand-printed photographs of children.

Helen Bartlett Photography 0845 603 1373
www.helenbartlett.co.uk

Kate Keenan Photography 07930 402 051
www.katekeenan.com
Kate Keenan takes natural and happy shots of babies and children that can be kept as treasured memories forever.

Marten Collins Photography 01442 871 010
www.martencollins.co.uk
With over 40 years experience between them Anne and Marten travel to client's homes bringing all the lights and background with them. The studio specialises in black & white, hand printed photographs and as they maintain their own darkroom they can also offer hand painted, sepia and other colour toning techniques.

Mary Dunkin 020 8969 8043
www.marydunkinphotography.co.uk
Mary Dunkin is an experienced family photographer who has delighted the families who have commissioned her. Her relaxed style reflects the individuality of her sitters and examples of her photographs can be seen on her website.

RebeccaLouise Photographics 020 7702 9280
www.rebeccalouise.com
Rebecca Portsmouth captures your child just the way they are, in your own home or close by using natural light.

Robin Farquhar-Thomson 020 7622 3630
www.robinft.co.uk
Wonderful pictures of children.

Stacey Mutkin 020 7221 0503
www.mutkinphoto.com
Black and white portrait photography at home or on location.

CHARLES TETON
child photographer
www.shootingangels.com
0778 660 5026

pram and buggy repairs

Barnes Buggy Repair Centre   020 8543 0505
278 Upper Richmond Road, SW15

Beryl Gerwood   01732 847 790
Restores and sells traditional coach prams.

Infantasia   020 8889 1494
103 Wood Green Shopping Centre, N22

Kiddi Centre   020 8809 4251
147 Clapton Common, Stamford Hill, E5

London Nursery Supplies   020 8889 3003
Hardy Passage, Berners Road, N22

Mamas & Papas Repairs   01604 597 700

Maclaren Repairs   01327 841 300
www.maclarenbaby.co.uk

Nanny's Prams Restoration   01953 884 164
30 Swaffam Road, Watton, IP25 6LA
Traditional coach built pram repairs

Soup Dragon   020 8348 0224
N8 & SE22

WJ Daniel & Co   020 8567 6789
96-122 Uxbridge Road, W13

rocking horses

Quality Rocking Horses   01326 231 053
www.qualityrockinghorses.co.uk
We like their Western saddle and removable tack with
coloured numnah. Prices from £825.

Robert Mullis   01793 813 583
www.rockinghorsesmaker.com
Robert Mullis is a craftsman producing traditional rocking
horses. In addition to the dappled greys made from
hardwoods you can also choose Muffin the Mule, a duck,
tortoise or The Loch Ness Monster.

Stevenson Brothers   0808 108 6120
www.stevensonbros.com
Take your pick from the Golden Jubilee dappled grey
complete with the Queen's racing colours, or a limited edition
of the Serengeti Zebra. Prices start from £700. Website also
includes antique rocking horse sales.

shoes: online

Babyworld   01491 821 877
www.babyworld.co.uk
Babyworld stocks lovely Starchild baby shoes, Kaloo boots
and TOGZ overboots for when you're out and about. Order
online for delivery within 2 working days (see ad pg 65).

Birkenstock   0800 132 194
www.birkenstock.co.uk

Hippychick   01278 434 440
www.hippychick.com
Their Shoo Shoos are imaginative and refreshingly different,
soft leather baby shoes 0-24 months (see ad pg 63).

Jester Boots   01243 790 009
www.jester-boots.co.uk
Designer stay-on, machine-washable, hand-made bootees.
Design your own colour scheme. Matching hats also
available.

Papillon Shoes   020 7834 1504
www.papillon4children.com
Ballerinas, moccasins, Jack Rogers flip flops and canvas mules.

Start-rite   0800 783 2138
www.start-rite.co.uk

Starchild Shoes   01509 817 600
www.starchildshoes.co.uk
Handmade soft leather shoes that stay on. Wonderful
designs for boys and girls (0-4yrs).

shoe shops

NORTH LONDON

Kiddie Shoes   020 8809 5059
8 Amhurst Parade, N16 5AA

Shoe & Fashion Boutique   020 8806 5581
28 Stamford Hill, N16 6XZ

NORTH WEST LONDON

Instep   020 8458 3911
117 Golders Green Road, NW11
www.instepshoes.co.uk

Brians Children's Shoes   020 8455 7001
2 Hallswelle Parade, Finchley Road, NW11 0DL

Look Who's Walking   020 7433 3855
78 Heath Street, NW3 1DN

Pom d'Api   020 7431 9532
33 Rosslyn Hill, NW3 1NH
www.pomdapi.fr

Sole Mates   020 8959 3649
42B The Broadway, Mill Hill, NW7 3LH

Instep   020 7722 7634
45 St John's Wood High Street, NW8 7NJ

EAST LONDON

Clarks Shoes   020 8534 7118
6 The Mall, E15
www.clarks.com

SOUTH EAST LONDON

Merlin Shoes   020 8771 5194
44 Westow Street, SE19 3AH

David Thomas   **020 8670 8100**
8 Croxted Road, SE21 8SW

Pares Footwear   **020 8297 0785**
24 Tranquil Vale, Blackheath, SE3 0AX

SOUTH WEST LONDON
Instep   **020 8741 4114**
80 Church Road, SW13 0DQ

One Small Step, One Giant Leap   **020 8487 1288**
409 Upper Richmond Rd West, East Sheen, SW14
www.onesmallsteponegiantleap.com

Pied Piper   **020 8788 1635**
234 Upper Richmond Road, SW15 6TG

Instep   **020 8767 3395**
11 Bellevue Road, SW17

Footsies   **020 8947 3677**
15 High Street, Wimbledon, SW19

Elys of Wimbledon   **020 8946 9191**
16 St George's Road, SW19 4DP
Stocks Clarks shoes and toys.

Start-rite   **020 8946 9735**
47 High Street, Wimbledon, SW19 5AX
www.start-rite.co.uk

Pollyanna   **020 7731 0673**
811 Fulham Road, SW6 5HG

French Sole   **020 7736 4780**
184 Munster Road, SW6 6AU

Footsies   **020 7589 4787**
27 Bute Street, SW7 3EY

The Shoe Station   **020 8940 9905**
3 Station Approach, Kew Gardens, TW9 3PS
www.theshoestation.co.uk

CENTRAL & WEST LONDON
Buckle My Shoe   **020 7935 5589**
19 St Christopher's Place, W1M 5HD

Pieton Shoes   **020 7792 0707**
9 Westbourne Grove, W2

Chiswick Shoes   **020 8987 0525**
1 Devonshire Road, W4 2EU

Stepping Out   **020 8810 6141**
106 Pitshanger Lane, W5 1QX

Millie Claude   **020 7313 4634**
202 Kensington Park Road, W11 1NR

One Small Step, One Giant Leap   **020 7243 0535**
3 Blenheim Crescent, Notting Hill, W11 2EE

swimwear and sun stuff

Everyone knows how important it is to protect babies' and children's delicate skin from the sun's rays. Their skin can be easily damanged and they can overheat. Overexposure can also damage their eyesight

SUN SUITS
These give excellent protection on the beach, by the pool or in the garden/park. Look for the UVPF50 (Ultra Violet Proection Factor) to gauge the strength - cost is usually relevant to this.

The Beach Factory   **020 8332 7467**
www.beachfactory.com
The Beach Factory leads the way with a wide choice of UV swimwear and sunsuits to protect babies, children and adults from the sun. Select from a range of styles and fabrics offering UVF50+ protection by Lion in the Sun, Sposh or Gul. They also have fun beach bags, pool toys, aqua shoes, wet suits and a variety of swimming aids.

Lion in the Sun   **01483 565 301**
www.lioninthesun.com

Konfidence.co.uk   **01566 777 720**
www.konfidence.co.uk

Sun-Togs   **01733 765 030**
www.sun-togs.co.uk

Bump to 3   **0870 606 0276**
www.bumpto3.com

Babyworld   **01491 821 877**
www.babyworld.co.uk
Arm bands, buoyancy aids, sun protection suits and caps, wraps and snugs, Happy Nappy, Shade a Babe and Auto Shade brands. Order online, fast delivery.

Incy Wincy   **0118 377 3581**
www.incywincy.org
Comprehensive catalogue and website selling buoyancy aids and swimming accessories.

Kidsafe Lifejacket
www.hellyhansen.com
A revolutionary lifejacket for babies and kids. A must-have for all boating families.

Kool Sun   **01483 417 753**
www.koolsun.com
Sun protective clothing and accessories for children 6mths-12yrs.

SUNGLASSES
Sunglasses needn't be expensive (£5-£15) but they must have UV protection . Some come with adjustable headbands to help keep them on babies and young toddlers.

Baby Banz   01460 281 229
www.babybanz.co.uk
UV protective clothing and sunglasses.

Babies R Us   0800 138 7777
www.babiesrus.co.uk

Kids Banz from Sunproof   01460 281 229
www.esunproof.co.uk

toy shops

EAST LONDON

Play   020 8510 9960
89 Lauriston Road, Victoria Park, E9 7HJ
www.playtoyshops.com
Lego, Galt and playmobil are a few of the many branded toys
as well as dressing-up and art materials, books and musical
instruments.

NORTH LONDON

Soup Dragon   020 8348 0224
27 Topsfield Parade, Tottenham Lane, N8 8TT
www.soup-dragon.co.uk

Fagin's Toys   020 8444 0282
84 Fortis Green Road, N10 3HN
A large shop with all the classics including Sylvanian Families,
Lego, Brio and Playmobil. Arts and craft materials, with Galt
and Crayola leading the way. Lots of animals, cars and
brightly coloured stationery.

Never Never Land   020 8883 3997
3 Midhurst Parade, Fortis Green, N10 3JE
Lots of baby-friendly toys sit alongside this specialist dolls
house toy shop.

Rainbow Toys   020 8340 9700
253 Archway Road, N6 5BS
www.rainbow-toys.co.uk
A good little online site supports this popular toy shop, with
expertise on quality wooden puzzles and toys, dolls houses
and furnishings as well as dressing-up clothes and
accessories.

Route 73 Kids   020 7923 7873
92 Stoke Newington Church Street, N16 0AP
All sorts of toys ranging from pocket money to classic
Christmas gifts. Galt activity kits, Brio trains and tracks,
friendship bracelets and lots of outdoor toys in the summer.

Word Play   020 8347 6700
1 Broadway Parade, Crouch End, N8 9TN
This local toyshop has an excellent children's book collection
as well as art and craft supplies, farm animals, cars and
castles complete with knights and dragons.

NORTH WEST LONDON

Harvey Johns   020 7485 1718
16-20 Parkway, NW1 7AA

Toys 'R' Us   020 8209 0019
Tilling Road, NW2
Branches in Croydon, Enfield, Hayes Road

Happy Returns   020 7435 2431
36 Rosslyn Hill, Hampstead, NW3 1NH
Good selection of party-bag toys and a helium balloon
service, as well as board games, arts and crafts materials and
dressing-up clothes.

Kristin Baybars   020 7267 0934
7 Mansfield Road, Gospel Oak, NW3 2JD
For any dolls house and miniaturist afficionardos, trek to this
unique emporium of tiny things. There's everything from
fixtures and fittings as well as kits.

Toy Wonderland (Toymaster)   020 7722 9821
10-11 Northways Parade, Finchley Road, NW3 5EP

Early Learning Centre   020 8202 6948
Brent Cross Shopping Centre, NW4 9FE

J.J.Toys   020 7722 4855
138 St John's Wood High Street, NW8 7SE

Mystical Fairies   020 7431 1888
12 Flask Walk, Hampstead, NW3 1HE
www.mysticalfairies.co.uk

SOUTH EAST LONDON

2nd Impressions   020 8852 6192
10 Montpellier Vale, Blackheath, SE3

Dulwich Village Toy Shop   020 8693 5938
31 Dulwich Village, SE21 7BN
Tucked behind the art stationers this little Alladins cave has
an excellent selection of toys, board games, dolls houses,
castles and knights, lego and brio as well as pocket-money
treats and party-bag fillers.

Early Learning Centre   020 8294 1057
7 St Mary's Place, High Street, SE9 1DO

110 High Street, SE13 4TJ   020 8318 3930

Cheeky Monkeys   020 8655 7168
4 Croxted Road, SE21 8SW
www.cheekymonkeys.com

Just Williams   020 7733 9995
18 Half Moon Lane, London, SE24
This shop never seems to disappoint with an excellent
selection of the current trends, as well as high quality animals
and knights, dressing up, dolls and accessories and a small
selection of paints, glue and art materials.

Soup Dragon   020 8693 5575
106 Lordship Lane, SE22 8HF
www.soup-dragon.co.uk
This is the sister shop to that in Crouch End, but the range
includes many classics such as puppets and full-scale
marionettes, fancy dress and accessories, as well as
nursery goods and a selection of clothing.

SOUTH WEST LONDON

Fun Learning 020 8974 8900
Bentall's Centre, Clarence Street, Kingston-upon-Thames, KT1 1TP
Brent Cross, NW4 020 8203 1473
Extremely popular and highly regarded toy shops, selling a wide range of early leaning toys as well as outdoor games, puzzles, ride-on and pull-along toys.

Traditional Toys 020 7352 1718
53 Godfrey Street, SW3 3SX
Tucked into Chelsea Green this is stuffed full of toys, games, books and more. Lots of farm animals, ride-on toys, soft teddies and dolls. Also a range of good-quality dressing-up clothes with accessories.

Early Learning Centre 020 7581 5764
36 King's Road, SW3 4HD

Daisy & Tom 020 7352 5000
181 King's Road, SW3 5EB
www.daisyandtom.com
Great range of toys ranging from lots of art and craft activities, as well as puzzles, brio trains, dolls (ie Baby Annabel), dolls houses and ride-on cars. At Christmas they do late night shopping - and dad's only night (see ad pg 59).

Patrick's Toys & Games 020 7385 9864
107-111 Lillie Road, SW6 7SX
www.patrickstoys.co.uk
Excellent shop for Hornby and Scalextric's fans, but also good for garden games, dolls' houses as well as Barbies and Bratz etc.

Tridias 020 7584 2330
25 Bute Street, SW7 3EY
www.tridias.co.uk
This shop stocks a small selection from it's extremely successful catalogue. Lego and Brio, cars and farm animals and wooden rocking horses to name a few. Also good for books, innovative gift ideas and stocking-fillas.

Q.T.Toys 020 7223 8637
90 Northcote Road, SW11 6QN
Huge range of toys, art materials, board games, educational CDs, storytapes, animals, knights and castles - as well as push-along trucks and doll's prams. Also available seasonally are paddling pools, sandpits and swings.

The Farmyard 020 8332 0038
63 Barnes High Street, Barnes, SW13 9LF
54 Friar's Stile Road, Richmond, TW10 6NQ
www.thefarmyard.co.uk
Traditional toyshop for babies to 7yr olds. Personalised wooden toys, and lots of fairy/princess pink things amongst many other classics.

Early Learning Centre 020 8780 1074
8 Putney Exchange Centre, SW15 1TN

Havanas Toy Box 020 8780 3722
Ground floor, Putney Exchange Centre, SW15 1TW
Baby clothes, shoes and toys.

Early Learning Centre 020 8944 0355
111 Centre Court Shopping Centre, 4 Queen's Road, SW19 1YE

Little Wonders 020 8255 6114
3 York Street, Twickenham, TW1 3JZ

Little Rascals 020 8542 9979
140 Merton Road, Wimbledon, SW19 1EH

CENTRAL & WEST LONDON

The Disney Store 020 7491 9136
360-366 Oxford Street, W1N 9HA
www.disney.co.uk

Hamleys 0870 333 2455
188-196 Regent Street, W1R 6BT
www.hamleys.com
Also branches in Covent Garden and Heathrow Airport.

Snap Dragon 020 8995 6618
56 Turnham Green Terrace, W4 1QP

Cheeky Monkeys 020 7792 9022
202 Kensington Park Road, W11 1NR
www.cheekymonkeys.com
Unusual and traditional children's toys and gifts, furniture, china, dressing-up, etc

Barnetts Toys 020 7727 7164
14 Elgin Crescent, Notting Hill, W11 2HX

toys: early development

Baby Einstein 020 8222 1571
www.babyeinstein.co.uk
Baby Einstein is an award-winning range of DVDs, videos, music CDs, books and toys that parents can share with their baby for early play and discovery.

Brainy Baby Company 01678 762 1100
www.brainybaby.com
Educational videos for children aged 6mths-5yrs.

Bright Minds 0870 442 2144
www.brightminds.co.uk
Educational toys for young children.

Babyworld 01491 821 877
www.babyworld.co.uk
Babyworld stocks a massive range of cot, soft, wooden, ride-on and rocking toys. Order online for delivery within 2 working days.

Child's Play 01793 616 286
www.childs-play.com
Child's Play has developed an award-winning series of baby books which help contribute to a lifelong love of reading.

Smart Baby Zone   0845 060 7786
www.smartbabyzone.co.uk
Smart Baby Zone is a new online company specialising in developmental and educational products for 0-5yrs.

toys: online

Cheeky Monkeys   020 7792 9022
www.cheekymonkeys.com
Unusual and traditional children's toys and gifts, furniture, china, dressing-up etc with birthday reminders.

Hawkin's Bazaar   0870 429 4000
www.hawkin.co.uk
Best selection of stocking fillers, tricks, educational and science-based toys from £1 up.

Hippychick wheelybugs   01278 434 440
www.hippychick.com
Award winning ride on toys.

Loddon Valley Garden Toys   0845 644 1546
www.lvgt.co.uk
Leading brands of outdoor toys, including wooden playsets, sandpits, tampolines and more.

Wooden Train Sets   02380 898 085
& Accessories
www.woodentrainsets.co.uk
Brio compatible train sets (at half the Brio prices), bridges, tunnels, trains, track, buildings, competitive prices, fully secure website.

Win Green Company   01622 746 516
www.wingreen.co.uk
Little Gretels will be the envy of their pals with Win Green's Gingerbread Play House, made from appliquéd and embroidered cotton, with lace curtains. Perfect for bedrooms and playrooms, and can move outside for the summer. Many more designs.

travel and changing bags

Groovy Mummy   020 8650 1286
www.groovymummy.co.uk
Refreshingly stylish accessories for you and your baby including luxurious changing bags and exquisite blankets. We love their contemporary fabrics (see pg 29).

Hippychick Health Back   01278 434 440
Baby Bag
www.hippychick.com
A totally organised ergonomic shaped bag with contours to the body.

Caboodle Bags   01795 590 664
www.caboodlebags.co.uk
Nappy changing bags designed with great flair and practicality.

travel cots

You might ask whether this is a really necessary purchase. Everyone we spoke to had one and felt that it was perfect during those early years of not having to find a babysitter. The pop-up models are even better for holidays as they weigh next to nothing and act both as a playpen and a cot

Babyworld   **01491 821 877**
www.babyworld.co.uk
Babyworld supplies carrycots from Bébé Confort and Quinny and travel cots and beds from BabyDan, Hauck and LittleLife. Order online, delivery within 2 working days (see ad page 65).

Graco   **0870 909 0501**
www.graco.co.uk
Two models, the Compact and the Contour. Very easy to assemble and relatively compact when folded away. Wheels help you manoeuvre them around and they can double-up as a playpen. The Contour comes with a bassinet which acts as a changing unit - very helpful for holidays abroad.

Samsonite Pop-Up Bed   **01746 769 676**
www.baby-travel.com
From 0-6mths this pop-up travel cot is perfect for weekends or when dining with friends. It's very lightweight and folds away into its own hand carry bag.

twins and multiples

One of your major purchases will be a double pushchair where you will need to consider the needs of your lifestyle over the demands of the pushchair. But there is no doubt that you need to take advantage of all the special discounts that stores offer - ie join up to TAMBA (see helplines)

Twins Things   **01600 715 146**
www.twinsthings.co.uk
This is an excellent website with a great range of innovative and practical products for parents of twins or multiples. They also have a number of beautiful gift ideas as well as useful information and links to other twin and multiple websites.

Although many houses and flats cannot accommodate the classic carriage pram, this does offer parents a supremely elegant and old-fashioned appeal. Otherwise you can opt for the lightweight pushchair frame with a carrycot that can be swapped for a pushchair seat or car seat (a 3-in-1). Or a pushchair with a reclining seat (a 2-in-1).

SilverCross Balmoral

This classic hand-made pram will give your baby the most luxurious childhood experience. And will no doubt maintain or double its value over the years.

- Rigid steel body
- Hand sprung chassis
- Leather suspension
- Chrome shopping tray
- Mattress & changing bag

£850
www.silvercross.co.uk
Stockists: 0870 840 6727

Quinny Buzz

This has the contemporary feel of an all-terrain pushchair with the elegance of a traditional carrycot. It is easy to fold and has removable wheels.

- 3-in-1
- Reversible seat
- Air tyres
- Mesh shopping basket

£289
www.quinny.com
Stockists: 020 8236 0707

Hauck Mini Star M360

This has a carrycot, and a car seat/pushchair frame to complete the travel system. Mid-size swivel wheels makes for easy manoeuvring around town.

- 3-in-1
- Pneumatic tyres
- Multi-position seat
- Large shopping basket

£225
www.hauckuk.com
Stockists: 0870 840 6727

Chicco Cortina

This carrycot, car seat and pushchair fit together very easy with one click, and with twist handles which rotate to 8 different positions' it's very comfortable to push

- 3-in-1
- Adjustable handle
- Large pneumatic tyres
- Thermo regulation system

£380
www.chicco.co.uk
Stockists: 01623 750 870

Mamas & Papas Pliko Pramette

An effortless transformation from pram into pushchair makes this a smart choice. Lightweight, versatile and suitable from birth through to toddler years.

- 4 position reclining seat
- Adjustable handlebar
- Compact folding

£300
www.mamasandpapas.co.uk
Stockists: 0870 830 7700

Graco Quattro Tour TS

This spacious travel system has a bigger than usual (and easy to access) shopping basket and folds down simply and easily. One click to add their AutoBaby car seat.

- 2-in-1
- 5 position backrest
- Washable fabric
- Fits Britax 0+ car seat

£190
www.graco.co.uk
Stockists: 0870 909 0501

Other brands

Britax www.britax.co.uk	01264 386 034
Bebecar www.bebecar.co.uk	020 8201 0505
Cosatto www.cosatto.com	0870 050 5900
Emmaljunga www.emmaljunga.co.uk	0800 652 8007
Johnston Prams www.johnstonprams.co.uk	02890 770 779
Mamas & Papas www.mamasandpapas.co.uk	0870 830 7700

Top online pushchair stockists:

www.babyworld.co.uk

www.babymunchkins.com

www.pushchairs.co.uk

www.londonprams.co.uk

www.practicalpushchairs.co.uk

www.pramsdirect.co.uk

www.twoleftfeet.co.uk

www.vanblanken.co.uk

This is probably your biggest purchase, and the choice is large. Many lifestyles will dictate two (city pushchair that fits easily into the back of a car or bus and an all-terrain for those living in the country). Below are our favourites based on style, practicality and value. Most of these models come as prams and evolve into pushchairs as your baby matures.

Bugaboo Frog

Simple, smart and very contemporary with all the essential accessories and multi-tasking wheels.

- 3 position reclining seat
- Reversible handlebar
- Compact folding

£499
www.bugaboo.nl/uk
Stockists: 020 7385 5338

Stokke Xplory

Cutting edge design makes this pushchair the most stylish on the market, with your baby no longer having to look at the back of everyone's legs

- 5 sitting positions
- Reversible handle
- 2 wheel position for stairs

£469
www.stokke.com
Stockists: 01753 655 873

Hauck i'coo

Suitable from birth, this lightweight aluminium framed pushchair has lockable, front swivelling wheels and a height adjustable handle.

- 3 position reclining seat
- Removable bumper bar
- Easy and compact folding

£355
www.hauckuk.com
Stockists: 0870 840 6727

Silver Cross Compact

The first contemporary pushchair from this classic brand does not disappoint. Well designed and stylish with quality fittings and finishes.

- Multi-position backrest
- Rotating handles
- Compact folding

£199
www.silvercross.co.uk
Stockists: 01756 702 412

Maclaren Techno Classic

Comfort and style minus the bulk makes this one of the top selling pushchairs across London. Suitable from 3mths in great sporty designs.

- 4 position reclining seat
- Compacts with one hand
- Ergonomic foam handles

£170
www.maclarenbaby.com
Stockists: 01327 841 320

Mamas & Papas Pulse Vibe

An effortless, folding pushchair makes this a smart choice. Lightweight, versatile and suitable from birth through to toddler years.

- 5 position reclining seat
- Soft grip handles
- Compact folding

£89
www.mamasandpapas.co.uk
Stockists: 0870 830 7700

OTHER MANUFACTURERS

Bebe Confort — 01484 401 802
www.bebeconfort.com

Bebecar — 020 8201 0505
www.bebecar.co.uk

Britax — 01264 386 034
www.britax.co.uk

Chicco — 01623 750 870
www.chicco.com

Cosatto — 01268 722 811
www.cosatto.com

Graco — 0870 909 0510
www.graco.co.uk

Maclaren — 01327 841 320
www.maclarenstrollers.com

Mamas & Papas — 01484 438 226
www.mamasandpapas.co.uk

Mountain Buggy — 01276 502 587
www.mountainbuggy.com

The appeal of the all-terrains has grown enormously in recent years. They not only cope well with the wet and muddy UK climate, but are surprisingly versatile through shopping malls and on pavements. They're heavier, bulkier and take up more boot space than lightweight pushchairs – so if you've got a small car do experiment first.

Mountain Buggy Breeze

Suitable from birth, this lightweight aluminium framed pushchair folds easily, quickly and compactly with no need to remove the wheels.

• 3 position reclining seat
• No puncture tyres
• Very lightweight
• Fits into small cars

£355
www.mountainbuggy.co.uk
Stockists: 01404 815 555

Graco Expedition

This 3-wheeler folds easily, quickly and compactly and has

• 2 position reclining seat
• Soft-grip handlebar
• Handbrake and tether
• Large shopping basket
• Soft seat pad

£120
www.graco.co.uk
Stockists: 0870 909 0501

We like this rugged design and the automatically tilting steering wheel which can be locked. Hand and foot brake.

Quinny Zapp

• Aluminium wheels
• Adjustable handlebar
• Smooth suspension
• Integrated folding

£140
www.quinny.com
Stockists: 020 8236 0707

Suitable from birth with quick release wheels for easy transportation, and storage. Also fits with car seat for 3in1versatility.

Urban Detour Glacier

• Multi-seat positioning
• Covered bumper bar
• Pneumatic tyres/pump
• Viewing window in hood

£160
www.mothercare.com
Stockists: 0845 330 4030

Maclaren MX3

This award winning stroller folds down to the smallest size and is fine even for small cars.

• 2 position reclining seat
• Lightweight chassis
• Adjustable hand brake
• Quick release wheels
• Storage in hood

£200
www.maclarenbaby.com
Stockists: 01327 841 320

Red Castle Shop 'n' Jogg

This light aluminium framed 3-wheeler with a lockable front swivel wheel has a 3 position seat and disc brakes.

• Removable cushion pad
• Integral rain cover
• Zip storage pocket
• Wheel covers

£299
www.bettacare.co.uk
Stockists: 01293 851 896

Other Brands

Phil and Teds
www.philandteds.com

Baby Jogger   01455 550 600
www.babyjogger.co.uk

Babies R Us   0800 038 8899
www.babiesrus.co.uk

Babystyle   01509 816 444
www.babystyle.co.uk

Accessories
Abstract   01273 693 737
www.abstractuk.com
Fleecy blankets.

Baby Direct   0113 225 0505
www.baby-direct.com
Wide range of 3 wheelers for sale including accessories.

Buggysnuggle Co   01869 340 694
www.buggysnuggle.com
Funky fleeces and fake fur buggysnuggles to keep your child warm and snug.

childcare

Finding the right childcare is a potential minefield. Full-time nanny, mother's help or au pair? Through word of mouth, small ad in the local paper or a scribbled card in a shop window? While such methods of finding help may yield happy results, childcare is one area where you don't want to take risks. In this section we recommend professional agencies that will find you a nanny, maternity nurse or other carer with proper qualifications, experience and references.

au pair agencies

The majority of au pairs are aged between 17 -25, and are admitted from EC countries, and work for around 6 months. Expect to pay between £40-£55 per week, in exchange for around 25hrs of light housework, childcare and 2 evenings of babysitting. They are not suitable for sole care of babies and young children. The agencies below will do a lot of the hard work for you in terms of selecting suitable and reliable candidates and verifying all their details.

Au Pair International   020 7370 3798
www.apni.co.uk
The professional childcare agency since 1992 providingaupairs, mother's helps and nannies throughout the UK. Please visit our website for the full list of childminders.

Childcare International   0800 652 0020
www.childint.co.uk
Established for more than 20 years, we offer a caring professional service throughout the UK to host families and applicants. Au Pairs from the EU, Mother's Helps and Nannies from Australia, Canada and South Africa. Full ongoing support throughout the stay. We are founder members of the British Au Pair Agencies Association (BAPAA), the International Au Pair Association (IAPA) and members of the Childcare Division of the REC.

Euro Pair Agency   020 8421 2100
www.euro-pair.co.uk
Au pairs: French mainly. Short-term in summer. Long-term from September. References verified, police checked.

Just Help   01460 30775
www.just-help.co.uk
Voted 'Best agency for personal service,' Evening Standard.

Peek-a-boo Childcare   020 7778 0720
www.peekaboochildcare.com
Peek-a-boo matches the most suitable au-pairs and nannies with families in the UK and around the world. Specialise in Scandinavian and British carers although they welcome all nationailities who hold a valid UK work visa).

CONGRATULATIONS...

A new baby on the way!

Make those first weeks happy and memorable by
booking your very own MATERNITY NURSE from...

Established in 1996, we are London's leading MATERNITY NURSE AGENCY.
We satisfy the needs of over 500 families a year, most of whom have
approached us through recommendation.

All our MATERNITY NURSES are personally interviewed, are of the
highest calibre, with verified references. They will ensure you have plenty of
rest, 'show you the ropes', settle your baby into that all important routine and
leave you feeling confident for the future.

Whether you are a first-time mother, have a sibling on the way or
are expecting twins, please call one of our experienced consultants
to discuss your particular needs.

TELEPHONE: +44(0)20 7795 6299 FAX: +44(0)20 7937 8100
OR VISIT OUR WEBSITE AT: www.maternally-yours.com

MATERNALLY YOURS, 17 RADLEY MEWS, KENSINGTON, LONDON W8 6JP

babysitters

Hopes and Dreams   **020 7833 9388**
www.hopesanddreams.co.uk
A professional 24 hour, 7 days a week babysitting agency
with all members of staff fully reference checked and
interviewed in person. For extra reassurance, a detailed
profile can be provided prior to booking. We service many
top London hotels and have an excellent reputation as a
professional and reliable babysitter service.

maternity nurses and nannies

Specialising in the care of newborns, a maternity nurse will look
after your baby on return from hospital, allowing you to rest.
Normally, they are on call 24hrs a day with one day off per week

Maternally Yours   **020 7795 6299**
17 Radley Mews, London, W8 6JP
www.maternallyyours.co.uk

Mayfair Maternity   **08704 423 262**
www.mayfairmaternity.com
Maternity nurses, baby nurses, breastfeeding and sleep
training consultants. Placing in the UK and overseas. The
experienced professionals in the recruitment and placement
of infant specialists.

Nannies Incorporated   **020 7593 5898**
www.nanniesinc.com
Specialists in maternity care.

Newborn Nannies   **01689 898 484**
www.newbornnannies.co.uk
Exceptionally high quality maternity nurses and night nannies.
Flexible services from an agency managed by midwives. Also
offers babycare and first aid training courses.

Regency Nannies and   **020 7225 1055**
Maternity Nurses
50 Hans Crescent SW1X 0NA
A premier maternity agency. Friendly but professional service.
Listed by the Portland Hospital.

Sleeping Babies   **07767 446 000**
www.sleepingbabies.co.uk
Sleeping Babies maternity nurses and night nannies offers a
unique package of support to suit individual family

requirements. As well as giving you a good night's sleep they
will help with establishing breast feeding and routines, colic
and reflux as well as supporting twins and multiples.

The Maternity Nurse Company 01423 709 679
www.maternitynurse.co.uk
Specialists in maternity nurse placements offering an
experienced and truly personal service. UK and International.

The Nanny Service   **020 7935 3515**
www.nannyservice.co.uk
Specialists in maternity nurses and maternity nannies since
1975. All candidates personally interviewed and references
thoroughly checked.

Tinies International   **020 7384 0322**
Central London
www.tinies.com
Most progressive agency with more nannies, maternity
nurses, part-time and emergency carers

nanny agencies

Abbeville Nannies   **020 7627 3352**
www.abbevillenannies.co.uk
A selection of the best nannies, mothers' helps and maternity
nurses across London.

BB's Au Pairs & Nannies   **020 8480 9461**
www.bbs-aupairsandnannies.co.uk
BB's agency offers continual support for au pairs and nannies
and prior to the placement helps to lay down groundwork
rules to ensure that the placement is as smooth as possible.
The agency is open Mon to Fri from 9:30-6pm and messages
are accessed during weekends (except bank holidays).

Bellamy of Mayfair   **020 7569 6734**
www.bellamyofmayfair.com
Bellamy of Mayfair is a professional Household recruitment
consultancy.

Burlington Nannies   **020 7821 9911**
www.burlingtonnannies.com
We are a team of professionals who seek out high calibre
Nannies, Governesses, Maternity Nurses and Private Tutors
for families in London and Overseas.

Eden Nannies   **020 7569 6771**
www.eden-nannies.co.uk
The complete childcare solution.

Elite Nannies   **020 7801 0061**
22 Rowena Crescent, London, SW11 2PT
www.elitenannies.co.uk
An excellent agency - highly recommended by clients,
nannies and maternity nurses.

Greycoat Placements   **020 7233 9950**
35-37 Grosvenor Gardens, London, SW1W 0BS
www.greycoatplacements.co.uk
Personal, professional service for all permanent and
temporary childcare needs.

Hyde Park International   **01962 841 234**
www.hydeparkint.com
One of the UK's leading agencies established in 1983.
Friendly, professional, through and efficient.

Ideal Nannies   020 7917 1862
212 Picadilly, London W1V 9LD
www.idealnannies.com

Imperial Nannies   020 7795 6220
www.imperialnannies.co.uk
Providing the very best for your children all over London and throughout the UK

Just Help   01460 30775
www.just-help.co.uk
Voted 'Best agency for personal service,' Evening Standard

Kensington Nannies   020 7937 2333/3299
www.kensington-nannies.com
Nanny agency who knows about childcare needs from good experience.

KiwiOz Nannies   020 7229 6547
www.kiwioznannies.co.uk
London's No 1 source for Australasian nannies and mother's helps! Friendly staff and fantastic services including the KiwiOz 'Grow' Program- ongoing teamwork between nanny, family and agency to ensure the best for your children. View some of our currently available candidates now on our easy-to-use website.

Knightsbridge Nannies   020 7610 9232
London House, 100 New Kings Road, SW6 4LX
www.knightsbridgenannies.com
Providing a personal childcare service in the UK and overseas for professionals looking for high calibre nannies.

Les Papillotes   020 7589 8755
10 Exhibition Road, SW7 2HF
www.lespapillotes.com
The French Nannies Agency of London. The Papillotes Method is a fun and active method for babies and children. Nannies, Mother's Helps, Maternity Nurses, Au Pairs.

London Nanny Company   020 7368 1603
Vicarage House, 58-60 Kensington Church St, W8
www.londonnannycompany.co.uk
Nanny, maternity nurse, nanny agency, governess, baby sitters, jobs overseas

Marianna Domestic Placements   0845 058 1116
www.marianna-agency.com
Specialist providers of nannies, nanny-housekeepers, mothers help and au pairs. Live in and daily, full and part time. All applicants screened and personally interviewed. Covering London and the Home counties.

Nannies Incorporated   020 7593 5898
Suite 7, 2 Caxton Street, London, SW1H 0QE
www.nanniesinc.com
A well-established agency supplying maternity nurses, nannies both in the UK and overseas.

Nannies of St James   0870 300 0824
100 New King's Road, London, SW6 4LX
www.stjamesandtemporarynannies.com
The professional agency providing professional nannies and maternity nurses.

Night Nannies London   020 7731 6168
www.night-nannies.com
Night Nannies is Britain's leading overnight maternity service. Fully vetted, interviewed and qualified nannies will sweep in, full of reassurance and confidence, and take over the care of your child overnight. Established 4 years ago in London, they now have 8 branches nationwide.

North London Nannies   020 8444 4911
www.northlondonnannies.co.uk
Established 16yrs ago, North London Nannies is a leading provider for all your childcare requirements. Permanent, temporary and emergency placements. Very experienced agency understanding the needs of parents and their children's welfare and happiness.

Occasional & Permanent Nannies   020 7225 1555
2 Cromwell Place, SW7 2JE
www.nannyworld.co.uk
Occasional and Permanent nannies was founded over 50 years ago and has helped several generations of clients find the most appropriate childcare support. Whether that's a temporary nanny, housekeeper-nanny, or a governess with special teaching experience. They can also provide maternity nurses with considerable experience both in the UK and abroad.

Riverside Nannies   020 7374 6363
29 Milligan Street, Limehouse, E14 8AT
Experienced agency placing excellent candidates with families in London and outside.

Swansons   020 8994 5275
www.swansonsnannies.co.uk
Anne Babb has run this West London agency for over 21yrs and is known for her efficient and approachable way with clients and nannies. She supplies both daily and live-in nannies as well as keeping a list of local families who wish to share. She also has a part-time nanny register and is scrupulous about checking references.

The Nanny Agency   020 8883 3162
www.thenannyagency.co.uk
All employers and nannies met, providing a personal, thorough and understanding service for families.

The Nanny Service   020 7935 3515
17 Nottingham Street, SW1
www.nannyservice.co.uk
Specialists in maternity nurses and maternity nannies since 1975. All candidates personally interviewed and references thoroughly checked.

Tinies International Childcare   020 7384 0322
www.tinies.com
Most progressive agency with more nannies, maternity nurses, part-time and emergency carers

Richmond	**020 8876 4391**
South East London	**0845 600 3590**
North London	**020 7544 8620**
South West London	**020 7720 2045**

NANNIES INCORPORATED
Specialists in Maternity Care

Nannies Incorporated was established in 1989. We have 17 years experience in providing professional and experienced maternity nurses and nannies in London, County and Overseas.

We have a long and successful record of fulfilling our clients expectations. We achieve this through:

- *In depth interviewing of each candidate.*
- *Careful matching of clients and candidates profiles.*
- *Thorough reference checks, including checks carried out by the Criminal Record Bureau.*
- *Providing a generous refund policy.*

Please ask for a copy of our complimentary childcare guide for parents and consult our website for further information.

MATERNITY NURSES

Our maternity nurses are trained or experienced nurses/nannies, registered nurses or midwives who specialise in the care of the newborn, including multiple births.

A maternity nurse will advise you in all aspects of feeding (breast/bottle), care and hygiene and assist you in establishing a suitable routine. They are on call 24 hours a day, 6 days a week. Advance bookings advisable.

LIVE IN AND DAILY NANNIES

Nannies Incorporated believe that creating a loving and stimulating environment for your children can only be achieved by adopting a professional interview and selection procedure. We always seek to provide for different needs and circumstances of families.

Our nannies will either hold the CACHE diploma, BTEC or similar qualification and will have considerable experience. They will either be British citizens, come from Eastern European countries or the southern hemisphere.

SUITE 7, 2 CAXTON STREET, LONDON SW1H 0QE
TEL: 020 7593 5898 FAX: 020 7593 5899   E-MAIL: nanniesinc@aol.com
WEBSITE: www.nanniesinc.com

IMPERIAL NANNIES

Providing the very best for your children

We specialise in placing qualified and experienced childcarers
with families in London, the country and overseas. We aim to
ease the difficult process of nanny selection by providing
an individual, tailor-made service for your particular needs.
All our nannies are fully reference checked, with at least
two years private household experience and are personally
interviewed by our dedicated consultants.

We provide an excellent selection of:

DAILY NANNIES
*Four to five days per week. Candidates are available with
years of excellent service.*

LIVE-IN NANNIES
Flexible childcare based in the privacy of your own home.

OVERSEAS NANNIES
Experienced nannies looking for an exciting challenge.

NANNY/GOVERNESSES
Working towards developing the mind and skills of your children.

NANNY/HOUSEKEEPERS
*Combining the abilities of childcare and domestic chores
in the home.*

MOTHERS HELPS
Young people to assist with childcare and light housekeeping.

---

17 RADLEY MEWS, KENSINGTON, LONDON W8 6JP
TELEPHONE: +44(0)20 7795 6220 FACSIMILE: +44(0)20 7937 2251
www.imperialnannies.com

ideal nannies

- All staff personally interviewed
- References thoroughly checked
- Nannies, Nanny/Governesses, Nanny/Housekeepers, Mothers Helps & Maternity Nurses
- Live in & Live out
- Full time & Part time
- Permanent & temporary
- First Aid courses

Karen Murphy of Ideal Nannies has been running this flourishing agency since 1988. It is manned by sensible, careful staff who are easy to talk to and have practical experience in the childcare world

212 Piccadilly London W1V 9LD
Tel: **020 7917 1862**

4 Stilehall Parade Chiswick High Road London W4 3AG
Tel: **020 8994 5888**

www.idealnannies.com
info@idealnannies.com

GREYCOAT
PLACEMENTS

We have an excellent selection of
permanent and temporary
NANNIES
MATERNITY NURSES
MOTHER'S HELPS
TUTORS & GOVERNESSES
NANNY/ HOUSEKEEPERS
On a Live In or Daily basis
In London, the UK & Internationally

All candidates are personally interviewed by our
trained consultants and references are fully checked.

Our friendly, experienced staff listen carefully to the
needs of the family and offer a discreet, professional service.
They can also provide post-placement help and advice.

We are registered with the CRB enabling us to conduct
the necessary disclosure procedures on our candidates.

Telephone: 020 7233 9950
Email: childcare@greycoatplacements.co.uk
Website: www.greycoatplacements.co.uk
Greycoat Placements Ltd,
Grosvenor Gardens House,
35-37 Grosvenor Gardens,
London, SW1W 0BS

Recruitment &
Employment
Confederation

Burlington Nannies

Experienced Professionals in the Recruitment of Nannies and Governesses for the UK and Overseas

Burlington Nannies have a team of dedicated professional consultants who will seek out high calibre Nannies, Governesses and Maternity Nurses for families within the UK and Overseas. We believe our success is down to the personal service we offer our clients.

Burlington Nannies Ltd
Grosvenor Gardens House
35 - 37 Grosvenor Gardens
London, SW1W 0BS

Telephone 020 7821 9911
Website www.burlingtonnannies.com
Email enquiries@burlingtonnannies.com

I am more than happy to recommend Burlington Nannies who take the time to get to know their clients. If you are a Nanny seeking a position or a Client needing a Nanny then this agency stands out above the rest. Burlington Nannies will attend to your requirements and do their very best to satisfy your needs.

Cynthia Powell – Client

new clients please quote SN1 for a 10% discount

Bellamy
of Mayfair
Domestic & Corporate Recruitment

A PERSONAL SERVICE IN YOUR SEARCH FOR

Nannys / Housekeepers

Housekeepers • Dailies • Porters

Domestic Couples

Cooks • Chefs

Butlers • Chauffeurs

Gardeners • Handypersons

Estate Managers

Personal Assistants

118 PICCADILLY • MAYFAIR
LONDON • W1J 7NW

Tel: **0207 569 6734** Fax: **0207 569 6772**

Email: info@bellamyofmayfair.com

www.nurturer.co.uk

nurtur⊖r
A Lifestyle Management Company

Services range from,
Baby massage | prenatal yoga |
housecleaning | babysitting |
garden maintenance | dog-walking |
pedicures ...and more.

0141 3373328
info@nurturer.co.uk
www.nurturer.co.uk

Taking Care of You from conception, birth and beyond

nanny payroll services

If you've never seen the small binder that encompasses the PAYE tax tables then we do recommend you value your time highly and delegate all responsibility for calculating tax to one of the services below. Sanity could at least be your upside

Nanny Paye   **0845 466 0044**
www.nannypaye.co.uk
Comprehensive nanny payroll service.

Nanny Tax   **0845 226 2203**
www.nannytax.co.uk
Nannytax is the UK's leading payroll service for parents employing a nanny.

Taxing Nannies   **020 8882 6847**
www.taxingnannies.co.uk
London's leading payroll agency for employers of nannies.

nanny training

The new Government Nanny Approval Scheme allows you access to tax relief on your childcare costs, with Employer-led Childcare Vouchers. You need to find a CACHE accredited course to enable your childcarer to comply with the requirements of the scheme.

The Riverside   **020 7374 6364**
Training Company
Offering a 12 hour training course recognised by the Childcare Approval Scheme as well as wokshops for both parents and childcarers on health, nutrition, behaviour managament and play. Delivered by experienced lecturers with extensive knowledge and practical experience in childcare. Led by Jill Wheatcroft NNEB RSCN MSC; University Lecturer in Child Health.

your health visitor

After your baby arrives much of your time will be spent sleeping and feeding. You will also be visited by your health visitor, who will come to weigh your baby and ensure that you have all the support you need. And now there's a new online service that has a whole host of FAQs as well as a personal advisory service, covering sleep routines, feeding, weaning, development and other ideas at www.healthvisitors.com

HEALTHVISITORS.COM

Ask A Health Visitor

about

your infants, toddlers and small children

These days, education starts young. Here you'll find everything from day nurseries caring for almost-newborns, to formal nursery schools and pre-preps. We have listed all independent (ie private) nursery schools, day nurseries, montessori and bilingual nurseries, in postcode order to help parents find places that offer high quality childcare and an early education. Compulsory education in the UK starts at 5yrs, but before that the following categories of care are on offer:

Day Nurseries: ages 3mths-5yrs; open 8am-6pm and for 48 or more weeks of the year. This includes catering for breakfast, lunch and tea, following the sleep routines set by parents, and gradually being introduced to a more structured day of music, play, painting, stories and outdoor games.

Nursery Schools: ages 2-5yrs; offers sessional care (ie 9am-12pm and/or 2pm-4pm), and are open on a termtime basis. Often attached to pre-prep schools.

Activities include music, play, painting, stories, games as well as early number and letter learning.

Montessori: many nurseries use Montessori methods, a system devised by Maria Montessori in 1907, which emphasises training of the senses and encouragement rather than a rigid academic curriculum

Bilingual Nurseries: these offer care either on a day nursery or nursery school basis, but have the additional advantage of your child being exposed to two languages. Children are gradually introduced to their second language through songs and simple instructions and within a term are happily conversing in either language.

Pre-Prep Schools which prepare your child for big school at 7, have an S alongside their listing.

We have not listed **playgroups** as the parent or carer remains in attendance. For registered parent and toddler groups contact your local Council (see page 204).

For nearly all nurseries and schools in the private sector, early registration is highly recommended, so ring, visit with babe in arms and register ahead of time, even if you later decide not to pursue that option. For a list of state-run nurseries ie state primary schools with nursery classes contact your local Council.

NORTH LONDON POSTCODES

N1

Floral Place Nursery   020 7354 9945
2 Floral Place, Northampton Grove, N1 2PL
www.brighthorizons.com
3mths- 5yrs. Full day

Pentland Nursery   020 8970 2441
224 Squires Lane, Finchley, N3 2QL
www.brighthorizon.com
3mths-5yrs. 8am-6pm. 50 wks.

Beckett House Montessori Nursery   020 7278 8824
98 Richmond Avenue, N1 0HR
2½-5yrs. 8.30am-5.30m. 52wks.

Bentham U5's Centre   020 7354 3589
135 Bentham Court, Ecclesbourne Road, Islington
2-5yrs. 8am-5.45pm. 51wks.

Essex Road Pre-School   020 7354 3944
Sir Walter Sickert Hall, Canonbury Crescent,
Islington, N1 2FE
2-5yrs. 9.30am-12pm and 12.30-3pm. Termtime.

Mars Montessori Nursery   020 7704 2805
4 Collins Yard, Islington Green, N1 2XQ
2-5yrs. 8am-6pm. 52wks.

Rosemary Works Early   020 7613 5500
Years Centre
2a Branch Place, Southgate Road, N1 5PH
3mths-3yrs. 8am-6pm or 10am-4pm. 51wks.

St Andrew's Montessori   020 7700 2961
St Andrew's Church, Thornhill Square, N1 1BQ
3-5yrs

S St Paul's Steiner Project   020 7226 4454
1 St Paul's Road, Islington, N1 2QH
3-12yrs.

The Children's House   020 7354 2113
77 Elmore Street, N1 3AQ
2½-7yrs. 9am-3.15pm. Termtime.

The Grove Pre-School & Nursery   020 7226 4037
Shepperton House, 91 Shepperton Road, N1 3DF
3mths-5yrs. Full day

N2

Annemount Nursery &   020 8455 2132
Pre-Prep School
18 Holne Chase, N2 0QN
2 3/4-5yrs. 9am-12pm. Termtime.

Fortis Green Nursery   020 8883 1266
70 Fortis Green, N2 9EP
6mths-5yrs. 8.30am-5.30pm. 51wks.

S Kerem School   020 8455 0909
Norrice Lea, N2 0RE
Co-ed 4-11yrs.

N4

Asquith Nursery Crouch Hill   020 7561 1533
33 Crouch Hill, Islington, N4 4AP
3mths-5yrs. 8am-6pm. 51wks

Asquith Nursery Finsbury Park   020 7263 3090
Dulas Street, Islington, N4 3AF
3mths-5yrs. 8am-6pm. 51wks

Crouch Hill Day Nursery   020 7561 1533
33 Crouch Hill, N4 4AP
3mths-5yrs. 8am-6pm. 51wks.

Holly Park Montessori   020 7263 6563
Holly Park Methodist Church Hall, Crouch Hill, N4 4BY
2-7yrs. 9.15am-3.15pm. Termtime.

Little Jewel Pre-School   020 8341 2733
St Paul's Church Hall, Cavendish Road, N4 1RT
18mths-5yrs. 8am-6pm. 50wks.

St Marks Playgroup   020 7263 6035
1 Moray Road, N4 3LD
2-5yrs. 9am-1.45pm. Termtime.

St Thomas Playgroup   020 7354 9347
St. Thomas's Church, Monsell Road, Islington, N4 2QY
2-5yrs. 9.30am-12pm. Termtime.

N5

Aberdeen Park Nursery   020 7226 2610
143 Highbury New Park, N5 2LJ
2-5yrs. 8am-6pm. 48wks.

Christchurch Playgroup   020 7354 3117
Christ Church, 155 Highbury Grove, N5 1SA
2.5-5yrs. 9.30am-12pm and 1-3pm Mon-Thurs, 9.30am-
12pm Fri. Termtime.

Little Angels Day Nursery   020 7354 5070
& Pre-School
217 Blackstock Road, N5 2LL
3mths-5yrs. 8am-6pm. 50wks.

Martineau Community Nursery   020 7359 9911
1 Elwood Street, N5 1EB
2½-4½yrs. 8am-5.30pm. 50wks.

New Park Montessori School   020 7226 1109
& Nursery
67 Highbury New Park, N5 2EU
4mths-5yrs. 7.30am-6.30pm. 50wks.

St Augustines Playgroup   020 7704 8003
108 Highbury New Park, N5 2DR
9.30am-12pm. Termtime.

N6

Avenue Nursery School   020 8348 6815
2 Highgate Avenue, N6 5RX
2½-5yrs

S Channing School   020 8340 2328
Highgate, N6 5HF
Girls 4-18yrs

Highgate Activity Nursery   020 8348 9248
1 Church Road, N6 4QH
2-5yrs. 8am-6pm. 51wks.

S Highgate Pre-paratory School   020 8340 9196
7 Bishopswood Road, N6 4PH
Co-ed 3-7yrs.

Ladybird Montessori   020 7586 0740
The Scout Hall, Sheldon Avenue, N6 4ND
2¹/₂-5yrs. 9.30am-12.30pm. Termtime.

Rainbow Montessori School   020 7328 8986
Highgate United Reform Church, Pond Square, N6
6BA
2¹/₂-5yrs. 9am-12.15pm and 12.15-3pm. Termtime.

N7

Monkey Puzzle Nursery   020 7619 3624
Whittington Park Community Centre, Yerbury Road,
Tufnell Park, N19 4RS
www.monkeypuzzlenursery.co.uk
0-4yrs. 8am-6pm. 51wks. Full and part-time day care for
children aged 3mths-5yrs in a warm and caring environment.
50wks per year. 8am-6pm. Mon-Fri. See website for full
details.

First Steps Playgroup   020 7700 4721
16 Bride Street, Islington, N7 8RP
2-4yrs. 9.15am-1.15pm. Termtime.

Kidsunlimited Nurseries   0845 850 0222
Camden & Islington Health Authority, Tollington
Way, N7 6QX
3mths-5yrs. 7.30am-6pm. 51 wks.

Manor Gardens Pre-School   02075 615 261
Manor Gardens Centre, 6-9 Manor Gardens, N7
6LA
2-5yrs. 9am-4.30pm (or sessional 9.30am-12pm and 1.30-
4pm). Termtime.

Market Road Playgroup   020 7609 6088
55 Tealby Ct, Roman Way, Islington, N7 8HW
2¹/₂-5yrs. 9.30am-3.30pm. 39wks.

Sam Morris Centre Nursery   020 7609 1735
Parkside Crescent, Isledon Road, N7 7JG
6mths-5yrs. 8am-6pm.

Spanish Sisters of Charity   020 7607 3974
Day Nursery
95 Huddleston Road, Islington, N7 0AE
2-5yrs. 8am-5pm.

N7
The Gower School   020 7700 2445
18 North Road, N7 9EY
www.thegowerschool.co.uk
3mths-7yrs. Where little people matter.

N8
Active Learning Nursery   0800 081 1620
Tivoli Road, Crouch End, N8 8RG
3mths-5yrs. 8am-6pm. 51wks.

Adventure Land Day Nursery   020 8347 6951
18 Gisburn Road, N8 7BS
2-5yrs. 8am-6pm. 52wks.

Bowlers Community Nursery   02072 812 832
81 Crouch Hill, N8 9EG
0-5yrs. 8.30am-5.30pm. 48wks.

Claremont Day Nursery   020 8340 3841
7 Harold Road, N8 7DE
2-5yrs. 8am-6pm. 51wks.

Hollybush Nursery   020 8348 8537
5 Redston Road, N8 7HL
2-5yrs. 8am-5.45pm. 51wks.

Little Tree Montessori   020 8342 9231
143 Ferme Park Road, N8 9SG
2-5yrs. 9am-3.30pm. Termtime.

North London Rudolf Steiner School   020 8341 3770
Campsbourne Baptist Church, Hornsey High Street

Playland Day Nursery   020 8341 5199
40 Tottenham Lane, N8 7EA
2-5yrs.

Ruff 'N' Tumble   020 8348 2469
51 Crouch Hall Road, N8 8HH
2-5yrs. Full day

Starshine Nursery   020 8348 9909
Hornsey Club, Tivoli Road, N8 8RG
2-5yrs. Full day

N9
Edmonton Community Day Nursery   020 8807 9649
24 Cyprus Road, N9 9PG
2-5yrs. 8am-6pm. 51wks.

New Horizons Nursery   020 8351 8280
Walbrook House, 1 Huntingdon Road, N9 8LS
2-5yrs. Full day

Rainbow Nursery Firs Farm   020 8807 9078
1-4 Kipling Terrace, Great Cambridge Road, N9 9UJ
2¹/₂-5yrs. 9.15-11.45am and 12.30-3pm or 9.15-3pm.

Tara Kindergarten   020 8804 4484
310-314 Hartford Road, N9 7HB
3mths-5yrs. Full day

N10
3-4-5 Pre-School   07966 541 889
Church Crescent 345, Friends Meeting House,
Muswell Hill, N10 3NE
2-5yrs. 9.15am-12pm and 12.45-3.15pm. Termtime.

3-4-5 Pre-School   07930 340 557
Tetherdown 345, United Reform Church Hall,
Tetherdown, N10 1NB
2-5yrs. 9.15am-12pm and 12.45-3.15pm. Termtime.

Grey Gates Nursery   020 8883 5640
182 Muswell Hill Road, N10 3NG
6mths-5yrs. 8.10am-5.45pm. 51 wks

Montessori House   020 8444 4399
5 Princes Avenue, Muswell Hill, N10 3LS
Full Montessori education for ages 2-5yrs+ in Central Muswell Hill

s Norfolk House Prep School   020 8883 4584
10 Muswell Avenue, N10
Co-ed 4-11yrs

Nursery Montessori   020 8883 7958
24 Tetherdown, Muswell Hill, N10 1NB
2-5yrs. Full day

s Prince's Avenue School   020 8444 4399
5 Prince's Avenue, N10 3LS
Co-ed 5-7yrs

Rosemount Nursery School   020 8883 5842
6 Grosvenor Road, Muswell Hill, N10 2DS
2-5yrs. 8am-6pm. 50wks.

N11
Teddies Nurseries New Southgate   0800 980 3801
60 Beaconsfield Road, New Southgate, N11 3AE
3mths-5yrs. 8am-6pm. 51wks

N12
Busy Bees Nursery   020 8343 8500
c/o David Lloyd Leisure, Leisure Way, Finchley High
Road, N12 0QZ
3mths-5yrs. 9am-6pm. 51wks.

Primary Steps Day Nursery   020 8446 9135
37 Moss Hall Grove, N12 8PE
From 16mths-5yrs. 8am-6pm. 52wks.

s Woodside Park Intl School   020 8920 0600
88 Woodside Park Road, N12 8SH
Co-ed 2¹/₂-7yrs.

Asquith Nursery Salcombe   020 8882 2136
33 The Green, Southgate, N14 6EN
2-5yrs. 8am-6pm. 51wks

s Salcombe Prep School   020 8441 5282
224-226 Chase Side, Southgate, N14 4PL
Co-ed 4-11yrs

Shining Eyes & Busy Minds   020 8350 4584
West Grove Primary School, Chase Road, N14 4LR
2-5yrs. Full day

Southgate Day Nursery   020 8886 2824
25 Oakwood Avenue, N14 6QH
3mths-5yrs. Full day

Tara Kindergarten   020 8886 6163
2-16 Burleigh Parade, Burleigh Gardens, N14 5AD
3mths-5yrs. Full day

N15
Sugar Plum Nursery   020 8800 7560
255 West Green Road, N15 5JN
2-5yrs. Full day

Tottenham Green Under 5s Centre   020 8808 9194
The Green, Phillips Lane, N15 4GZ
2-5yrs. 8.30am-5.30pm. 50wks.

N16
Coconut Nursery   020 7923 0720
133 Stoke Newington Church Street, N16 0UH
10mths-5yrs. 8am-6pm. 51wks.

Mini Home   020 7249 0725
14 Allen Road, N16 8SD
3mths-5yrs. Full day 8am-6pm. 51 wks

Sunrise Nursery   020 8806 6279
1 Cazenove Road, N16 6PA
2-4¹/₂yrs. Full day

The Factory Community Nursery 020 7241 1520
107 Matthias Road, N16 8NP
2-4yrs. 8am-6pm. 49wks.

Thumbelina Nursery 020 7354 1278
169-171 Green Lanes, N16 9DB
2-5yrs. 8am-6pm. 48wks.

N17
Assure Day Nursery 020 8808 7373
33 Forster Road, N17 6QD
2-5yrs. 8am-6pm. 50wks.

Blossoms Nursery 020 8808 0178
Unit 10, Imperial House, 64 Willoughby Lane, N17 0SP
18mths-5yrs. 7.30am-6.15pm. 52wks.

Sunrise Nursery 020 8885 3354
55 Coniston Road, N17 0EX
2$^1/_2$-5yrs

N18
Ashland Private Day Nursery 020 8345 5752
36 Weir Hall Road, N18 1EJ
2-5yrs. 8am-6pm. Termtime.

Tinkerbells Nursery 020 8372 7682
2 Amersham Avenue, N18 1DT
3mths-5yrs. 8am-6pm. 52wks.

N19
Chameleon Nursery 020 7272 9111
76 Dartmouth Park Hill, N19 5HU
3mths-5yrs. 8.30am-6pm. 51wks. High quality childcare in a friendly environment for children aged 3mths-5yrs. A wide range of extra curricular activities are available for children. Organic food is used for our healthy home-cooked meals.

Hanley Crouch Playgroup 020 7263 1067
The Laundry, Sparsholt Road, Islington, N19 4EL
2$^1/_2$-5yrs. 9.30am-12.30pm. Termtime.

Highgate New Town Community 020 7281 7031
Play Group
Highgate New Town Community Centre, 25 Bertram Street, N19 5DQ
2-5yrs. 9.30am-12.30pm.

Konstam Nursery Centre 020 7272 3594
75 Chester Road, N19 5DH
0-5yrs. 8am-6pm. Termtime.

Montpelier Nursery 020 7485 9813
115 Brecknock Road, N19 5AH
3-5yrs. Full day

St John's Playcentre 020 7272 2780
Pemberton Gardens, N19 5RR
4-11yrs. 4.30-6.30pm. Termtime.

N21

Bumble Bees Montessori Nursery   020 8364 3647
8 Uplands Way, Winchmore Hill, N21 1DG
2-5yrs. 8am-6pm. 51wks.

S Keble Prep School   020 8360 3359
Wades Hill, Winchmore Hill, N21 1BG
Boys 4-13yrs

Leapfrog Day Nursery   020 8360 6610
2 Florey Square, Highlands Village, N21 1UJ
3mths-5yrs. 7am-7pm. 52 wks

S Palmers Green High School   020 8886 1135
Hoppers Road, Winchmore Hill, N21 3LJ
Girls 3-16yrs

Palmers Green High School Nursery   020 8360 1964
Holy Trinity Church Hall, Green Lanes, N21
3-5yrs. 9am-12pm. Termtime. Admissions are on a first-
come, first-served basis so do register early and visit the
school with your baby.

Teddys Day Nursery   020 8364 3842
18 Green Dragon Lane, N21 2LD
3mths-5yrs. 8am-6pm. 52wks.

Woodberry Day Nursery   020 8882 6917
63 Church Hill, Winchmore Hill, N21 1LE
6wks-5yrs, 8am-6pm, 52 week per year.

N22

3-4-5 Pre-School   07778 739 319
Springfield 345, c/o The Actual Workshop, The
Grove, Alexandra Park, N22 4AY
2-5yrs. 9.15am-12pm. Termtime.

Alexandra Nursery School   020 8374 9492
189 Alexandra Park Road, N22 7BJ
2-5yrs

Bowes Park Nursery   020 8888 1142
63-65 Whittington Road, N22 8YR
6mths-5yrs. 7.30am-6.30pm. 51wks.

Rainbow Corner Nursery   020 8888 5862
24 Elgin Road, N22 7UE
2-5yrs. 8am-6pm. 48wks.

NW1

Daisies Day Nursery   020 7498 2922
& School - Regents Park
15 Gloucester Gate, NW1
www.daisiesdaynurseries.co.uk
3mths-5yrs. 8am-6pm. 50 wks.

Agar Community Nursery   020 7485 5195
Wrotham Road, NW1 9SU
2-5yrs. 8.30am-5pm. Termtime.

Auden Place Community Nursery   020 7586 0098
1 Auden Place, Manley Street, NW1 8LT
2-5yrs. 8.30am-6pm. 51wks.

Camden Chinese Community Nursery   020 7485 4156
United Reformed Church, Buck Street, NW1 8NJ
2-5yrs. 8.30-5.50pm. Termtime currently, possibly going full time.

Dolphin Montessori School   020 7267 3994
Luther Tyndale Church Hall, Leighton Crescent,
NW1 2QY
2$^{1}/_{2}$-4$^{1}/_{2}$yrs

Hampden Nursery Centre   020 7387 1822
80 Polygon Road, NW1 1HQ
0-3yrs. 8am-6pm. 48wks.

Kidsunlimited Nurseries   0845 850 0222
Regents Place
1 Triton Mall, Regents Place, Longford Street, NW1 3FN
3mths-5yrs. 7.30am-6pm. 51 wks.

Ready Steady Go   020 7722 2488
29 Hopkinsons Place, Camden, NW1 8TN
2-3yrs. 9.30am-12.30pm. Termtime. For admissions details
call head office on 020 7586 5862.

Ready Steady Go   020 7267 4241
123 St Pancras Way, NW1 0SY
2-5yrs. 9.15am-12.15pm. Termtime. For admissions details
call head office on 020 7586 5862.

Regents Park Nursery Centre   020 7387 2382
Augustus Street, NW1 3TJ
0-5yrs. 8am-6pm. 50wks.

Regents Place Nursery   020 7383 7176
1 Triton Mall, Regents Place, Longford Street, NW1 3FN
0-4yrs. 7.15am-6pm. 51wks.

St Christopher's Community Nursery   020 7388 5545
4th Floor, St. Christopher flats, Bridgeway Street
2-5yrs. 9.30am-4pm. 46wks.

St Mark's Square Nursery School   020 7586 8383
St Mark's Church, St Mark's Square, NW1 7TN
2-5yrs. Full day

S The Cavendish School   020 7485 1958
179 Arlington Road, NW1 7EY
Girls 3-11yrs

The Speech Language   020 7383 3834
and Hearing Centre
1-5 Christopher Place, Chalton Street, NW1 1JF
0-5yrs. 9am-12pm and 2-3.15pm. Termtime.

Westminster Kingsway College   020 7391 6412
Nursery
Regents Park Centre, Longford Street, NW1 3HB
2-5yrs.

Woodentots Montessori School   020 7485 0053
6 Rochester Road, NW1 9JH
2$^{1}/_{2}$-5yrs. 9am-3pm. Termtime.

NW2

s Mulberry House School   020 8452 7340
7 Minster Road, NW2 3SD
www.mulberryhouseschool.com
Co-ed 2-8yrs. Admissions: names down early as the school
is well subscribed.

Fordwych Nursery   020 8208 2591
107 Fordwych Road, NW2 3TL
2-5yrs. 9am-3pm. Termtime.

Hoot Lane Montessori   020 8209 0813
St Cuthberts Church, Fordwych Road, NW2 3TG
2½-5yrs

Little Ark Montessori Nursery School   020 7794 6359
80 Westbere Road, NW2 3RU
2-5yrs. 8am-6pm. 50wks.

Neasden Montessori   020 8208 1631
St Catherine's Church Hall, Dudden Hill Lane, NW2 7RX
2-5yrs

NW3

s Devonshire House School   020 7435 1916
69 Fitzjohn's Avenue, Hampstead, NW3 6AE
www.devonshirehouseschool.co.uk
Co-ed 3-13yrs.

Oak Tree Nursery   020 7435 1916
2 Arkwright Road, NW3 6PD
www.devonshirehouseschool.co.uk
2½-11yrs Girls, 13yrs Boys. Part of Devonshire House
School.

Peter Piper Nursery School   020 7431 7402
St Luke's Church Hall, Kidderpore Avenue, NW3 7SU
2-5yrs. 9am-1pm. Established 1967. A friendly and
stimulating spacious nursery environment.

Belsize Square Synagogue   020 7431 3823
Nursery School
51 Belsize Square, NW3 4HX
2 1/4-5yrs. 9.15am-12.15pm plus afternoon sessions.
Termtime.

Chalcot Montessori Nursery School   020 7722 1386
9 Chalcot Gardens, NW3 4YB
2-5yrs. 9am-1pm. Termtime.

Cherryfields Preschool Nursery   020 7431 0055
523 Finchley Road, NW3 7BD
2-5yrs. 9am-3pm. Termtime.

Church Row Nursery   020 7431 2603
Hampstead Parish Church, Church Row, NW3 6UP
2½-5yrs. 9.15am-12.15pm. 36wks.

Eton Nursery Montessori School   020 7722 1532
45 Buckland Crescent, NW3 5DJ
2-5yrs. 9am-3.30pm. Termtime.

Friends Pre-School 07745 104 996
120 Heath Street, NW3 1DR
3-5yrs. 9am-12.30pm. Termtime.

S Hall School 020 7722 1700
23 Crossfield Road, NW3 4NU
Boys 4-13yrs

Hampstead Activity Nursery 020 7435 0054
Christ Church, Hampstead Square, NW3 1AB
1-5yrs. 8am-6pm. 51wks.

Hampstead Hill Nursery School 020 7435 6262
St. Stephens Hall, Pond Street, NW3 2PP
2-5yrs. 7.45am-5.30pm. 51wks.

S Heathside Preparatory School 020 7794 5857
16 New End, NW3 1JA
Co-ed 2¹/₂-11yrs

S Hereward House School 020 7794 4820
14 Strathray Gardens, NW3 4NY
Boys 4-13yrs

S Lyndhurst House Prep School 020 7435 4936
24 Lyndhurst Gardens, Hampstead, NW3 5NW
Boys 7-13yrs. New admittance for boys aged 4yrs from
September 2006.

Maria Montessori Children's House 020 7435 3646
26 Lyndhurst Gardens, NW3 5NW
2¹/₂-6yrs. Full day

Octagon Nursery School 020 7586 3206
Saint Saviour's Church Hall, Eton Road, NW3 4SU
2¹/₂-5yrs. 9am-12pm. Termtime.

Olivers Montessori Nursery School 020 7435 5898
52 Belsize Square, NW3 4HN
2-5yrs

S Phoenix School 020 7722 4433
36 College Crescent, NW3 5LF
Co-ed 3-7yrs

Primrose Nursery (Rudolph Steiner) 020 7794 5865
32 Glenilla Road, NW3 4AN
3-5yrs. 9.30am-12.30pm.

Puss in Boots Nursery School 020 7281 5485
Agincourt Road, NW3 2NT
2-8yrs. 9am-3.30pm. Termtime.

Ready Steady Go 020 7586 6289
12a King Henry's Road, NW3 3RP
3-5yrs. 9am-2pm. Termtime. For admissions details call
head office on 020 7586 5862.

S Royal School Hampstead 020 7794 7708
65 Rosslyn Hill, NW3 5UD
Girls 3-18yrs (boarders from 11yrs+).

S Sarum Hall 020 7794 2261
15 Eton Avenue, NW3 3EL
Girls 3-11yrs

S South Hampstead High School 020 7794 7198
5 Netherhall Gardens, NW3 5RN
Girls 4-18yrs.

S Southbank International School 020 7431 1200
16 Netherhall Gardens, NW3 5TH
Co-ed 3-14yrs

S St Anthony's School 020 7435 0316
90 Fitzjohns Avenue, NW3 6NP
Boys 5-13yrs

S St Christopher's School 020 7435 1521
32 Belsize Lane, NW3 5AE
Girls 4-11yrs

S St Margaret's School 020 7435 2439
18 Kidderpore Gardens, NW3 7SR
Girls 5-16yrs

S St Mary's School, Hampstead 020 7435 1868
47 Fitzjohn's Avenue, NW3 6PG
Boys 2-7yrs, Girls 2-11yrs

Stepping Stone Nursery 020 7435 9641
(North Bridge House School)
33 Fitzjohn's Avenue, NW3 5JY
2¹/₂-5yrs. Sessional. Termtime 9am-3.30pm.

Swiss Cottage Pre-School 020 7916 7090
19 Winchester Road, NW3 3NR
3-4yrs.

Three Acres Pre-School 020 7722 3812
29-31 Parkhill Road, NW3 2YH
3-5yrs. 9.30am-1.30pm. Termtime.

S Trevor-Roberts Prep School 020 7586 1444
55-57 Eton Avenue, NW3 3ET
Co-ed 5-13yrs

S University College School (Jnr) 020 7435 3068
11 Holly Hill, NW3 6QN

S Village School 020 7485 4673
2 Parkhill Road, NW3 2YN
4-11yrs

NW4

S Hendon Preparatory School   020 8203 7727
20 Tenterden Grove, NW4 1TD
www.hendonprep.co.uk
Co-ed 4-13yrs.

NW5

Bringing Up Baby: 020 7284 3600
Kentish Town Day Nursery
37 Ryland Road, NW5 3EH
www.bringingupbaby.co.uk
3mths-5yrs. 8am-6.15pm. 50 wks.

Highgate Children's Centre   020 7485 5252
Highgate Studios, 53-79 Highgate Road, NW5 1TL
www.brighthorizons.com
3mths-5yrs. 8am-6pm. 51wks. Also after school and holiday
clubs for 4-10yrs.

York Rise Nursery   020 7485 7962
St Mary Brookfield Church Hall, York Rise, NW5 1SB
2-5yrs. 9am-4pm. 49wks.

Gospel Oak Nursery Centre   020 7267 4517
5 Lismore Circus, NW5 4RA
6mths-5yrs. 8am-6pm. 51wks (also an after school club).

Bluebells Nursery   020 7284 3952
Our Lady Help of Christians Church Hall, Lady
Margaret Road, NW5 2NE
2¹/₂-5yrs

Caversham Centre Nursery   020 7974 3377
Vadnie Bish House, 33-43 Caversham Road, NW5 2DR
2-5yrs. 9.30am-3.30pm. 48wks.

Chaston Nursery & Pre-prep School   020 7482 0701
Chaston Place, off Grafton Terrace, NW5 4JH
3mths-7yrs. 8.30am-6pm. 51wks.

Cresswood Nursery   020 7485 1551
215 Queen's Crescent, NW5 4DP
2-5yrs. 8am-5.30pm. 51wks.

Elfrida Rathbone Nursery   020 7424 1601
7 Dowdney Close, Bartholomew Road, NW5 2BP
0-5yrs. 10am-2pm and 12.30-3pm. Termtime.

Rooftops Nursery   020 7267 7949
Priestly House, Athlone Street, Kentish Town, NW5 4LN
2-5yrs. 8am-6pm. 51wks.

The Dolphin Montessori School   020 7267 3994
Luther Tyndale Church Hall, Leighton Crescent
2-5yrs. 9am-3pm. Termtime.

NW6

Sunshine Playgroup   020 7328 0713
Hashomer House, 37A Broadhurst Gardens, NW6 3QT
www.sunshineplaygroup.com
Play, music, art & crafts and cookery classes for 6 mths-5yrs
in South Hampstead. Small groups 8 - 10 children
with/without carers. Open every day, half terms, summmer
workshops in July, birthday parties.

Acol Nursery Centre   020 7624 2937
16 Acol Road, NW6 3AG
0-7yrs. 8am-6pm. 51wks.

Asquith Nursery West Hampstead   020 7328 4787
11 Woodchurch Road, West Hampstead, NW6 3PL
18mths-5yrs. 8am-6pm. 51 wks

Beehive Montessori   020 8969 2235
147 Chevening Road, NW6
2-5yrs. .40am-4.30pm (closes at 3pm on Fridays). Termtime.

S Broadhurst School   020 7328 4280
19 Greencroft Gardens, NW6 3LP
Co-ed 2¹/₂ -7yrs. 8.45am-11.45am and 12.45-3.45pm or full
day 8.45am-2.45pm. Termtime.

Centro Infantil Menchu   020 7624 9398
Priory House, Kingsgate Place, NW6 4TA
2-5yrs. 9am-5pm. 49wks.

Chaston Nursery School   020 7372 2120
30-31 Palmerston Road, NW6 2JL
3mths-5yrs. Full day

Crickets Montessori   07811 102 085
Nursery School
South Hampstead Cricket Club, Milverton Road
2¹/₂-5yrs. 9am-3pm. Termtime only.

Happy Child Day Nursery   020 7625 1966
St Anne's & St Andrew's Church Hall, 125
Saulsbury Road, NW6 6RG
2-5yrs. 8am-6pm. 51wks.

Happy Child Day Nursery   020 7328 8791
2 Victoria Road, NW6 6QG
3mths-5yrs. 8am-6pm. 51wks.

S Islamia Primary School   020 7372 2532
Salusbury Road, NW6 6PE
Co-ed 4-16yrs.

Kingsgate Pre-School & Creche   020 7625 1743
Kingsgate Community centre, 107 Kingsgate Road
Pre-school 9.30am-12pm. Creche 1-3pm. Termtime.

Mackenzie Day Nursery   020 7624 0370
St Mary's Church Hall, Abbey Road, NW6 4SR
2-5yrs. Full day

S Rainbow Montessori   020 7328 8986
Junior School
13 Woodchurch Road, NW6 3PL
Co-ed 5-12yrs.

Rainbow Montessori School   020 7328 8986
St James's Hall, Sherriff Road, NW6 2AP
2¹/₂-5yrs. 9am-12.15pm and 12.15-3pm. Termtime.

Sington Nursery   020 7431 1279
Portakabins Community Centre, 160 Mill Lane, NW6 1TF
3-5yrs. Full day

Teddies Nurseries   020 7372 3290
West Hampstead
2 West End Lane, NW6 4NT
3mths-5yrs. 8am-6pm. 51wks

The Learning Tree Nursery   020 7372 7213
Quex Road, Methodist Church, NW6 4PR
2-5yrs. 9am-12pm or 9am-1.30pm. Termtime.

West Hampstead Pre-School   020 7328 4787
(Asquith Court School)
11 Woodchurch Road, NW6 3PL
18mths-5yrs. Full day

NW7
S Belmont   020 8959 1431
Mill Hill, NW7 4ED
Co-ed 7-13yrs

S Goodwyn School   020 8959 3756
Hammers Lane, Mill Hill, NW7 4DB
Co-ed 3-11yrs.

Leapfrog Day Nursery   020 8906 9123
30 Millway, Mill Hill, NW7 3RB
3mths-5yrs. 7am-7pm. 52 wks

S Mill Hill Pre-Prep School   020 8959 6884
Winterstoke House, Wills Grove, NW7 1QR
3-7yrs. 8.30am-3.15pm. Termtime.

S Mount School   020 8959 3403
Milespit Hill, Mill Hill, NW7 2RX
Girls 4-18yrs

NW8
S Abercorn School   020 7286 4785
28 Abercorn Place, NW8 9XP
Co-ed 2¹/₂-13yrs. 8.45-11.45am and 12.30-3.30pm.
Termtime.

Al Madina Nursery School   020 7724 7971
Regents Park Mosque, 146 Park Road, NW8 7RG
From 3yrs+. 9am-3pm. 51wks. (For Muslim children only).

S American School in London   020 7449 1200
1 Waverley Place, NW8 0NP
An independent co-educational day school for students aged
4-18yrs

S Arnold House   020 7266 6982
1 Loudon Road, NW8 0LH
Boys 5-13yrs

Barrow Hill Pre-School   020 7722 5455
Allisten Road, NW8 7AT
2-5yrs. 9.30am-3.15pm. Termtime.

Carlton Hill Day Nursery   020 7641 4491
86 Carlton Hill, NW8 0ER
6mths-5yrs. 8am-6pm. 51wks.

Independent Mothers Pre-School   020 7723 4852
Broadley Street Gardens, Broadley Street, NW8 8BN
2¹/₂-5yrs. 9.30am-3.15pm. 38wks.

Langtry Nursery Centre   020 7624 0963
11-29 Langtry Road, NW8 0AJ
0-3yrs. 8am-6pm. 51wks..

Ready Steady Go   020 7722 0007
St. John's Wood Terrace, NW8 6LP
3-5yrs. 9am-2pm. Termtime. Register early as usually
oversubscribed. For admissions details call head office on
020 7586 5862.

S St Christina's RC   020 7722 8784
Preparatory School
25 St Edmund's Terrace, NW8 7PY
Boys 3-7yrs, Girls 3-11yrs+

s St John's Wood Junior   020 7722 7149
Prep School
St John's Hall, Lord's Roundabout, NW8 7NE
Co-ed 3-8yrs

St John's Wood Synagogue   020 7286 3859
Kindergarten
37/41 Grove End Road, NW8 9NA
2-5yrs

The Vestry Pre-School   020 7624 2705
St. Marks Church, Abercorn Place, NW8 9YD
2-5yrs. 9.30am-12pm. Termtime.

Toddler's Inn Nursery School   020 7586 0520
Cicely Davies Hall, Cochrane Street, NW8 7NX
2-5yrs. 9am-3.30pm. Termtime (with a summer programme).

NW9
Gower House School & Nursery   020 8205 2509
Blackbird Hill, NW9 8RR
2-11yrs. 8.50am-3.30pm plus a breakfast and after school club. Termtime.

Joel Nursery   020 8200 0189
214 Colindeep Lane, NW9 6DF
2-5yrs. 8am-6pm. 48wks.

s St Nicholas School   020 8205 7153
22 Salmon Street, NW9 8PN
Co-ed 2-11yrs

NW10
Andrew Memorial Day Nursery   020 8459 2184
Seventh Day Adventist Church, Glebe Road, NW10 2JD
2-5yrs. 8.15am-5.30pm. 51 wks.

Christchurch Nursery School   020 8961 9250
St Albans Road, NW10 8UG
18mths-3yrs. 8am-6pm. 51wks.

Domino Playgroup   020 8459 3487
Kings Hall Centre, 155 Harlesden Rd, NW10 2BS
2-5yrs. 9am-12pm on Mon, Tues, Thurs and Fri. 51wks.

Fairhaven Nursery   020 8459 4845
Longstone Avenue, NW10 3UE
18mths-5yrs. 8.30am-5.30pm. 51wks.

Happy Child Day Nursery   020 8961 3485
15 Longstone Avenue, NW10 3TY
3mths-5yrs. 8am-6pm. 51wks.

Harlesden Angels Nursery   020 8961 4927
25-27 High Street, NW10 4NE
2-5yrs. 8am-6pm. 49 wks.

Jubilee Clock Pre-School   020 8838 0085
All Souls Church Hall, Station Road, NW10 4UJ
1-4yrs. 8am-6pm. Full year.

Kensal Green Under 5s   020 8968 6095
130 Mortimer Road, NW10 5SN
2-5yrs. 8am-5.30pm. 48wks.

Kindercare Montessori   020 8838 1688
Bridge Park Sports Centre, Harrow Road, NW10 0RG
2-5yrs. 8am-6pm. 51wks.

Little Acorn Nursery   020 8451 1705
Scout House, Strode Road, NW10 2NN
2-5yrs. 8am-6pm. 52wks.

St Mary's Nursery   020 8459 8578
The Parish Centre, Neasden Lane, NW10 2TS
2-5yrs. 8am-6pm. 52wks.

St Michael's Nursery   020 8961 6399
St Matthews Church, St Marys Road, NW10 4AU
2-5yrs. 8am-6pm. Full year.

The Children's Centre   020 8961 6648
40 Nicoll Road, NW10 9AB
18mths-5yrs. 8am-6pm. 51wks.

The Children's Centre   020 8961 9250
Christ Church, St Albans Road, NW10 8UG
18mths-5yrs. 8am-6pm. 51wks.

The Heritage Family Centre   020 8830 1993
161 Pitfield Way, NW10 0UW
6mths-5yrs. 8am-6pm. 50wks.

NW11
Asquith Nursery Golders Green   020 8458 7389
212 Golders Green Road, NW11 9AT
18mths-5yrs. 8am-6pm. 51 wks

Clowns   020 8455 7333
153 North End Road, Golders Green, NW11 7HX
1-5yrs. 8am-6pm. 51wks.

s Goldershill School   020 8455 2589
666 Finchley Road, NW11 7NT
Co-ed 2-7yrs

Hellenic College Bi-Lingual   020 8455 8511
Montessori Nursery
Greek Orthodox Cathedral of Holy Cross & St
Michael, The Riding, NW11 8HL
2^1/$_2$-5yrs.

Hoop Lane Montessori School   020 8209 0813
31.5 Hoop Lane, Unitarian Church Hall, NW11 8BS
2-5yrs. Mornings only. Termtime.

s King Alfred School   020 8457 5200
Manor Wood, North End Road, NW11 7HY
Co-ed 4-18yrs

Pardes House Kindergarten   020 8458 4003
Golders Green Synagogue, 41 Dunston Road,
NW11 8HG
2-4. Full day

East London Postcodes

E1

Spitalfields Nursery　020 7375 0775
21 Lamb Street, E1 6EA
www.brighthorizons.com
3mths-5yrs. 8am-6pm. 51wks.

Alice Model Nursery　020 7790 5425
14 Beaumont Grove, E1 4NQ
3-5yrs. 9.15am-3.15pm. Termtime.

Dreammaker Day Nursery　020 7480 7166
65 Cartwright Street, E1 8NB
3mths-5yrs. 7am-6pm. 52wks.

Green Gables Montessori School　020 7488 2374
St Paul's Institute, 302 The Highway, E1 3DH
3mths-5yrs. 8am-6pm. 51wks.

The Nursery　020 7265 0098
St. Paul's Church, Dock St, Wapping, E1 8JN
3mths-5yrs. 7am-7pm. 52wks.

E2

Bethnal Green Montessori School　020 7739 4343
68 Warner Place, E2 7DA
2-6yrs. Mon-Thurs 8.45am-3pm and Fri 8.45am-12pm.
Termtime. Also summer school.

Columbia Market Nursery School　020 7739 4518
Columbia Rd, E2 7PG
3-5yrs. 9.30am-3.30pm. Termtime.

Noah's Ark　020 7613 6346
within Mildmay Hospital, Hackney Road, E2 7NA
1mth-4yrs. 8.30am-6pm. 52wks.

Rachel Keeling Nursery School　020 8980 5856
Bullards Place, Morpeth Street, E2 0PS
3-5yrs. 9.15am-3pm. Termtime.

The Happy Nest Nursery　020 7739 3193
Fellows Court Family Centre, Weymouth Terrace, E2 8LR
2-5yrs. 8.30am-5.30pm. 51wks.

E3

Bow Nursery Centre　020 8981 0483
1 Bruce Rd, Bromley by Bow, E3 3HN

Overland Day Nursery　020 8981 1619
60 Pardell Rd, E3 2RU

Pilla Box Gardens Nursery　020 8983 7431
49 Fairfield Road, E3 2QA
3mths-2yrs. 8am-6pm. 52wks.

Pillar Box Montessori Nursery School　020 8980 0700
107 Bow Road, E3 2AN
0-7yrs. Full day

E4

Billet's Corner Nursery　020 8523 3823
adj. Sainsbury's, 11 Walthamstow Avenue, E4 8ST
www.brighthorizons.com
3mths-5yrs. 8am-6pm. 50 wks.

Ainslie Wood Nursery　020 8523 9910
140 Ainslie Wood Road, Chingford, E4 9DD
3-5yrs. 9-11.30am and 1-3.30pm. Termtime.

Amhurst Nursery　020 8527 1614
13 The Avenue, E4 9LB
2-5yrs. 8am-6pm. 52wks.

Buttercups　020 8527 2902
22 Marborough Road, Chingford, E4 9AL
3mths-5yrs. 8am-6pm. 51wks.

College Gardens Nursery School　020 8529 3885
College Gardens, E4 7LQ
3-5yrs. 8am-6pm. 51wks.

Leapfrog Day Nursery　020 8524 7063
2 Larkswood Leisure Park, 175 New Road,
Chingford, E4 9EY
3mths-5yrs. 7.30am-6.30pm. 51wks.

Merryfield Montessori Nursery　020 8524 7697
76 Station Road, Chingford, E4 7BA
2-5yrs. Full day.

s Normanhurst School　020 8529 4307
68-74 Station Road, Chingford, E4 7BA
Co-ed 2-16yrs.

Tiny Tots　020 8523 5046
101 Higham Station Avenue, E4 9AY
3mths-5yrs. 8am-6pm. 52wks.

Woodlands E4 Day Nursery　020 8531 0713
16a Handsworth Avenue, E4 9PJ
3mths-5yrs. 7.45am-6.30pm. 52wks.

E5

Belz Nursery　020 8800 6186
96 Clapton Common, E5 9AL
2-5yrs. 9.30am-3.30pm. Termtime.

Harrington Hill Nursery School　020 8806 9643
Wrens Park Estate, Warwick Grove, E5 9LL
3-5yrs. 9.10am-3.10pm. Termtime.

Nightingale Nursery School　020 8985 5937
Rendlesham Road, E5 8PA

North London Rudolf Steiner Nursery　020 8986 8968
89 Blurton Road, Hackney, E5 0NH

St Michael's Nursery　020 8985 2886
59 Thistlewaite Road, E5 0QG

E6

Heritage Children's Day Nursery   020 7473 3522
116 Evelyn Dennington Road, E6 5YU
0-5yrs. 7.30m-6.30pm. 51wks.

Oliver Thomas Nursery School   020 8552 1177
Mathews Avenue, E6 6BU
9am-3pm. Termtime.

St Stephens Nursery School   020 8471 1366
St. Stephens Road, E6 1AX

s **Grangewood School**   020 8472 3552
Chester Road, Forest Gate, E7 8QT
Co-ed 4-11yrs

Kaye Rowe Nursery School   020 8534 4403
Osborne Road, E7 0PH
3-5yrs. 9.15am-3.15pm. Termtime.

E8

Independent Place Nursery   020 7275 7755
Units 26/27 Independent Place, Shacklewell Lane
3mths-5yrs. 8am-6pm. 51wks.

Market Nursery   020 7241 0978
Wilde Close, Hackney, E8 4JS

New Generation   020 7249 9826
179 Haggerston Road, Haggerston, E8 4JA

Teddy Bear School House Nursery   020 7249 4433
The Trinity Centre, Beechwood Road, E8 3DY
2-4yrs. 8am-6pm. 52wks.

E9

Little Saint Nursery School   020 8533 6600
Wally Foster Community Centre, Homerton High
Road, E9 5QB
2mths-5yrs. 7.30am-6.30pm. 50wks.

Wentworth Nursery School   020 8985 3491
Cassland Road, E9 5BY

E10

Alertkids Community Nursery   020 8558 8503
806 High Road, Leighton, E10 6AE
3mths-5yrs. 8am-6pm. 51wks.

Beaumont Nursery Unit   020 8518 7203
192 Vicarage Road, E10 5DX
3 1/2-5yrs. 9.10-11.40am and 12.55-3.25pm. Termtime.

Bright Kids Day Nursery   020 8558 0666
2 Leyton Mills, Marshall road, E10 5NH
4mths-5yrs. 8am-6pm. 51wks.

Bright Kids Day Nursery   0800 298 2633
71 Vicarage Road, E10 5EF
12mths-5yrs. 8am-6pm. 51wks.

Hillcrest Nursery   020 8558 9889
Trinity Methodist Church, 274 High Road, Leyton
1-5yrs. 7.30am-6pm. 51wks.

Smilers Nursery   020 8558 1810
29 Vicarage Road, Leyton, E10 5EF

The Nappy Gang Nursery   020 8539 8359
100 Oliver Road, E10 5JY
2-5yrs. 7.30am-6.30pm (breakfast and afterschool clubs).
48wks.

E11

Acacia Nursery School   020 8558 4444
Cecil Road, E11 3HE
6mths-5yrs. 8am-6pm. 48wks.

Humpty Dumpty Nursery   020 8539 3810
24/26 Fairlop Road, Leytonstone, E11 1BN
1-5yrs. 8am-6pm. 48wks.

Just Learning Nursery   020 8988 0818
Whipps Cross University Hospital, Whipps Cross
Road, E11 1NR
3mths-5yrs. 6.45am-7pm. 51wks.

Kiddy Care Day Nursery   020 8556 1732
62 Hainault Road, Leytonstone, E11 1EQ
3mths-5yrs. 8am-6pm. 51wks.

Little Green Man Day Nursery   020 8539 7228
15 Lemna Road, E11 1HX
0-5yrs. 7am-7pm. 51wks.

Sunbeams day Nursery   020 8530 2784
10 Bushwood, E11 3AY

Sunshine Day Nursery   020 8556 6889
167 Wallwood Road, E11 1AQ

E12

Happy Faces   020 8478 2805
524 High Street, E12 6QN
2-5 yrs

Sheringham Nursery School   020 8553 2479
Sheringham Avenue, E12 5PB

E13

Coccinelle   020 8552 3340
663 Barking Road, E13 9EX
1 1/2-5yrs. 8am-6.30pm. 51wks.

Foundation for Learning   020 7476 5123
Foster Road Nursery, Foster Road, Plaistow, E13 8BT
3mths-5yrs. 7.30am-6pm. 51wks.

Smarty Pants Day Nursery   020 8471 2620
1 Plashet Road, E13 0PZ

Stepping Stones Childcare   020 7476 8321
Kingsford Community School, Woodside Road, E13
4mths-5yrs. Full day, termtime only

E14

Bushytails Private Day Nursery   020 7537 7776
Wood Wharf Business Park, Docklands, E14 9LZ
0-5yrs. Full day

Elizabeth Lansbury Nursery School 020 7987 4358
Cordelia Street, E14 6DZ
3-5yrs. 9.15am-3.30pm. Termtime.

Lanterns Nursery & Pre-School 020 7363 0951
F2-F7 Lanterns Court, Millharbour, E14 9TU
0-5yrs. 8am-6pm. 51wks.

Unicorn Day Nursery 020 7513 0505
13 Columbus Courtyard, Canary Wharf, E14 4DA
3mths-5yrs. Full day

E15
Rebecca Cheetham Nursery School 020 8534 3136
Marcus Street, E15 3JT

Ronald Openshaw Nursery 020 8534 6196
Henniker Road, Stratford, E15 1JP
2-4yrs. 8am-6pm or sessional. 48wks.

Stepping Stones Childcare 020 8534 8777
Brickfields Centre, Welfare Road, E15 4HT
6mths-5yrs. Full day

Ultimate Montessori Day Nursery 020 8519 2100
9 Brydges Road, E15 1NA
3mths-5yrs. 8am-6pm. 52wks.

E16
Abrahams Nursery & Kids Club 020 7476 3672
1 Radland Road, E16 1LN
3mths-5yrs. 8am-6pm. 52wks.

Ceylon Cottage Nurseries 020 7511 0759
Ceylon Cottage, Butchers Road, E16 1PH
0-5yrs. 7.30am-6.30pm. 51wks.

Foundations for Learning 020 7473 1412
Kimberley Road, E16 4NT
3mths-5 yrs. 8am-6pm. 51wks.

Leapfrog Day Nursery 0207 474 7487
Royal Victoria Docks, E16 1XL
3mths-5yrs. 7am-7pm. 52 wks

Mayflower Nursery School 020 7474 5263
Burke Street, Canning Town, E16 1ET

Rosecare Nursery 020 7474 0881
Custom House Baptist Church, Prince Regent
Lane, E16 3JJ

E17
Carville Day Nursery 020 8521 7612
43a West Avenue Road, E17 9SF
0-4¹/₂yrs. 8am-6.30pm. 51wks.

Chapel End Early Years Centre 020 8527 9192
Brookscroft Road, E17 4LH
2-5yrs. 8am-6pm. 51wks.

Church Hill 020 8520 9196
Woodbury Road, E17 9SB

ⓢ Forest Pre-prep School 020 8520 1744
Snaresbrook, E17 3PY
Co-ed 4-11yrs.

Happy Child Pre-School Nursery 020 8520 8880
The Old Town Hall, 14b Orford Road, E17 9NL

Just Learning Day Nursery 020 8527 9711
20 Sutton Road, Higham Hill, Walthamstow, E17 5QA
0-5yrs. 7am-7pm. 51wks.

Koala Bear Day Nursery 020 8520 0762
1 Church Hill, E17 3AB
3mths-5yrs. 9am-6pm. 51wks.

Magic Roundabout Nursery 020 8523 5551
161 Wadham Road, E17 4HU
3mths-5yrs. 7.30am-7pm. 52wks.

Rascals Day Nurseries 020 8520 2417
34 Verulam Avenue, E17 8ER
0-5yrs. 7.45am-6pm. 52wks.

Tinkerbells Nursery 020 8520 8338
185 Coppermill Lane, Walthamstow, E17 7HU
3mths-5yrs. 8am-6pm. 52wks.

Tom Thumb Nursery 020 8520 1329
20 Shirley Close, 1-7 Beulah Road, E17 9LZ
2-5yrs. 8am-6pm. 48wks.

Walthamstow Montessori School 020 8523 2968
Penrhyn Hall, Penrhyn Avenue, E17 5DA
2¹/₂-5yrs. 8am-3pm. Termtime.

E18
Cleveland's Day Nursery 020 8518 8855
71 Cleveland Road, E18 2AE
3mths-5yrs. 8am-6pm. 51wks.

Fareacres Nursery 020 8505 3248
1 Chelmsford Road, South Woodford, E18
3mths-5yrs. 8am-6.30pm. 51wks.

Fullers Hall Community Nursery 020 8505 5779
64a Fullers Road, South Woodford, E18 2QA
2-5 rs. 8am-6pm. 51wks.

Heritage Children's Day Nursery 020 8530 8688
52-54 Chigwell Road, E18 1NN
2-5yrs. 7.30-6pm. 51wks.

Rainbow Kids Nursery 020 8504 1036
2 Malmesbury Road, E18 2NN
3mths-5yrs. 8am-6.30pm. 52wks.

ⓢ Snaresbrook College 020 8989 2394
75 Woodford Road, E18 2EA
Co-ed 3-11yrs

The Hertiage Day Nursery   **020 8530 8688**
52-54 Chigwell Road, South Woodford, E18 1NN
2-5yrs. 7.30am-6pm. 51wks.

Woodlands Babies   **020 8559 1247**
194 Maybank Road, South Woodford, E18 1EL
3mths-2yrs. 7.45am-6.30pm. 52wks.

EC1

Bright Horizons Family Solutions   **020 7253 9620**
Morelands, 5-23 Old Street, EC1V 9HL
www.brighthorizons.com
3mths-5yrs. 8am-6pm. 50wks)

Hopes and Dreams   **020 7833 9388**
339-341 City Road, EC1V 1LJ
www.hopesanddreams.co.uk
3mths-5yrs. 7am-7pm. Award-winning montessori nursery
school with a reputation for excellent childcare.

East West Community Nursery   **020 7490 1790**
Mitchell Street, Islington, EC1V 3QD
2-5yrs. 8.30am-5.30pm.48wks.

Kidsunlimited Nurseries Mango Tree   **0845 850 0222**
62-66 Farringdon Road, EC1R 3GA
3mths-5yrs. 7.30am-6pm. 51 wks.

Leapfrog Day Nursery 020 778 0100
Weddel House, 13-21 West Smithfield, EC1A 9HU
3mths-5yrs. 7am-7pm. 52 wks

EC2
Broadgate Nursery 020 7247 3491
21 Curtain Road, EC2A 3LW
www.brighthorizons.com
3mths-5yrs. 8am-6pm. 50wks (see advert pg X)

Daisies Day Nursery 020 7498 2922
& School - City
1 Bridgewater Square, EC2Y 8AH
www.daisiesdaynurseries.co.uk
3mths-5yrs. 8am-6pm. 50wks.

Leapfrog Day Nursery 020 7422 0088
49 Clifton Street, EC2A 4EX
3mths-5yrs. 7am-7pm. 52 wks

Barbican Playgroup 020 7638 2718
Level 1& 2, Andrewes House, Barbican, EC2Y 8AX
2 ¹/₂-5yrs. 9.30am-12.30pm. Termtime.

s City of London School for Girls020 7628 0841
St Giles Terrace, Barbican, EC2Y 8BB
Girls 7-18yrs

Newpark Childcare Centre 020 7638 5550
1 St Giles' Terrace, Barbican, EC2Y 8DU
4mths-5yrs. 7am-7pm. 50 wks.

EC3
Tower Hill Nursery 020 7320 1780
100 Minories, EC3N 1JY
2-4yrs. 8.30am-5.30pm. Termtime.

EC4
s St Paul's Cathedral School 020 7248 5156
2 New Change, EC4M 9AD
Boys 7-13yrs, Girls 4-7yrs

SOUTH EAST POSTCODES

SE1
Bright Horizons at 020 7407 2068
Tabard Square
10-12 Empire Square, Tabard Street, SE1 4NA
www.brighthorizons.com
3mths-5yrs. 8am-6pm. 50wks.

Coral Day Nursery 020 7928 0597
Windmill House, Wootton Street, SE1 8LY
0-5yrs. 8am-6pm. 51wks.

Kintore Way Nursery 020 7237 1894
Grange Road, SE1 3BW
3-5yrs. 9.15am-3.05pm. Termtime.

La Providence 020 7928 9293
1a Kennington Road, SE1 7QP
3mths-5yrs. 8am-6pm. 50wks.

St Patrick's Creche, Nursery 020 7928 5557
and Montessori School
91 Cornwall Road, SE1 8TH
3mths-5. Full day.

St Thomas' Day Nursery 020 7188 7188
Gassiot House, Lambeth Palace Road, SE1 7EH
0-5yrs. 7am-7pm. 51wks.

SE2
Croft Day Nursery 01322 431 045
75 Woolwich, SE2 0DY
4mths-5yrs. 8am-6pm. 51wks.

Thamesmead Children's Centre 020 8311 5291
Harrow Manorway, Thamesmead, Abbeywood, SE2 9XH
2¹/₂-4yrs. 7.45am-6pm. 51wks.

SE3
Blackheath Day Nursery 020 8305 2526
The Rectory Field, Charlton Road, SE3 8SR
6mths-5yrs. 8am-6pm. 52wks.

s Blackheath High: Junior 020 8852 1537
Department
Wemyss Road, SE3 0TF
Girls 3-11yrs

Blackheath Montessori Centre 020 8852 6765
Independents Road, Blackheath, SE3 9LF
Co-ed 3-5yrs. 8am-6pm. Termtime (4 terms).

s Blackheath Nursery and Prep 020 8858 0692
4 St German Place, SE3 0NJ
3-11yrs. 9am-3.30pm. Termtime.

Brooklands Pre-School Playgroup 020 8297 1816
The Clubhouse, Richmount Gardens, SE3 9AE
2-5yrs. 9.15-11.45am. Termtime.

Ferrier Phase 2 Pre-School 020 8856 6550
Community Hall, Telemann Square, SE3 9YR
2¹/₂-5yrs. 9.15am-11.45pm. Termtime.

First Steps Nursery 020 8852 1233
1 Pond Road, Blackheath, SE3 9JL
2¹/₂-5yrs. 9.30am-3pm. Termtime.

Flintmill Pre-School 020 8319 8336
Flintmill Community Hall, Flintmill Crescent,
Kidbrooke, SE3 8LU
3-5yrs. 9.30am-12pm. Termtime.

Greenwich Steiner School 020 8318 9790
St Georges Church, Kirkside Road, SE3 7SQ
3¹/₂-6¹/₂. Mornings.

Just Two's Pre-Nursery Group 020 8856 0677
90 Mycenae Road, Blackheath, SE3 7SE
2-3¹/₂yrs. 9.30am-12pm. Termtime.

Kids & Co Nursery 020 8858 6222
41 Westcombe Park Road, Blackheath, SE3 7RE
2-5yrs. 8.30am-6pm. 51wks.

Lingfield Day Nursery   020 8858 1388
37 Kidbrooke Grove, SE3 0LJ
18mths-5yrs. 8am-6pm. 51wks.

Lollipops Childcare   020 8294 0546
12 Southwood Road, New Eltham, SE3 3TH
0-5yrs. 8am-6pm. 51wks.

S Pointers Pre-Prep School   020 8293 1331
19 Stratheden Road, Blackheath, SE3 7TH
Co-ed 3-11yrs. Full day

The Park Nursery   07775 911 601
St. John's Hall, Vicarage Avenue, St. John's Park
2-5yrs. 9am-12pm. Terimtime only.

SE4
Catherine House Day Nursery   020 8692 5015
71 Tressillian Road, Brockley, SE4 1YA
3mths-5yrs. 7.30am-6.30pm. 51wks.

Chelwood Nursery School   020 7639 2514
Chelwood Walk, St Norbert Road, SE4 2QQ
3-5yrs. 9.15am-3.15pm. Termtime.

Cherry Li Nursery   020 8691 0497
40 Tyrwhitt Road, Brockley, SE4 1QT
2-5yrs. 8am-6pm. 51wks.

Hillyfields Day Nursery   020 8694 1069
41 Harcourt Road, Brockley, SE4 2AJ
3mths-5yrs. 8am-6pm. 51wks.

Lillingtons' Montessori   020 8690 2184
Nursery School
20 Chudleigh Road, Ladywell, SE4 1JW
$2^1/_2$-5yrs. 8am-4pm. 48wks.

SE5
Our Precious Ones   020 7701 9857
Clemance Hall, Brisbane Street, SE5 7NL
2-5yrs. Full day

South East Montessori   020 7737 1719
40 Ivanhoe Road, SE5 8DJ
2-5yrs. Full day

St John's Montessori Nursery   020 7737 2123
Crawford Tenants Hall, Denmark Road, SE5 9EW
2-5yrs. Full day

The Nest Pre-School   020 7978 9158
Longfield Hall, 50 Knatchbull Road, SE5 9QY
$2^1/_2$-5yrs. 9.30am-12.15pm (Mon-Fri) and open until 3pm
(Tues & Thurs). Also a mother and toddler group on Wed
from 1-3pm. Termtime.

SE6
Little Learners Day Nursery   020 8291 3994
Rubens Street, Catford, SE6 4TH
3mths-5yrs. 8.15am-6pm. 51wks.

S St Dunstan's College   020 8516 7200
Stanstead Road, SE6 4TY
Co-ed 4-18yrs

Thornsbeach Day Nursery   020 8697 7699
10 Thornsbeach Road, Catford, SE6 1DX
2-5yrs. 7.30am-6pm. 52wks.

SE7
Charlton Family Centre   020 8856 9906
41-43 Shirley House Drive, Charlton, SE7 7EL
1-5yrs. 9.30am-3.30pm. Termtime.

Joyful Gems Day Nursery   020 8355 8464
90 Maryon Road, Charlton, SE7 8DJ
3mths-5yrs. 8am-6pm. 51wks.

Pound Park Nursery School   020 8858 1791
Pound Park Road, Charlton, SE7 8AS
$3-4^1/_2$yrs. Part time

SE8
Bunny Hop Day Nursery   020 8691 7171
1 King Fisher Square, Wooton Road, SE8 5TW
$2-4^1/_2$yrs. 8am-6pm. 52wks.

Clyde Nursery School   020 8692 3653
Alverton Street, Deptford, SE8 5NH
0-3yrs. 8am-5.45pm. 51wks. Then 3-5yrs. 9.15am-3.15pm.
Termtime.

Rachel McMillan Nursery School   020 8692 4041
McMillan Street, Deptford, SE8 3EH
0-5yrs. 8am-6pm 48wks (up to 3yrs - thereafter termtime).

Rainbow Nursery   020 8692 1224
44 Alverton Street, SE8
2-5yrs. 8am-6pm. 52wks.

SE9
Asquith Nursery Elizabeth Terrace   020 8294 0377
18-22 Elizabeth Terrace, Eltham, SE9 5DR
3mths-5yrs. 8am-6pm. 51wks

Asquith Nursery New Eltham   020 8851 5057
699 Sidcup Road, New Eltham, SE9 3AQ
18mths-5yrs. 8am-6pm. 51 wks

Coombe Nursery   020 8850 4445
467 Footscray Road, New Eltham, SE9 3UH
6mths-5yrs. 8am-6pm. 51wks.

Eltham Green Nursery   020 88 50 4720
Queenscroft Road, Eltham, SE9 5EQ
3mths-5yrs. 7.45am-5.30pm. Termtime.

Lollipops Childcare   020 8859 5832
Bramble House, 88 Southwood Road, New Eltham
3mths-5yrs. 8am-6pm. 51wks.

Maryfield Pre-School   020 8851 4874
73 Leysdown Road, SE9 4UB
$2^1/_2$-5yrs. 9.30am-12pm and 12.30-3pm. Termtime.

New Eltham Pre-School   020 8851 5057
& Nursery (Asquith Court)
699 Sidcup Road, SE9 3AQ
3mths-5yrs. Full day

Nikki's Day Nursery   020 8265 1584
164 Footscray Road, SE9 2TD
3mths-4yrs. 8am-6.30pm. 51wks.

Peter Pan Pre-School   020 8850 3740
Middle Park Rear Hall, Middle Park Avenue, Eltham,
SE9 5SD
2¹/₂-5yrs. 9.20-11.50am. Termtime.

Playwell Pre-School   020 8859 7740
32a Westmount Road, SE9 1JE
9.15-11.50am and 12.30-3pm. Termtime.

Royal Eltham Pre-School   020 8859 7718
Westmount Road, Eltham, SE9 1XX
2-5yrs. 9.30am-12pm. Termtime.

S St Olave's Prep School   020 8829 8930
106-110 Southwood Road, New Eltham, SE9 3QS
Co-ed 3-11yrs

St Saviours Playgroup   020 8850 0511
98 Middle Park Avenue, Eltham, SE9 5JH
3-4yrs. 9.15-11.45am. Termtime.

Village Nurseries   020 8850 5019
98 Sparrow Lane, SE9 2BU
9.15am-12pm. Termtime.

Willow Park Day Nursery   020 8850 8988
19 Glenlyon Road, SE9 1AL
2-5yrs. Full day

Willow Park Day Nursery   020 8850 8988
13 Glenesk Road, Eltham, SE9 1AG
5mths-2yrs.

SE10
Courtyard Nursery   07903 238 445
Small Hall, St.Alfege Church, Roan Street, SE10
3-5yrs. 9.15am-12.15pm. Termtime.

Kings & Queens Day Nursery   020 8858 3608
51 Armitage Road, SE10 0HN
2-5yrs. 7am-6pm. 50wks.

Mrs Bartlett's Nursery   020 8692 1014
The Church of the Ascension, Dartmouth Row,
SE10 8AW
2¹/₂-5yrs

Sommerville Day Nursery   020 8691 9080
East Side Stage, Sparta Street, Greenwich, SE10 8DQ
2-4yrs. Full day

St Mark's Church Playgroup   020 8853 0563
22 Greenwich South Street, Greenwich, SE10 8TY
2-5yrs. 9.30am-12pm. Termtime.

Teddies Nurseries Greenwich   0800 980 3801
Chevening Road, Greenwich, SE10 0LB
3mths-5yrs. 8am-6pm. 51wks

SE11
Ethelred Nursery School   020 7582 9711
10 Lollard Street, Lollard Street, SE11 6UP
3-4yrs. 9.15am-3.15pm. Termtime.

Hurley Pre-School   020 7582 1838
Hurley House, Kempsford Road, Kennington, SE11 4PB
2¹/₂-5yrs. 9-11.30am and 1.30-4pm. 50wks.

James Kane Day Nursery   020 7820 0054
Tyers Terrace, SE11 5LY
2-5yrs. 8am-5.45pm. 50wks.

Lambeth Walk Day Nursery   020 7735 6317
Longton House, Lambeth Walk, SE11 6LU
6mths-5yrs. 8am-6pm. 51wks.

Toad Hall Nursery School   020 7735 5087
37 St Mary's Gardens, SE11 4UF
2mths-5yrs. 8am-6pm. 48wks.

Vauxhall Christian   020 7582 2618
Centre Pre-School
105 Tyers Street, SE11 5HS
2¹/₂-5yrs. 9.10am-3.10pm. Termtime.

William Wilberforce Day Nursery   020 7735 6317
Longton House, Lambeth Walk, SE11 6LU
6mths-5yrs. 8am-6pm. 52wks.

SE12
Asquith Creche Kidbrooke   020 8856 1328
David Lloyd Club, Weigall Road, SE12 8HG
18mths-5yrs. 8am-6pm. 51 wks

Colfe's Pre-prep School   020 8852 0220
Horn Park Lane, Lee, SE12 8AW
Co-ed 3-11yrs. Admission by examination at 3, 4, and 7+.
The nursery has a large waiting list, so early registration is
essential.

Grove Park Pre-School   020 8857 8258
353 Baring Road, Grove Park, SE12 0EE
3mths-5yrs. 8am-6pm. 51wks.

Lingfield Day Nursery   020 8851 7800
155 Baring Road, SE12 0LA
18mths-5yrs. 8am-6pm. 51wks.

S Riverston School   020 8318 4327
63-69 Eltham Road, Lee, SE12 8UF
Co-ed 1-16yrs

St Francis Pre-School   020 8857 8141
96 Sibrhorpe Road, SE12 9DP
2-5yrs. 9.15-11.45am. Termtime.

SE13

Little Gems Day Nursery   020 8692 0061
Clare Road, Brockley, SE13 6PX
3mths-5yrs. 8am-6pm. 50wks.

Mother Goose Nursery   020 8694 8700
113 Brooke Bank Road, SE13
1-5yrs. Full day

Sandrock Day Nursery   020 8692 8844
10 Sandrock Road, SE13 7TR
2-5yrs. Full day

Saplings Day Nursery   020 8852 8071
83a Belmont Hill, Lewisham, SE13 5AX
4mths-5yrs.

Scallywags 11   020 8692 7772
120 Lewisham Road, SE13 7NL
0-5yrs. 8am-6pm. 51wks.

Step by Step Day Nursery   020 8297 5070
Dindon House, Monument Garden, SE13 6TP
3mths-5yrs. Full day

The Coach House Montessori   020 8297 2021
30 Slaithwaite Road, Lewisham, SE13 6DL
2-5yrs. 8am-6pm. 51wks.

Village Nursery   020 8690 6766
St Mary Centre, Ladywell Road, SE13 7HU
2-5yrs. 8am-6pm. 52wks.

SE14

Stars of Hope Nursery   020 7639 1777
74 Wildgoose Drive, SE14 5LL
2-5yrs. Full day

Stepping Stones   020 7277 6288
Montessori Nursery
Church of God of Prophecy, Kitto Road, SE14 5TW
6mths-5yrs. Full day

Woodpecker Early Years   020 8694 9557
20 Woodpecker Road, SE14 6EU
2-5yrs. 8am-5.45pm. 52wks.

SE15

Asquith Nursery Peckham   020 7635 5501
24 Waveney Avenue, Peckham Rye, SE15 3UE
3mths-5yrs. 8am-6pm. 51wks

Bellenden Day Nursery   020 7639 4896
198 Bellenden Road, SE15 4BW
2-5yrs. 8am-5.45pm. 52wks.

Colourbox Day Nursery   020 7277 9662
385 Ivydale Road, Peckham, SE15 3ID
6mths-5yrs. 8am-6pm. 51wks.

Goslings Day Nursery   020 7639 5261
106 Evelina Road, SE15 3HL
6mths-5yrs. 8am-6pm. 51wks.

Mother Goose Nursery   020 7277 5951
34 Waveney Avenue, Nunhead, SE15 3UE
18mths-5yrs. Full day

Mother Goose Nursery   020 7277 5956
54 Linden Grove, Nunhead, SE15 3LF
3mths-2yrs. Full day

Nell Gwynn Nursery   020 7252 8265
Meeting House Lane, Peckham, SE15 2TT
3-5yrs. Full and part-time places

Sankofa Day Nursery   020 7277 6243
14 Sharratt Street, SE15
2-5yrs. Full day

The Villa Pre-Prep School   020 7703 6216
54 Lyndhurst Grove, SE15 5AH
6mths-7yrs. Full day

SE16

5 Steps Community Nursery   020 7237 2376
31-32 Alpine Road, Rotherhithe, SE16 2RE
18mths-5yrs. 8.30am-5.30pm. 52wks.

Scallywags Day Nursery   020 7252 3225
St Crispin's Church Hall, Southwark Park Road
2-5yrs. Full day

Trinity Childcare   020 7231 5842
Holy Trinity Church Hall, Bryan Road, Rotherhithe
2-5yrs. Full day

SE17

Elephant & Castle Day Nursery   020 7277 4488
15 Hampton Street, SE17 3AN
6mths-5yrs. 8am-6pm. 51wks.

St Wilfrid's Montessori Pre-School   020 7701 2800
101-105 Lorrimore Road, Kennington, SE17 3LZ
Hours 8-6, 49 weeks, 'a home from home'

SE18

Brook Day Nursery: Early   020 8855 3716
Years Childcare
87 Antelope Road, Woolwich, SE18 5QG
0-5yrs. 7.30am-6pm. 52wks.

Earl Rise Pre-School   020 8317 2568
St.John's Church Hall, Earl Rise, SE18 7NF
3-5yrs. 9-11.30am. Termtime.

East Plumstead Pre-School   020 8855 6544
East Plumstead Baptist Church, Griffin Road, SE18 7PZ
3-5yrs. 9.30am-12pm. Termtime.

Plumstead Common Playgroup   020 8854 2870
65 Admaston Road, Plumstead, SE18 2TX
3-5yrs. 9.30am-12pm. Termtime.

Plumstead Manor Pre-school   020 8855 0124
Old Mill Road, SE18 1QF
3-5yrs.

Ripplings Playgroup　020 8854 3628
All Saints Church, Ripon Road, Plumstead
3-5yrs. 9.30am-12pm. Termtime.

Saplings Extended Day Pre-School　020 8317 7544
Willow-Dene School, Swingate Lane, Plumstead
2.10-5yrs. 9am-3pm. 51wks.

Shrewbury House Pre-School　020 8854 3895
Shrewsbury House, Bushmoor Crescent, SE18 3EG
3-5yrs. 9.45am-12.15pm. Termtime.

Simba Day Nursery　020 8317 0451
Artillery Place, Woolwich, SE18 4AB
2-4yrs. Full day

St Pauls Pre-School　020 8317 7809
Invicta Lodge, Strandfield Close, SE18
2-5yrs. 9.15-11.45am. Termtime.

St Peter's Playgroup　020 8317 2285
130 Brookhill Road, Woolwich, SE18 6UZ
9.30am-12pm. Termtime.

Thames Tiddlers Nursery　020 8317 2978
33 Westfield Street, Woolwich, SE18 5PH
2-5yrs. 8am-6pm. 51wks.

Victoria House Playgroup　020 8781 4387
405 Shooters Hill Road, Woolwich, SE18 4LH
9.30am-12pm Mon-Fri and 12.30-3pm Tues and Thurs.
Termtime.

Willow Tree Pre-School　020 8854 3695
Woolwich Common Road, SE18 4DJ
2¹/₂-5yrs. 9.30am-2.30pm. Termtime.

SE19

Crown Point Nursery　020 8766 7737
316 Beulah Hill, Upper Norwood, SE19 3HF
2-5yrs. 8am-6pm. 51wks.

Downsview Primary and　020 8764 4611
Nursery School
Biggin Way, Upper Norwood, SE19 3XE
3¹/₂yrs+. Sessional

Little Crystals Day Nursery　020 8771 0393
49 Maberley Road, Upper Norwood, SE19 2JE
2-5yrs. 8am-6pm. 50wks.

Norwood Playgroup　020 8766 6227
Crown Dale, SE19 3NX
2¹/₂-5yrs.

s **Virgo Fidelis Prep School**　020 8653 2169
Central Hill, Upper Norwood, SE19 1RS
Co-ed 3-11yrs

SE20

Anerley Montessori　020 8778 2810
45 Anerley Park, SE20
2-5yrs. Full day

Norris Day Nursery　020 8778 9152
1 Thornsett Road, Amerley, Amerley, SE20 7XB
2-5yrs. Full day

SE21

Asquith Nursery Dulwich　020 8761 6750
Chancellor Grove, West Dulwich, SE21 8EG
18mths-5yrs. 8am-6pm. 51 wks

Buds Pre-School　020 8299 2255
Marlborough Cricket Club, Cox's Walk, Dulwich
Common, SE21 7EX
2¹/₂-5yrs. Part time

Chellow Dene Day Nursery　020 8670 9001
134 Croxted Road, SE21 8NR
18mths-5yrs. 8am-6pm. 51wks.

Clive Hall Day Nursery　020 8761 9000
52 Clive Road, SE21 8BY
3mths-5yrs. 8am-6pm. 51wks.

Ducks in Dulwich　020 8693 1538
Eller Bank, 87 College Road, SE21 7HH
3mths-7yrs. 8am-4.30pm. Termtime.

Dulwich College Nursery　020 8693 4341
8 Gallery Road, SE21 7AB
Boys 3-13yrs, Girls 3-5yrs. 9am-3pm. Termtime.

Dulwich College Prep School　020 8670 3217
42 Alleyn Park, SE21 7AA
Boys 5-13yrs.

Dulwich Montessori　020 8766 0091
St Stephen's Church, College Road, College Road, SE21
2¹/₂-5yrs. 9am-3pm. Termtime.

Dulwich Village Pre-school　020 8693 2402
Old Alleynian Club, Dulwich Common, SE21 7HA
3-5yrs. Sessional 9.30am-12pm. And 12.45-3.15pm.
Termtime.

Nelly's Nursery　020 8761 4178
27 Turney Road, SE21 8LX
3mths-5yrs. 7.30-6:30pm. 48wks.

s **Oakfield Prep School**　020 8670 4206
125-128 Thurlow Park Road, SE21 8HP
Co-ed 2-11yrs.

s **Rosemead Preparatory School**　020 8670 5865
70 Thurlow Park Road, SE21 8HZ
Co-ed 2-11yrs. 9am-3.30pm. Termtime.

SE22

Dulwich Nursery　020 7738 4007
Adj Sainsburys, 80 Dog Kennel Hill, SE22 8BD
www.brighthorizons.com
3mths-5yrs. 8am-6pm. 51wks.

s **Alleyn's School**　020 8693 3457
Townley Road, Dulwich, SE22 8SU
Co-ed 4-18yrs

EATON SQUARE SCHOOL

Celebrating 25 years as one of
London's Premier Preparatory Schools

- For children aged 2½-13 years
- Fully co-educational
- Enriched curriculum and broad range of activities
- "Good teaching characterises lessons throughout the school" (ISC inspection report 2005)
- "Pupils are highly motivated, sustain concentration and are always well behaved" (ISC inspection report 2005)
- Pupils are well prepared for national, Common Entrance and Selective London Day School exams

Eaton Square Preparatory School is located in Belgravia, London SW1 (School bus covers SW1, SW3, SW6, SW7, SW10, W8)

Eaton Square School Nurseries are located in:
Rutland Gardens SW7, Fulham Road SW10, Lupus Street SW1, Eccleston Square SW1 and Eccleston Street SW1

Telephone 020 7951 9469

www.eatonsquareschool.com
Email: admissions@eatonsquare.westminster.sch.uk

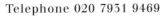

Bojangles Nursery School   **020 8693 2076**
New Life Assembly Church, Upland Road, East Dulwich, SE22 0DA
18mths-5yrs. 8am-6pm. 51wks.

First Steps Montessori Day   **020 8299 6897**
Nursery & Pre-School
254 Uplands Road, East Dulwich, SE22
2-5yrs. 8am-6pm. 51wks.

S James Allen's Prep School   **020 8693 0374**
East Dulwich Grove, SE22 8TE
Girls 4-11yrs, Boys 4-7yrs

Mother Goose Nursery   **020 8693 9429**
248 Upland Road, East Dulwich, SE22
1-5yrs. Full day

Puddleduck Nursery   **020 8291 4735**
Goose Green Centre, East Dulwich Road, SE22 9AT
2½-5yrs

SE23
Cottage Day Nursery   **020 8291 7117**
St Hilda's Church Hall, Courtrai Road, SE23 1PL
15mths-5yrs. 8am-6pm. 51wks.

SE24
2nd Step Nursery & Pre-School   **020 7274 9090**
St Johns Hall, Heron Road, SE24 0HZ
6mths-5yrs. 7.30am-6.30pm. 50 wks.

Halfmoon Montessori Nursery   **020 7326 5300**
The Methodist Church Hall, 155 Half Moon Lane
2½-5yrs. 8am-3.30pm. Termtime.

S Herne Hill School   **020 7274 6336**
127 Herne Hill, SE24 9LY
Co-ed 3-7yrs.

Little Fingers Montessori Nursery **020 7274 4864**
The Edward Alleyn Club, Burbage Road, Herne Hill
2-5yrs. 9am-4pm. Termtime.

Ruskin House School   **020 7737 4317**
48 Herne Hill, SE24 9QP
3mths-5yrs. 7am-7pm. 51wks. Also provides after-school club for 6 of the local Dulwich Schools.

The Whitehouse Day Nursery   **020 8671 7362**
331 Norwood Road, SE24 9AH
2-5yrs. 8am-6pm. 51wks.

SE25
Children's Paradise Day Nursery **020 8654 1737**
2-4 Crowther Road, South Norwood, SE25 5QW
3mths-5yrs. 8am-6pm. 51wks.

SE26
Cornerstone Day Nursery   **020 8676 0478**
& Pre-school
2 Jews Walk, Sydenham, SE26 6PL
6mths-5yrs. 9am-6pm. 51wks.

Crystal Day Nursery 020 8659 6417
202 Venner Road, Sydenham, SE26 5HT
3mths-5yrs. 8am-6pm. 51wks.

Little Cherubs Nursery 020 8778 3232
2a Bell Green Lane, Lower Sydenham, SE26 5TB
3mths-5yrs. 8am-6pm. 51wks.

Puzzle House Nursery 020 8291 9844
Trinity Path, Sydenham, SE26 4EA
2-5yrs

S Sydenham High School 020 8778 8737
15 & 19 Westwood Hill, SE26 6BL
Girls 4-18yrs

Sydenham Hill Kindergarten 020 8693 6880
Community Hall, Sydenham Hill, SE26 6TT
2^1/$_2$-5yrs

SE27
Dunelm Grove Pre-School 020 8670 2498
23 Dunelm Grove, West Norwood, SE27 9JP
2^1/$_2$-5yrs. 9.30am-3.30pm. Termtime.

Knights Hill Day Nursery 020 8761 7338
24 Eden Road, SE27 0UB
2-5yrs. 7.30am-5.45pm. 50wks .

Norwood Day Nursery Co-Operative 020 8766 6899
Gypsy Road, SE27 9TG
3mths-5yrs. 8am-5pm. 48wks.

Norwood Manor Nursery 020 8766 0246
48 Chapel Road, West Norwood, SE27 0UR

One World Nursery 020 8670 3511
11 Thurlby Road, SE27 0RL
2-4yrs. Full day

Rosemead School Early Years 020 8761 1307
St Cuthberts Church, Elmcourt Road, SE27 9BZ
3-6yrs. 9.15am-3.15pm. Termtime.

Teddies Nurseries Gipsy Hill 0800 980 3801
Gipsy Road Baptist Church, West Norwood, SE27 9RB
3mths-5yrs. 8am-6pm. 51wks

SE28
Heronsgate Pre-School 020 8317 4991
Whinchat Road, SE28 0DJ
2.5-5yrs. 9-11.30am. Termtime.

St Paul's Pre-School 020 8310 8118
St. Paul's Church, Bentham Road, SE28 8AS
2^1/$_2$-5yrs. 9-11.30am. Termtime.

Triangle Day Nursery 020 8331 0131
123 Battery Road, SE28 0JN
6wks-5yrs. 7am-6pm. 52wks.

Waterways Community Day Nursery 020 8311 5491
Southwood Road, SE28 8EZ
2-5yrs. 7.30am-6.15pm. 51wks.

SW1
Belgravia Bi-Lingual 020 7736 8645
Nursery School
77-79 Kinnerton Street, SW1X 8ED
Bi-lingual (English/French) nursery school . 2-5yrs plus a toddler group from 1-2yrs. Session from 9am-12pm. Termtime and an afternoon club (French or Spanish) all year round.

Daisies Day Nursery 020 7498 2922
& School - Pimlico
St James the Less School, Moreton Street, SW1V 2PT
www.daisiesdaynurseries.co.uk
3mths-5yrs. 8am-6pm. 50 wks.

S Eaton Square Preparatory 020 7931 9469
School & Nursery
79 Eccleston Square, SW1V 1PP
29 Belgrave Road, SW1V 1PP
30 Eccleston Street, SW1W 9PY
www.eatonsquareschool.com
Eaton Square School is one of the few co-educational day schools in Central London. With five locations the School offers nursery education (2^1/$_2$-4 yrs) through Pre-Prep (4-6yrs) to Preparatory (6-13yrs). With small classes and focused teaching the School embraces modern technology with new classrooms equipped with interactive whiteboards linked to a school-wide PC network.

Ringrose Kindergarten 020 7976 6511
32a Lupus Street, SW1V 3DZ
www.eatonsquareschool.com
2^1/$_2$-5yrs. 9am-12pm. Termtime. They also offer an afterschool club and holiday care. Part of Eaton Square Schools.

Thomas's Kindergarten, Pimlico 020 7730 3596
St Barnabas Church, 14 Ranelagh Grove, SW1W 8PD
www.thomas-s.co.uk
2^1/$_2$-4yrs. 8am-12pm (plus afternoon clubs). Termtime.
Caring environment in the heart of Pimlico. Government Early Years Curriculum.

Bessborough Nursery 020 7641 6387
1 Bessborough Street, SW1V 2JD
0-5yrs. 8am-6pm. 51wks.

Dolphins Nursery 020 7581 5044
67 Pont Street, SW1X 0BD
2-5yrs. 3 mornings per week. Termtime.

S Eaton House School 020 7730 9343
3-5 Eaton Gate, SW1W 9BA
Boys 4-9yrs.

S Francis Holland School 020 7730 2971
39 Graham Terrace, SW1W 8JF
Girls 4-18yrs

S Hill House School 020 7584 1331
17 Hans Place, SW1X 0EP
Co-ed 4-13yrs

Moreton Day Nursery   020 7233 8979
31 Moreton Street, SW1V 2PA
2¹/₂-5yrs. Full day. Also Moreton Day Pre-School

Moreton Day Nursery & Pre-School   020 7821 1979
18 Churton Street, SW1V 2NZ
0-5yrs.

Knightsbridge Kindergarten   020 7371 2306
119 Eaton Square, SW1W 9AL
2-5yrs. 9am-12pm and 1-3pm Termtime. They also have an after school club from 3.30-6.30pm, and offer holiday care between 8.15am-6.15pm.

Little House at Napier Hall   020 7592 0195
1 Hide Place, Vincent Square, SW1P 4NJ
18mths-5yrs

Miss Morley's Nursery School   020 7730 5797
Club Room, Fountain Court, Buckingham Palace Road, SW1W 9SU
2¹/₂-5yrs. 9am-12pm Mon-Fri and an extra session 1.30-3.45pm Mon/Wed/Thurs. Termtime.

s Sussex House   020 7584 1741
68 Cadogan Square, SW1X 0EA
Boys 8-13yrs

s Westminster Cathedral Choir School   020 7798 0981
Ambrosden Avenue, SW1P 1QH

s Westminster Under School   020 7821 5788
Adrian House, 27 Vincent Square, SW1P 2NN
Boys 7-18yrs.

Young England Kindergarten   020 7834 3171
St Saviour's Hall, St George's Square, SW1V 3QW
2¹/₂-5yrs

SW2
Cherubins Day Nursery   020 8671 3256
Chestnut Lodge, 48 Palace Road, SW2 3NJ
3mths-5yrs. 7.30am-7pm. 52 wks.

Clapham Park Pre-School   020 8674 3869
19 Lycette House, New Park Road, SW2 4UZ
2-5yrs. 9.30am-12pm and 12.15-14.43pm. Termtime.

Elm Park Montessori Nursery School
Brixton Hill Methodist Church, Elm Park, SW2 2TX
2-5yrs

Lily's Day Nursery   020 8674 8678
Brixton Hill Methodist Church, Elm park, SW2 2TX
2-5yrs. 8am-6pm. 50wks. They also have a baby unit 0-2yrs at 131 Rear of Briston Hill, Elm Park SW2.

Little Trees Nursery   020 8677 8400
Wavertree Road, SW2 3SR
Co-ed 3-5yrs. 8.30am-3.30pm. Termtime.

Nursery Schools

Clapham & Clapham Park Montessori

- Children 2-6 years
- Morning and/or afternoon sessions
- Large Gardens
- French/ Spanish, Music and Drama available

Rectory Grove, SW4 0DX
020 7498 8324

Infant Community
Children 1-2½ years
Hambalt Road SW4 9EH

West Road, SW4 7DN
020 7627 0352

Home from Home
Parsons Green

Personal Homely Childcare
in a fun interactive learning environment

Full & Part time childcare from 6mths

Please contact: Charlotte Winham (NNEB)
OFSTED Approved
56 Quarrendon Street, SW6
Telephone: 020 7736 9029

Mini Stars Day Nursery   020 8678 8600
St Margarets Church, Barcombe Avenue,
Streatham Hill, SW2 3BH
6mths-5yrs. 8am-6pm. 51wks.

Streatham Montessori Nursery   020 8674 2208
66 Blairderry Road, SW2 4SB
2½-5yrs. Full day

SW3
S Cameron House   020 7352 4040
4 The Vale, SW3 6AH
Co-ed 4-11yrs

S Garden House School   020 7730 1652
Turks Row, SW3 4TW
Separate boys and girls school on the same site aged 3-11yrs.

Ringrose Kindergarten   020 7352 8784
St Luke's Church Hall, St Luke's Street, SW3 3RP

Violet Melchett Family Centre   020 7352 1512
30 Flood Street, SW3 5RR
1-4yrs. 8am-5.30pm. 51wks.

SW4
Clapham Montessori   020 7498 8324
St Paul's Church Hall, Rectory Grove, SW4 0DX
Clapham and Clapham Park Montessori. Well-established schools in interesting buildings with great gardens, offering real Montessori education. Experienced staff. Morning sessions are from 9.15am-12.15 pm afternoons from 1.15 - 3.45. ME(UK) registered and accredited. New Infant Community in spacious hall. 2-6yrs. 9.15am-3.45pm. 34 wks

Clapham Park Montessori   020 7627 0352
10 West Road, SW4 7DN
2½-6yrs. 9.15am-12.15pm with some afternoons. Termtime.

Daisies Day Nursery & School - Stockwell   020 7498 2922
Stockwell Methodist Church, Jeffreys Road, SW4 6QX
www.daisiesdaynurseries.co.uk
3mths-5yrs. 8am-6pm. 50 wks.

Anglo Spanish   020 7622 5599
152 Clapham Manor Street, SW4 6BX
18mths-4yrs. 8am-6pm. 51wks.

S Eaton House, The Manor   020 7924 6000
58 Clapham Common Northside, SW4 9RU
Co-ed 2½-5yrs; Boys 5-13yrs.

Elm Park Nursery   020 8678 1990
90 Clarence Avenue, Clapham, SW4 8JR
6mths-5yrs. 8am-6pm. 48wks.

L'Ecole du Parc   020 8671 5287
12 Rodenhurst Road, SW4 8AR
1-5yrs. 8.15am-3pm with after school care until 5pm. Termtime.

Magic Mind Nursery   020 8674 5544
4 Helby Road, SW4 8BU
1-5yrs. 8am-6pm. 50wks.

Magic Roundabout Day Nursery   02074 981 194
Binfield Road, Clapham, SW4 6TB
3mths-5yrs. 7.30am-7pm. 50wks.

S Oliver House   020 8772 1911
7 Nightingale Lane, Clapham, SW4 9BG
Pre-prep school newly opened for 2-5yr olds for the September 2004 intake.

S Parkgate House School   020 7350 2452
80 Clapham Common Northside, SW4 9SD
Co-ed 2½-11yrs

Parkgate Montessori School   020 7350 2452
80 Clapham Common Northside, SW4 9SD
2½-5yrs.

Pixies Nursery School   020 7720 7095
William Wilberforce Centre, Clapham Common North Side, SW4 0NT
2½-5yrs. 9.15am-12.15pm. Termtime.

Squirrels Pre-School   020 8673 1277
Agnes Riley Gardens, Poynders Road, SW4 8PR
Play and fun are the best way to learn

SW5
Ladybird Nursery School   020 7244 7771
St Jude's Church, 24 Collingham Road, SW5 0LX
3-5yrs. 9.25am-12.30pm Mon, Fri and 12.45-2.45pm. Tues & Thurs.

SW6
Home From Home   020 7736 9029
56 Quarrendon Street, SW6 3SU
6mths-3yrs. 8am-6pm. Full or part-time quality childcare.

Peques Nursery School   020 7385 0055
St John's Church, Waltham Green, North End
Road, Fulham Broadway, SW6 1PB
3mths-5yrs. 8am-6pm. 50 weeks per year. For a safe,
happy, secure, learning and developing environment.

Pippa Pop-ins   020 7385 7476
165 New Kings Road, Fulham, SW6 4SN
1-5yrs. Sessional am and pm. Termtime.

Pippa Pop-ins   020 7385 2458
430 Fulham Road, SW6 1DU
1-5yrs. Sessional am or pm. Termtime. Also creche facilities
and creative holiday activities.

Playhouse Nursery School   020 7385 6053
17 Burnthwaite Road, Fulham, SW6 5BQ
www.theplayhousenursery.co.uk
3mths-5yrs. First class teaching and care in a homely
environment with lots of love and fun.

S Thomas's Fulham   020 7751 8200
Hugon Road, SW6 3ES
www.thomas-s.co.uk
Co-ed 4-11yrs. Termtime. Thomas's Fulham opened its
doors in September 2005. This flourishing and energetic co-
educational day school has excellent facilities and resources.

Happy Times   0800 652 2424
57 Filmer Road, Fulham, SW6 7FJ
www.happytimes.co.uk
3mth-5yrs. Full Day.

The Studio Day Nursery   020 7736 9256
93 Moore Park Road, SW6 2DA
The studio day nursery offers excellent all year round care
combined with strong educational programme including
special needs. Montessori and traditional methods taught by
qualified teachers. 2-5yrs. 8am-7pm. 52wks.

Bobby's Playhouse   020 7384 1190
16 Lettice Street, Fullham, SW6 4EH
www.bobbysplayhouse.co.uk
3mths-5yrs. 8am-6.15pm.

Bumpsa Daisies   020 7736 7037
Broomhouse Lane, Fulham, SW6 3DR
3mths-4yrs. Full day

Dawmouse Montessori Nursery   020 7381 9385
34 Haldane Road, SW6 7EU
2-5yrs

S Eridge House   020 7371 9009
1 Fulham Park Road, SW6 4LJ
Co-ed 4-8yrs

S Fulham Prep   020 7371 9911
47a Fulham High Street, SW6 3JJ
Co-ed 5-13yrs

S Kensington Prep School for Girls   020 7731 9300
596 Fulham Road, SW6 5PA
Girls 4-11yrs

Kiddi Caru Day Nursery   0800 028 4500
2 Piazza Buildings, Empress State, Lillie Road, SW6 1TR

L'Ecole des Petits   020 7371 8350
2 Hazlebury Road, Fulham, SW6 2NB

Little Lillies   07939 405 635
80 Lillie Road, SW6 1TN
2½-5yrs. Mornings. Termtime.

Little People of Fulham   020 7386 0006
250A Lillie Road, SW6 7PX
6mths-5yrs. 8am-6pm. 51wks.

New Era Community Day Nursery   020 7731 6131
196 Munster Road, Fulham, SW6 6AU
2-5yrs. 8am-6pm. 50wks.

Puffins Nursery School   020 7736 7442
60 Hugon Road, SW6 3EN
3-5yrs. Sessional 9am-12pm and 1pm-3.30pm. Termtime.

Rising Star Montessori   020 7381 3511
Nursery School
286 Fulham Palace Road, SW6 6HP
2-5yrs. 9.30am-12.30pm (Mon, Wed, Thurs, Fri) 9.30am-
3pm (Tues). Termtime.

Roche School   020 7731 8788
70 Fulham High Street, SW6 3LG
3-11yrs

Saplings Nursery   020 7610 6900
219 & 233 New Kings Road, Parsons Green, SW6 4XE
3mths- 5yrs. 8am-6pm. 48 wks.

Saplings Nursery   020 7610 6900
233 New Kings Road, SW6 4XE
3mths- 5yrs. 8am-6pm. 48 wks.

Scribbles 2   020 7381 8794
St Peter's Church Hall, 2 St Peter's Terrace, SW6 7JS
1-5yrs

Seahorses Montessori Nursery I   020 7385 7173
William Thompson Memorial Hall, Burnthwaite
Road, SW6 5BQ
2½-5yrs. Full day

Situated in South Kensington - Queen's Gate, SW7 has access to a magnificent garden.

Knightsbridge-off Wilton Place, SW1 has access to a lovely garden.

For a brochure please contact Marie-Laurence Edmonstone
020 7259 21 51

The Spanish out of school club for children from 2 to 5 years old Toddler Group from 1 year old

---

Seahorses Montessori Nursery II   020 7385 7173
St Etheldreda's Church Hall, Cloncurry Street, SW6
2-5yrs. Full day

s Sinclair House School   020 7736 9182
159 Munster Road, Fulham, SW6 6DA
2-8yrs. Probably the most adventurous Pre-Prep in south west London

The Little Tug Boat Day Nursery   020 7731 6648
3 Finlay Street, Fulham, SW6 6HE
3mths-5yrs. 8am-6.30pm. 52wks.

Twice Times Montessori School   020 7731 4929
The Cricket Pavilion, South Park, Fulham, SW6 3AF
2½-5yrs. 9am-12.30pm. Termtime.

Zebedee Nursery School II   020 7371 9224
Sullivan Hall, Parsons Green, SW6 4TN
2-5yrs. Mornings

SW7
Knightsbridge Kindergarten   020 7371 2306
Rutland Gardens, SW7 1BX
2-5yrs. 9am-12pm and 1-3pm. Termtime. They also have an after-school club from 3.30-6.30pm, and offer holiday care between 8.15am-6.15pm. Part of the Eaton Square schools group. Small classes, focused teaching and modern facilities.

Pooh Corner Kindergarten   020 7373 6111
St Stephens Church Hall, 48 Emperor's Gate, SW7 4HJ
2-5yrs

s Ravenstone House   020 7225 3131
Elvaston Place
24 Elvaston Place, SW7 5NL
2mths-11yrs. Open 8am-6.30pm. 46 wks.

The French Nursery School   020 7259 2151
65-67 Queen's Gate, SW7 5JS
2-5yrs plus a toddler group from 1-2yrs. 9am-12pm and 1.30-4.30pm. Termtime.

The Italian Nursery School   020 7259 2151
65-67 Queen's Gate, SW7 5JS
2-5yrs plus a toddler group from 1-2yrs. 9am-12pm and 1.30-4.30pm. Termtime. Additional groups in SW1.

Asquith Creche Kensington   020 7259 2425
David Lloyd Club, Point West, 116 Cromwell Road
3mths-5yrs. 8am-6pm. 51wks

s Falkner House Girls School   020 7373 4501
19 Brechin Place, SW7 4QB
Co-ed 3-4yrs, Girls 4-11yrs

s Glendower Preparatory School   020 7370 1927
87 Queen's Gate, SW7 5JX
Girls 4-12yrs

Hampshire School Early Years   020 7370 7081
5 Wetherby Place, SW7 4NX
3-6yrs. Sessional 8.55am-3.25pm. 35 wks.

S Hampshire School Pre-prep 020 7584 3297
63 Ennismore Gardens, SW7 1NH
Co-ed 5-8yrs.

Knightsbridge Nursery School   020 7584 2766
51 Thurloe Square, SW7 2SX
2½-5yrs.

S Lycée Francais   020 7584 6322
Charles de Gaulle
35 Cromwell Road, SW7 2DG
Co-ed 4-18yrs

Miss Willcocks' Nursery School   020 7937 2027
Holy Trinity Church, Prince Consort Road, SW7 2BA
2½-5yrs. 9.15am-12pm Mon-Fri and Tues/ Thurs/Fri 1.30-
3.45pm. Termtime.

Ovenstone Fhollan Park   020 7584 7955
House
22 Queensbury Place, SW7 2DZ
2-5yrs. Full day

S Queen's Gate School   020 7589 3587
133 Queen's Gate, SW7 5LE
Girls 4-18yrs

S St Nicholas Preparatory   020 7225 1277
School
23 Princes Gate, SW7 1PT
Co-ed 3-13yrs

S St Philip's School   020 7373 3944
6 Wetherby Place, SW7 4NE
Boys 7-13yrs

S Vale School   020 7584 9515
2 Elvaston Place, SW7 5QH
Co-ed 4-11yrs

Zebedee Nursery School I   020 7584 7660
St Pauls Church Hall, Onslow Square, SW7 3NX
2-5yrs

SW8
Bringing Up Baby: 020 7498 3167
Clapham Day Nursery
3 Peardon Street, SW8 3BW
www.bringingupbaby.co.uk
A day nursery for 72 children aged 3mths-5yrs. Open 8am-
6.15pm. 50wks.

Dorset Road Nursery   020 7582 1032
Fentiman Road, SW8 1BA
2-5yrs. 8am-6pm. 50wks.

Heath Road Day Nursery   020 7498 9324
119 Heath Road, Lambeth, SW8 3BB
3mths-5yrs. 8am-6pm. 50wks.

S Newton Prep   020 7720 4091
149 Battersea Park Road, SW8 4BH
Co-ed 3-13yrs

Oval Montessori Nursery   020 7735 4816
88 Fentiman Road, SW8 1LA
3-5yrs

Springtime Day Nursery   020 7720 5255
200 Wandsworth Road, SW8 2JU
2-5yrs. Full day

St Monica's Nursery   020 7582 0840
83-87 Clapham Road, SW8
2-5yrs. Full day

The Willow Nursery School   020 7498 0319
823-825 Wandsworth Road, SW8 3JL
2½-5yrs.

Victory Nursery   020 7793 0461
Mursell Tenants Hall, Mursell Estate, Portland
Grove, SW8 1JB
8.30am-6pm. 49wks.

SW9
Asquith Nursery Lambeth   020 7793 9922
50 Groveway, Lambeth, SW9 0AR
3mths-5yrs. 8am-6pm. 51wks

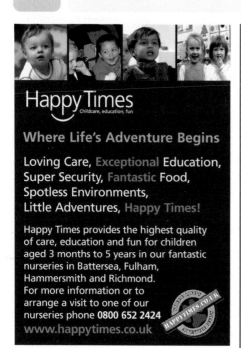

Bunnies on the Green   020 7738 4795
60 Stockwell Road, SW9 9JQ
2-5yrs. 8am-6pm.

Ferndale Road Day Nursery   020 7733 9779
Ground Floor Exbury House, Ferndale Road, SW9 8AZ
6mths-5yrs. 8am-6pm. 51wks.

Italian Day Nursery   020 7735 3058
174 Clapham Road, Stockwell, SW9 0LA
2-5yrs. 8.30am-4.30pm. Termtime.

Ladybird Nursery   020 7924 9505
9 Knowle Close, SW9 0TQ
2-5yrs. 7.30am-6pm. 50wks.

Latin American Community Nursery   020 7737 6494
29 Rhodesia Road, Stockwell, SW9 9DT
1-5yrs. 8.30am-5pm. Termtime.

Little Angels Nursery School   020 7274 8333
50 Gresham Road, Brixton, SW9 7NL
3mths-5yrs. 8am-6pm. 50wks.

St Michaels Pre-School   020 7274 0783
St. Michaels Church Hall, Stockwell Park Road
2¹/₂-5yrs. 9.45am-12.15pm. Termtime.

Vassal Road Pre-School   020 7735 4925
62a Vassall Road, SW9 6HY
2-5yrs. 9.30am-12pm and 12.30-3pm. Termtime.

Wiltshire Nursery   020 7274 4446
85 Wiltshire Road, SW9 7NZ
18mths-5yrs. 8am-6pm. 52wks.

Yours Truly Children's Centre   020 7737 4234
1 Corry Drive, SW9 8QS
1-5yrs. 8am-5.45pm. 51wks.

SW10
Paint Pots Montessori School   020 7376 4571
Chelsea Christian Centre, Edith Grove, SW10 0LB
2¹/₂-5yrs. Developing confidence, independence, self-esteem,
concentration social skills and self-discipline

Boltons Nursery School   020 7351 6993
262b Fulham Road, SW10 9EL
www.eatonsquareschool.com
2¹/₂-5yrs. 9.15am-4pm. Termtime. (Part of Eaton Square
Schools).

Ashburnham Day Nursery   020 7376 5085
Ashburnham Community Centre, Tetcott Road,
SW10 0SH
2-5yrs. 8.30am-5.30pm. 52wks.

S Parayhouse School   020 8740 6333
St John's, World's End, King's Road, SW10 0LU
Co-ed 5-17yrs with learning difficulties

S Redcliffe School   020 7352 9247
47 Redcliffe Gardens, SW10 9JH
Girls 2¹/₂-11yrs, Boys 2¹/₂-8yrs. 8.30am-4pm. Termtime.

Tadpoles Nursery School   020 7352 9757
Park Walk Play Centre, Park Walk, SW10 0AY
2¹/₂-5yrs

The Chelsea Kindergarten   020 7352 4856
St Andrew's Church, Park Walk, SW10 0AU
2-5yrs

Worlds End Pre-School   020 7351 1641
18 Blantyre Street, SW10 0DS
2¹/₂-5yrs. 9.30am-1.25pm. Termtime.

SW11
Happy Times   0800 652 2424
40 Park Gate Road, SW11 4NP
www.happytimes.co.uk
3mths-5yrs. Full day

S Thomas's Battersea   020 7978 0900
28-40 Battersea High Street, SW11 3JB
www.thomas-s.co.uk
Co-ed 4-13yrs. Termtime. A flourishing and energetic co-
educational day school with excellent facilities.

S Thomas's Clapham   020 7326 9300
Broomwood Road, SW11 6JZ
www.thomas-s.co.uk
Co-ed 4-13yrs. Termtime. A flourishing and energetic Co-
educational day school with excellent facilities.

Thomas's Kindergarten,   **020 7738 0400**
Battersea
St Mary's Church, Battersea Church Road, SW11 3NA
www.thomas-s.co.uk
2¹/₂-4yrs. 8am-12pm (plus afternoon clubs). Termtime.
Caring environment in beautiful riverside location.
Government Early Years Curriculum.

Alphabet Nursery School   **020 7924 2678**
Chatham Hall, Northcote Road, Battersea, SW11 6DY
9am-12pm. 1.15-3.45pm. Termtime.

Asquith Nursery Battersea   **020 7228 4722**
18-30 Latchmere Road, Battersea, SW11 2DX
18mths-5yrs. 8am-6pm. 51 wks.

Barnaby Bright Nursery School   **020 7978 4109**
St. Barnabas Church, 12 Lavender Gardens,
Clapham Common Northside, SW11 9BL
2¹/₂-5yrs. 9.30am-12.30pm. Termtime only.

Blundells Day Nursery   **020 7924 4204**
194-196 Sheepcote Lane, SW11 5BW
18mths-5yrs. 8am-6pm. 51wks.

Bridge Lane Nursery   **020 7978 4457**
18 Bridge Lane, Battersea, SW11 3AD
3mths-5yrs. 7am-7pm. 51wks.

Bumble Bee Nursery School   **020 7350 2970**
Church of the Ascension, Pountney Road, SW11 5TU
2-5yrs. 9am-12.15pm. Termtime.

Clapham Junction Nursery   **020 7924 1267**
Asda Precinct, 204 Lavender Hill, SW11 1JG
1-5yrs. 8am-6pm. 51wks.

S Dolphin School   **020 7924 3472**
106 Northcote Road, SW11 6QP
Co-ed 4-11yrs

Hummingbird Day Nursery   **020 7801 9296**
Christchurch & St. Stephens Hall, Cabul Road,
Battersea, SW11 2PN
6mths-5yrs. 8am-6pm. 51wks.

L'Ecole des Petits   **020 7371 8350**
Trott Street, Battersea, SW11 3DS

Little Red Hen Nursery School   **020 7738 0321**
2 Grant Road, SW11 2NU
2¹/₂-5yrs. 9.30am-12.30pm. Termtime.

Mini Me Montessori   **020 7622 7049**
6 Cupar Road, SW11 4JW
2¹/₂-4¹/₂yrs. 9.15am-12pm and 1.15pm-3.30pm. Timetime.

Mouse Hole Nursery   **020 7924 5325**
2a Mallinson Road, SW11 1BP
2-5yrs. 9am-12pm and 12.45-3.30pm. Termtime.

Mouse House Kindergarten   **01622 833 331**
25-27 Mallinson Road, SW11 1BW
2-5yrs. Sessional 9am-12.15pm and 1-3.30pm. Termtime.

Sparkies Nursery School
Where learning is a work of heart
OFSTED REGISTERED
Quality in Learning and Teaching Gold Award
Learning through discovery, in a heuristic environment
Two to rising five years
07939 268861
194, Ramsden Road, Balham, SW12 8QX

Noah's Ark Nursery School   **020 7228 9593**
St Michael's Church Hall, Cobham Close, SW11 6SP

S Northcote Lodge School   **020 8682 8888**
26 Bolingbroke Grove, SW11 6EL
Boys 8-13yrs.

Plantation Wharf Day Nursery   **020 7978 5819**
18 Cinammon Row, Plantation Wharf, SW11 3TW
6mths-5yrs. Full day

Somerset Nursery School   **020 7223 5455**
157 Battersea Church Road, SW11 3ND
3-5yrs

S South London   **020 7738 9546**
Montessori School
Trott Street, Battersea, SW11 3DS
2½-12yrs

Sparkies Playschool   **07939 268861**
St Vincent de Paul, 36 Altenburg Gardens, SW11 1JJ
2-5yrs

The Park Kindergarten   **01622 833 331**
St. Saviours Church Hall, 351 Battersea Park Road,
Battersea, SW11 4LH
2-4yrs. 9.30am-3.30pm. Termtime.

Victory Day School   **020 7207 1423**
140 Battersea Park Road, SW11 4NB
3mths-5yrs. Full day

Wakehurst Playgroup   **020 7787 6594**
Northcote Road Baptist Church, 53 Wakehurst
Road, SW11 6DT
9.45am-12.15pm. Termtime.

SW12
L'Ecole des Benjamins   **020 8673 8525**
Oldrige Road, Clapham, SW12 8PP
www.ecoledesbenjamins.com
Full day care from 7l30am-6.30pm for children aged 5mths-
5yrs. Schooling from 8.30am for children 2-6yrs. Alll non-
French speaking children are welcome.

Elmer Day Nursery   **020 8673 1166**
Balham Grove Hall, Aldridge Road, SW12 8BD
www.elmerdaynursery.com
5mths-3yrs. 7.30am-6.20pm. All year round.

Oaktree Nursery School   **020 8870 8441**
Ramsden Hall, 21 Ramsden Road, SW12 8QX
2½-5yrs. 9.15am-12.15pm. Mon-Fri. Termtime.

Sparkies Nursery School   **07939 268 861**
The St. Lukes Church Hall, Ramsden Road, SW12 8QX
2-5yrs. 9am-12.30pm. Termtime.

Abacus Early Learning Nursery   **020 8675 8093**
135 Laitwood Road, Balham, SW12 9QH
12mths-5yrs. 8am-6pm. 51wks.

Asquith Nursery Balham   **020 8673 1405**
36 Radbourne Road, Balham, SW12 0EF
18mths-5yrs. 8am-6pm. 51 wks

S Broomwood Hall School   **020 8682 8800**
74 Nightingale Lane, SW12 8NR
Boys 4-8yrs, Girls 4-13yrs

Caterpillar I Nursery School   **020 8673 6058**
74 Endlesham Road, SW12 8JL
2½-5yrs. 9.30am-12pm and 12.30-3pm. Termtime.

Caterpillar II Nursery School   **020 8265 5224**
14a Boundaries Road, SW12 8EX
2½-5yrs. 9.30am-12pm. Termtime.

Crescent Kindergarten III   **01622 833 331**
Grafton Tennis Club, 70a Thornton Road, SW12 0LE

Gateway House Nursery School   **020 8675 8258**
St Jude's Church Hall, Heslop Road, SW12 8EG
2½-4yrs. 9am-12pm. Termtime.

Nightingale Montessori   **020 8675 8070**
Nursery School
St Luke's Community Hall, 194 Ramsden Road
2-5yrs. Established 1976. Sessions or all day. OFSTED
registered. Call on number above or on 07958 567 210.

Nightingales Nursery   **020 8772 6056**
St Francis Xavier College, Malwood Road, SW12 8EN
3mths-5 yrs. Full day

Noah's Ark Nursery School   **020 7228 9593**
Endlesham Church Hall, 48 Endlesham Road, SW12 8JL

Rydevale Day Nursery   **020 8673 6633**
33 Little Dimmocks, Rydevale Road, SW12 9JP
18mths-5yrs. 8am-6pm. 49wks.

Second Step Day Nursery   **020 8673 6817**
60 Ravenslea Road, SW12 8RU

The White House Prep   **020 8674 9514**
& Woodentops Kindergarten
24 Thornton Road, SW12 0LF
2½-11yrs. 8.30am-4pm. 35wks.

Wainwright Montessori School 020 8673 8037
102 Chestnut Grove, SW12 8JJ
2¹/₂-5yrs.

s Woodentops Pre-Preparatory 020 8674 9514
School & Kindergarten
The White House, 24 Thornton Road, SW12 0LF
2¹/₂-11yrs

Yukon Day Nursery 020 8675 8838
Yukon Road, Balham, SW12 9DN
2-5yrs. 8.30am-6pm or sessional. 52wks.

SW13
s Colet Court 020 8748 3461
Lonsdale Road, SW13 9JT
7-13yrs. Junior St Paul's School

s Harrodian 020 8748 6117
Lonsdale Road, SW13 9QN
Co-ed 4-15yrs.

Ladybird Day Nursery 020 8741 1155
Montessori Pre-School
Trinity Church Road, SW13 8ES
2-5yrs. 8am-6pm. 51wks.

Montessori Pavilion 020 8878 9695
Vine Road Recreation Ground, SW13 0NE
3-5yrs. 9.15am-12.30pm. Termtime.

St Michael's Nursery School 020 8567 8037
Elmbank Gardens, SW13 0NX
2-5yrs. Mornings

The Ark Nursery School 020 8741 4751
Kitson Hall, Kitson Road, SW13 9HJ
3-5yrs

SW14
Primary Steps Day Nursery 020 8876 8144
459b Upper Richmond Road West, East Sheen,
SW14 7PR
From 16mths-5yrs. 8am-6pm. 52wks.

s Tower House School 020 8876 3323
188 Sheen Lane, SW14 8LF
Boys 4-13yrs

Working Mums Day Care 020 8392 9969
and Pre-School
Mortlake Green School, Lower Richmond Road
3mths-5yrs. 8am-6pm. 51wks.

SW15
Alton Community Playschool 020 8780 9100
Alton Road, SW15 4LJ
6mths-5yrs. 8am-5pm. Termtime.

Asquith Nursery Putney 020 8246 5611
107-109 Norroy Road, Putney, SW15 1PH
18mths-5yrs. 8am-6pm. 51 wks

Beehive Nursery School 020 8780 5333
Putney Park Lane, SW15
2-5yrs. 9.15am-12.15pm. Termtime.

Bees Knees Nursery School 020 8876 8252
12 Priory Lane, SW15 5JQ
2¹/₂-5yrs

Busy Bee Nursery 020 8780 1615
106 Felsham Road, SW15

Busy Bee Nursery School 020 8789 0132
19 Lytton Grove, SW15
2¹/₂-5yrs. 9.15am-12.15pm and 1-3.15pm. Termtime.

Gwendolen House Nursery School 020 8704 1107
39 Gwendolen Avenue, SW15 6EP
Montessori based teaching plus music, dance, yoga and
French. Nutritious menu (principally organic ingredients).
Beautiful large garden.

s Hall School Wimbledon 020 8788 2370
Stroud Crescent, Putney Vale, SW15 3EQ
Co-ed 4-11yrs. Senior school at 17 The Downs, SW20 8HF.
020 8879 9200. 11-16yrs

s Hurlingham School 020 8874 7186
122 Putney Bridge Road, SW15 2NG
Co-ed 4-11yrs

s Ibstock Place School 020 8876 9991
Clarence Lane, Roehampton, SW15 5PY
Co-ed 3-18yrs

Kingston Vale Montessori 020 8546 3442
St John's Church Lane, Robin Hood Lane, Kingston
Vale, SW15 3PY
2-5yrs. 9.30am-12.30pm. Termtime.

s Lion House School 020 8780 9446
The Old Methodist Hall, Gwendolen Avenue, SW15 6EH
Co-ed 2¹/₂-8yrs.

Little Fingers Nursery 020 8874 8649
St. Stephen;s Church, Manfred Road, Putney
2¹/₂-5yrs. 9.30am-12pm and 12.30-3pm. Termtime.

s Merlin School 020 8788 2769
4 Carlton Drive, Putney, SW15 2BZ
Co-ed 4-8yrs.

Noddy's Nursery School 020 8785 9191
2 Gwendolen Avenue, Putney, SW15 6EH
3mths-5yrs. 8am-6.30pm. 51wks.

s Prospect House School 020 8780 0456
75 Putney Hill, SW15 3NT
Co-ed 3-11yrs

s Putney High School 020 8788 4886
35 Putney Hill, SW15 6BH
Girls 4-18yrs

S Putney Park School 020 8788 8316
11 Woodborough Road, SW15 6PY
Boys 4-11yrs, Girls 4-16yrs

Riverbank Early Years 020 8785 3046
2-4 Clarendon Drive, Putney, SW15 1AA
2-5yrs. 9.15am-3pm. Termtime.

Riverside Montessori Nursery 020 8780 9345
95 Lacy Road, SW15 1NR
3mths-5yrs. Full time

Ro's Nursery 020 8788 5704
Putney Leisure Centre, SW15 1BL
6mths-5yrs. 8am-6pm or sessional.

Schoolroom Montessori 020 7384 0479
St Simon's Church Hall, Hazlewell Road, SW15 6LU
2½-5yrs.

Square One Nursery School 020 8788 1546
Lady North Hall, Ravenna Road, Putney, SW15 6AW
9.30am-12.15pm. Termtime.

Tiggers Nursery School 020 8874 4668
87 Putney Bridge Road, SW15 2PA
2-5yrs. 9am-3.15pm. Termtime.

SW16
Modern Montessori 020 8769 7539
International (MMI) Pre-school
MMI House, 142 Mitcham Lane, SW16 6NS
www.modernmontessori-intl.com
3mths-5yrs. 8am-6pm. 49wks.

Abacus Early Learning Nursery 020 8677 9117
7 Drewstead Road, Streatham, SW16 1LY
18mths-5yrs. 8.30am-6m. 51wks.

Allsorts Playgroup 020 8677 5376
Mitcham Lane Baptist Church, 230 Mithcam Lane,
Streatham, SW16 6NT
2-5yrs. 9.30am-12.15pm. Termtime. Also drop-in sessions.

S Beechwood School 020 8677 8778
55 Leigham Court Road, Streatham, SW16 2NJ

Blossomtime Montessori 020 7564 8295
Nursery School
130 Sunnyhill Road, Streatham, SW16 2UN

Carey Days Nursery 020 8679 4009
496 Streatham High Road, SW16 3QB
3mths-3yrs. Open 8am-6pm 51 wks.

Carmena Christian Day Nursery 020 8677 8231
47 Thrale Road, Streatham, SW16 1NT
6mths-5yrs. 8am-6pm. 51wks.

Early Learners Day Nursery 020 8764 8030
162 Eardley Road, SW16 5TG
3mths-5yrs. 8am-6pm. 51wks.

Heathfield Pre-School 020 8664 6114
39 Estreham Road, Scout Headquarters,
Streatham, SW16 6LS
2½-4yrs. 9.30am-12pm. Termtime.

Hyderi Nursery School 020 8696 9979
26 Estreham Road, Streatham, SW16 5PQ
2-5yrs. 9.30am-2.30pm. Termtime.

Lewin Pre-School 020 8677 9450
Streatham Baptist Church Hall, Natal Road,
Streatham, SW16
2½-5yrs. 9.15-11.45am and 12.30-3pm (Tues & Wed only).
Termtime.

Rainbow Day Nursery 020 8679 4235
34 Kempshott Road, SW16 5LQ
8am-6pm. 51wks.

Springtime Day Nursery 020 7622 7884
11 The Glebe, Prentis Road, Streatham, SW16 1QR
2-5yrs. 7am-6pm. 51wks.

Stepping Stones Day Nursery 020 8679 4009
496 Streatham High Road, SW16 3QF

S Streatham Hill & 020 8677 8400
Clapham High School
Abbotswood Road, SW16 1AW
Girls 3-18yrs

Streatham Vale 020 8764 5092
Holy Redeemer Church Hall, Churchmore Road,
Streatham Vale, SW16
2-5yrs. 9.15-11.45am. Termtime.

Teddies Nurseries Streatham 0800 980 3801
113 Blegborough Road, SW16 6DL
3mths-5yrs. 8am-6pm. 51wks

Waldorf School of 020 8769 6587
South-West London
16-18 Abbotswood Road, SW16 1AP
3½-14yrs

SW17
S Bertrum House School 020 8767 4051
290 Balham High Road, SW17 7AL
www.bertrumhouseschool.co.uk
Boys and girls from 2½-7yrs.

Blackshaw Nursery 020 8672 4789
Blackshaw Road, Tooting, SW17 0QT
3mths-5yrs. 7am-6.30pm. 51wks.

Buffer Bear at Springfield 020 8682 1108
61 Glenburnie Road, Tooting, SW17 7DJ
0-3yrs. 7.30am-6pm. 52wks.

Crescent Kindergarten I 01622 833 331
Flat 1, 10 Trinity Crescent, SW17 7AE
2-5yrs. Termtime.

Playdays Nurseries

Open - 8.00am to 6.00pm, 51 Weeks a Year
For children aged 3 months to 5 Years

At Playdays we are dedicated in providing the finest full-day care and education. We also offer before/after school programmes and holiday clubs, for when your child starts school.

West Kensington W14
13 Barton Road - Tel: 020 7386 9083
45 Comeragh Road - Tel: 020 7385 1955

Chiswick W4
15-19 Chiswick High Road - Tel: 020 8747 9599

Wimbledon SW19
100-102 Wimbledon Hill Road - Tel: 020 8944 8959
58 Queens Road - Tel: 020 8946 8139

Crescent Kindergarten II   01622 833 331
Holy Trinity Church Hall, 74 Trinity Road, SW17 7AR
3-5yrs. 9am-12.15pm.

Dolphin Nursery   02087 672 901
75 Macmillan Way, Tooting Bec., SW17 6AT
3mths-5yrs. 7.30am-6.30pm. 52wks.

Eveline Day Nursery School   020 8672 0501
1 Chillerton Road, SW17 9BE
3mths-5yrs. 7.30am-6.30pm. Termtime.

Eveline Day Nursery School   020 8672 7549
30 Ritherdon Road, SW17 8QD
3mths-5yrs. 7.30am-6.30pm. 51wks.

s Eveline Day School   020 8672 4673
14 Trinity Crescent, SW17 7AE
3-11yrs. 7.30am-6.30pm. 51wks.

s Finton House School   020 8682 0921
169-171 Trinity Road, SW17 7HL
Co-ed 4-11yrs. Termtime.

Headstart Montessori School   020 8947 7359
St Mary's Church Hall, 46 Wimbledon Road, SW17 0UQ
2-9yrs. 8.45am-3.30pm. Termtime.

Red Balloon   020 8672 4711
St Mary Magdalen Church, Trinity Road, SW17 7SD
2-5yrs. 8.45am-12.15pm and 1.30-4.15pm. Termtime.

Teddies Nurseries Balham   020 8672 4808
272 Balham High Road, SW17 7AJ
3mths-5yrs. 8am-6pm. 51wks

Toots Day Nursery   020 8767 7017
214 Totterdown Street, SW17 8TD
1-5yrs.

Wee Care Day Nursery   020 8767 5501
83 Beechcroft Road, SW17
6mths-3yrs. 8am-6pm. 50wks.

SW18
345 and 2 to 3 Nursery School   020 8870 8441
Fitzhugh Community Clubroom, Trinity Road, SW18 3SA
2-3yrs 1.15pm-3.15pm Tues-Thurs, and 3-5yrs 9.30am-12.30pm Mon-Fri. Termtime.

Eveline Day Nursery School   020 8870 0966
East Hill United Reformed Church Hall, Geraldine Road, SW18 2NR
3mths-5yrs. Full day

Jigsaw Day Nursery   020 8877 1135
Dolphin House, Riverside West, Smugglers Way, Wandsworth, SW18 1EG
Come and see for yourself why we are the best

The Launch Pad
Nursery School

At The Launch Pad we aim to give your child:

- A secure base where they feel safe, loved and respected
- The confidence to embark on a wonderful journey of exploration and learning
- A stimulating and happy environment where they can grow and develop at their own pace
- OFSTED Registered

We offer

- A spacious hall with secure outdoor play area
- Montessori and Early Years curriculum
- Qualified and experienced staff
- Opportunity to develop imagination and creativity

We take children aged 2-5 years. Morning, afternoon and all day sessions.

Call 020 8877 9554 for further information
Email: thelaunchpad@blueyonder.co.uk

All Saints Community Hall, Lebanon Road,
Wandsworth (off West Hill), London SW18 1RE

Launchpad Nursery School   **020 8877 9554**
All Saints Community Hall, Lebanon Road,
Southfields, SW18 1RE
2-5yrs. 9am-3pm. Termtime. Also holiday clubs for children aged 2-7yrs.

Little Bunnies   **020 8946 8330**
St. Andrews Church Hall, Waynflete Street,
Earlsfield, SW18 3QG
18mths-5yrs. 8am-6pm. 50wks.

Melrose House Nursery School   **020 8874 7769**
39 Melrose Road, SW18 1LX
2½-5yrs.

Noah's Ark Nursery School   **020 7228 9593**
Westside Church Hall, Melody Road, SW18 2QQ
2½-5yrs

Roche School   **020 8877 0823**
11 Frogmore, SW18 1HW
3-11yrs

Schoolroom Two   **020 8874 9305**
Gressenhall Road, SW18 1PQ
2½-5yrs

S St Michael Steiner School   **020 8648 5758**
5 Merton Road, Wandsworth, SW18 5ST
Co-ed 3-14yrs

Sticky Fingers Montessori   **020 8871 9496**
Day Nursery
St John the Divine Church Hall, Garratt Lane
18mths-5yrs. Full day

Teddies Nurseries Southfields   **0800 980 3801**
Duntshill Mill, 21 Riverdale Drive, SW18 4UR
3mths-5yrs. 8am-6pm. 51wks

The Colour Box Montessori   **020 8874 4969**
Nursery School
Magdelen Road, SW18 3NZ

The Gardens Nursery School   **020 8871 9478**
62 Standen Road, SW18 5TG
2½-5yrs. 8am-6pm. Termtime.

The Launch Pad Nursery School   **020 8877 9554**
All Saints Community Hall, Lebanon Road, SW18 1RE
2-5yrs. 9am-3.30pm. Termtime only.

The Park Gardens Nursery School   **020 8875 1277**
Wandle Recreation Centre, Mapleton Road
2½-5yrs. 9.30am-12.30pm. 32wks.

Wee Ones Nursery School   **020 8870 7729**
St Anne's Church Hall, St Ann's Hill, SW18
2½-5yrs

Wimbledon Park Montessori   **020 8944 8584**
Nursery School
206 Heythorp Street, SW18 5BU
2½-5yrs

SW19
Oak Tree Pre-School   **020 8715 1115**
St Mary's Church, 30 St Mary's Road, SW19 7BP
www.oaktree4kids.co.uk
Oak Tree Pre-School Nursery caters for children aged between 1 and 5 years old, open all year from 8am to 6pm, Monday to Friday, flexible sessions, safe, fun and stimulating environment, secure gardens.

Playdays
100 Wimbledon Hill Road, SW19   **020 8944 8959**
3mths-5yrs. 8am-6pm. 51wks.

58 Queens Road, SW19 8LR   **020 8946 8139**
3mths-5yrs. 8am-6pm. 51wks.

Apples and Honey, The Nursery   **020 8946 4836**
on the Common
1 Queensmere Road, Wimbledon, SW19 5QD
2-5yrs. 9.45am-12.30pm. Termtime. Wimbledon Jewish nursery.

Buffer Bear Nursery   **020 8944 5618**
Wimbledon Traincare Depot, Durnsford Road
3mths-5yrs. Full day

Castle Kindergarten   **020 8544 0089**
20 Henfield Road, SW19 3HU
2½-5yrs. 9.15am-12.15pm and 1-1.30pm. Termtime.

Cosmopolitan Day Nursery 020 8544 0758
65-67 High Street, Colliers Wood, SW19 2JF
0-5yrs. 8am-6pm. 51wks.

Crown Kindergarten 020 8540 8820
Coronation House, Ashcombe Road, SW19 8JP
1-5yrs. 9am-6pm. 51wks.

Dees Day Nursery 020 8944 0284
2 Mansel Road, SW19 4AA
3mths-5yrs. 8am-6.30pm. 51wks.

Dicky Bird's Day Nursery 020 8542 7416
52a Dundonald Road, SW19 3PH
3mths-5yrs. 8am-6.30pm. 51wks.

Dicky Birds Pre-School Nursery 020 8942 5779
27 Queens Road, Wimbledon, SW19 8NW
3mths-5yrs. 8am-6pm. 50wks.

Eveline Day Nursery School 020 8545 0699
89a Quicks Road, SW19 1EX
3mths-5yrs. 7.30am-6.30pm. 51wks.

S Kings College School 020 8255 5300
Southside, Wimbledon Common, SW19 4TT
Boys 7-13yrs

Little Hall Gardens Day Care 020 8947 7058
49 Durnsford Avenue, SW19 8BH
1-5yrs. 8am-7pm. 51wks.

Maria Montessori Nursery 020 8543 6353
St John's Ambulance Hall, 122-124 Kingston Road
2-5yrs. Mornings

Noddy's Nursery School 020 8785 9191
Trinity Church Hall, Beaumont Road, West Hill,
SW19 6SP
3mths-5yrs. 8am-6.30pm. 51wks.

Nutkins Nursery 020 8246 6400
Beaumont Road, (off West Hill), SW19 6TF
2-5yrs. Full day

St Mark's Montessori 07956 346938
St Mark's Church, St Mark's Place, SW19 7ND
2¹/₂-5yrs. Mornings

St Paul's Playgroup 020 8788 7734
23 Inner Park Road, Wimbledon, SW19 6ED
2-5yrs. 9.30am-12pm. Termtime.

S Study Preparatory School 020 8947 6969
Wilberforce House, Camp Road, Wimbledon
Common, SW19 4UN
Girls 4-11yrs

Sunny-side Nursery School 020 8337 0887
ATC Hall, 192 Merton Road, SW19
2¹/₂-5yrs. Mornings

S Willington School 020 8944 7020
Worcester Road, Wimbledon, SW19 7QQ
Boys 4-13yrs

S Wimbledon High School 020 8971 0900
Mansel Road, SW19 4AB
Girls 4-18yrs

S Wimbledon High School 020 8971 0902
(Junior School)
Mansel Road, SW19 4AB
Girls 4-10yrs.

SW20
Busy Bees Nursery 020 8543 9005
c/o David Lloyd Leisure Club, Bushey Road,
Raynes Park, SW20 8TE
3mths-5yrs. 7.45am-6pm. 51wks.

Coombe Day Nursery 020 8549 5543
Wimbledon College Playing Fields, 183 Coombe
Lane, SW20 0RW
2¹/₂-5yrs. Full day

Dicky Birds Pre-School Nursery 020 8942 5779
86 Pepys Road, Raynes Park, SW20 8PF
2-5yrs. Session from 9.15am-12.15pm and 1-4pm.
Termtime.

Eveline Day Nursery Schools 020 8672 7549
Grand Drive, Raynes Park, SW20 9NA
3mths-5yrs. 7.30am-6.30pm. 51wks.

Lollypops Nursery 020 8296 3731
Nelson Hospital, Kingston Road, SW20
3mths-5yrs. 7.30am-6pm. 51wks.

Teddies Nurseries Raynes Park 0800 980 3801
St Matthews Church, Spencer Road, Raynes Park
3mths-5yrs. 8am-6pm. 51wks

S The Rowans 020 8946 8220
19 Drax Avenue, SW20 0EZ
Co-ed 3-9yrs. 9am-3.30pm. Termtime.

Ursuline Convent Prep 020 8947 0859
18 The Downs, Wimbledon, SW20 8HR
Boys 3-7yrs. Girls 3-11yrs

TWs
Brentford Day Nursery 020 8568 7561
(Bringing up Baby)
Half Acre, Brentford, TW8 8BH
www.bringingupbaby.co.uk
A day nursery for 42 children aged 3mths-5yrs. Open 8am-
6.15pm.

Happy Times 0800 652 2424
Grena Road, Richmond, TW9 1XS
www.happytimes.co.uk
3mths-5yrs. Full day

S Kew College   020 8940 2039
Cumberland Road, Kew, Surrey TW9 3HQ
www.kewcollege.com
Kew College is a small independent co-educational school for children aged 3-11 years. We pride ourselves in the lively, happy and dynamic environment. Our teachers are enthusiastic, hardworking and dedicated. Excellent results for 11+ exams.

Twickenham Pk Day Nursery 020 8892 0872
Cambridge Road, TW1 2HN
www.eatonsquareschool.com
2mths-5yrs. 8am-6pm. All year round care.

S Newland House School   020 8892 7479
Waldegrave Park, Twickenham, TW1 4TQ
Co-ed 4-13yrs

Buttercups Day Nursery   020 8569 8046
The Garden House, Syon Park, Brentford, TW8 8JF
3mths-5yrs. 8m-6pm. 51wks.

The Little School   020 8568 4447
44 Boston Park Road, Brentford, TW8 9JF
3mths-5yrs. 8am-6pm. 51wks.

S Unicorn School   020 8948 3926
238 Kew Road, Richmond, TW9 3JX
Co-ed 3-11yrs

S Twickenham Preparatory   020 8979 6216
School
43 High Street, Hampton, Hampton, TW12 2SA
Boys 4-13yrs, Girls 4-11yrs

WEST LONDON POSTCODES
W1
Beginnings   020 7723 0330
West London Synagogue, 33 Seymour Place, W1H 5AU
0-5yrs. 8.30am-6.30pm. 51wks.

Great Beginnings Montessori   020 7258 1066
School
82a Chiltern Street, W1M 1PS
2-6yrs.

Jumbo Nursery School   020 7935 2441
St James's Church Hall, 22 George Street, W1U 3QY
2-5yrs. 9am-12.15pm. Termtime only.

S Queen's College Prep School   020 7291 0660
61 Portland Place, W1B 1QP
Girls 3-11yrs. 8.15am-3.20pm. Termtime.

S St Nicholas Pre-Preparatory   020 7493 0165
School
18 Balderton Street, W1
3-7yrs

W2
Daisies Day Nursery   020 7498 2922
& School - Hyde Park
St James's Church, Sussex Gardens, W2 3UD
www.daisiesdaynurseries.co.uk
3mths-5yrs. 8am-6pm. 50wks.

Paint Pots Montessori School 020 7792 0433
Bayswater United Reform Church, 12 Newton Road, W2 5LS
2^1/2-5yrs. Developing confidence, independence, self-esteem, concentration social skills and self-discipline.

Ravenstone House Hyde Park 020 7262 1190
The Long Garden, Albion Street, St George's Fields, W2 2AX
2mths-5yrs. Open 8am-6.30pm. 48 wks. First class education for children, first class service for parents.

S Connaught House School   020 7262 8830
47 Connaught Square, Hyde Park, W2 2HL
Boys 4-8yrs, Girls 4-11yrs

S Hampshire School   020 7229 7065
Prep School
9 Queensborough Terrace, W2 3TB
Co-ed 8-13yrs.

Linden Gardens Pre-School   020 7229 2130
73b Linden Gardens, W2 4HQ
2^1/2-5yrs. 9.30am-12.30pm. Termtime

Moorhouse Pre-School   020 7727 7483
Mickleton Lodge, Brunel Estate, Westbourne Park Road, W2 5UL
2-5yrs. 9.30am-12pm. Termtime.

Parkview Lodge Pre-School   020 7289 6714
Parkview Lodge, Senior Street, Westminster, W2 5TE
2-5yrs. 9.30am-3.15pm or sessional am/pm. Termtime.

S Pembridge Hall School   020 7229 0121
for Girls
18 Pembridge Square, W2 4EH
Girls 4-11yrs. 9am-3.30pm. Termtime. Very popular so you must put names down at birth to secure a place.

St James' Pre-School   020 7724 8640
Holy Trinity Hall, 170 Gloucester Terrace, W2 6HS
9.30am-12pm and 12.45-3.15pm.

St John's Montessori   020 7402 2529
Nursery School
St John's Church Hall, Hyde Park Crescent, W2 2QD
2-5yrs

Toddlers & Mums Montessori   020 7243 4227
St Stephens Church, Westbourne Park Road, W2 5QT
14mths-5yrs

Warwick Day Nursery   020 7641 4361
Cirencester Street, W2 5SR
10mths-5yrs. 8am-6pm. 51wks.

RAVENSTONE HOUSE
Pre-Preparatory School & Nursery

"First class education for children,
first rate service for parents"

HYDE PARK W2
Children from 2 months to 7 years
Telephone: 020 7262 1190
email: hydepark@ravenstonehouse.co.uk
The Long Garden, Albion Street, London, W2 2AX.

ELVASTON PLACE SW7
Children from 2 months to 11 years
Telephone: 020 7225 3131
email: elvastonplace@ravenstonehouse.co.uk
24 Elvaston Place, South Kensington, London, SW7 5NL.

S Wetherby School   020 7727 9581
11 Pembridge Square, W2 4ED
Boys 4-8yrs

W3

Bizzy Lizzy Day Nursery   020 8993 1664
Priory Community Centre, Acton Lane, W3 8NY
2-5yrs. 8am-6pm. 52wks.

Buffer Bear Nursery   020 8743 7249
10 Stanley Gardens, W3 7SZ
3mths - 5yrs. 8am-6pm. 51wks.

Buttercups Day Nursery   020 8749 9459
27 Old Oak Road, Acton, W3 7HN
3mths-4½yrs. Full day

Carousel Nursery   020 8993 2009
Acton Hill Church, Woodlands Avenue, W3 9BU
2-5yrs. 8am-6pm.

City Mission Nursery   020 8811 2540
St. Aidans Presbytery, 87-89 Old Oak Common
Lane, East Acton, W3 7DD
6mths-5yrs. 8am-6pm. 51wks.

Cybertots   020 8752 0200
1 Avenue Crescent, W3
2-5yrs. Full day

Ealing Montessori School   020 8992 4513
St Martin's Church Hall, 5 Hale Gardens, W3 9SQ
2¹/₂-5yrs. 9am-3pm. Termtime.

Happy Child Day Nursery   020 8992 0855
St Gabriel's Church, Noel Road, W3 0JE
6mths-5yrs. Full day

S Intl School of London   020 8992 5823
139 Gunnersbury Avenue, W3 8LG
Co-ed 4-18yrs. English + Arabic, etc.

S King Fahad Academy   020 8743 0131
Bromyard Avenue, W3 7HD
Muslim. Parallel classes for Boys and Girls 6-18yrs

Village Montessori Nursery   020 8993 3540
All Saints Church, Bollo Bridge Road, W3 8AX
Aged 2¹/₂-5yrs. Full day nursery. Walled garden area. Music,
art, French, dance. OFSTED registered.

W4
S Orchid Montessori School 077955 66978
Riverside Lands, Dukes Meadows, Chiswick, W4 2SH
www.orchidmontessorischool.co.uk
The school has been carefully structured to provide a
supportive and challenging environment to teach
independence and self-confidence. Ages 2-6 years.

Playdays Nurseries   020 8747 9599
15-19 Chiswick High Road, W4
3mths-5yrs. a8m-6pm. 51weeks.

Ark Montessori   020 8932 4766
Rugby Road, W4 1AT
2¹/₂-6yrs. Mornings

Buttercups Day Nursery   020 8742 8368
38 Grange Road, W4 4DD
3mths-5yrs. 8am-6pm. 51wks.

Caterpillar Montessori Nursery   020 8747 8531
St Albans Church Hall, South Parade, W4 5JU
2¹/₂-5yrs

S Chiswick and Bedford   020 8994 1804
Park Prep School
Priory House, Priory Avenue, W4 1TX
Boys 4-8yrs, Girls 4-11yrs

Chiswick Day Care   020 8995 2180
53 Barrowgate Road, W4 4QT
2-5yrs. 9.15am-2.45pm. Termtime.

Chiswick Toddlers World   020 8995 7267
St Paul's Church Hall, Pyrmont Road, W4 3NR
1-5yrs. 7.45am-6pm. 51wks.

Devonshire Day Nursery   020 8995 9538
2 Bennett Street, W4 2AH
6wks-5yrs, 8am-6pm, 52 weeks.

Elmwood Montessori   020 8994 8177
St Michaels Centre, Elmwood Road, W4 3DY
2¹/₂-5yrs. 9am-12pm and 1pm-4pm. Termtime.

S Falcons School for Boys   020 8747 8393
2 Burnaby Gardens, W4 3DT
Boys 3-8yrs.

Imaginations   020 8742 1658
Methodist Church Hall, Sutton Court Road, W4
2-5yrs. 9am-12pm. Termtime only.

Leapfrog Day Nursery   020 8742 0011
4 Marlborough Road, Chiswick, W4 4ET
3mths-5yrs. 7am-7pm. 52 wks

Meadows Montessori   020 8742 1327
Dukes Meadow Community Hall, Alexandra Gdns,
W4 2TD
2-5yrs. 9am-12pm Mon/Wed/Fri and 9am-3pm Tues/Thurs..
Termtime.

S Orchard House School   020 8742 8544
16 Newton Grove, W4 1LB
Co-ed 3-11yrs

Our Lady Queen of Peace   020 8994 2053
Day Nursery
10 Chiswick Lane, W4 2JE
2¹/₂-4yrs

Parkside Nursery School   020 8995 4648
Homefield Lodge, Chiswick Lane North, W4 2KA
2-6yrs. Mornings only

Pebbles Day Care Nursery   020 8994 6767
57 Harvard Road, Chiswick, W4 4ED

Primary Steps Day Nursery   020 8995 4648
Homefield Recreation Ground, Chiswick Lane, W4 2QA
From 2-5yrs. 8am-12pm. 52wks.

Riverside Children's Centre   020 8995 9299
Back of Cavendish School, Edensor Road, W4 2RG
2-5yrs. 8am-5.50pm. 51wks. They also run a sessional
playgroup from 8am-1pm or 1-3.30pm.

Tara House Nursery School   020 8995 5144
opposite 3 Wilson Walk, off Prebend Gardens, W4
2-5yrs

Westside Day Nursery   020 8742 2206
Steele Road, W4 5AF
3mths-2¹/₂ yrs. Full day

W5
S Aston House School   020 8566 7300
1 Aston Road, Ealing, W5 2RL
Co-ed. 2-11yrs

Buttercups Day Nursery   020 8840 4838
9 Florence Road, Ealing, W5 3TU
3mths-5yrs. 8am-6pm. 51wks.

Caterpillar Day Nursery   020 8579 0833
8th Ealing Scout Hall, Popes Lane, Ealing, W5 4NB
2-5yrs. 8am-5.30pm. 52wks.

s Clifton Lodge Prep School   020 8579 3662
8 Mattock Lane, W5 5BG
Boys 4-13yrs

s Durston House School   020 8997 0511
12 Castlebar Road, W5 2DR
Boys 4-13yrs.

s Falcons School for Girls   020 8992 5189
15 Gunnersbury Avenue, W5 3XD
Girls 2-12yrs.

Happy Child Day Nursery   020 8567 4300
2b The Grove, W5 5LH
3mths-5yrs. Full day

Happy Child Day Nursery   020 8992 0209
Woodgrange Avenue, W5 3NY
3mths-5yrs. 8am-6pm. 51wks.

Happy Child Day Nursery   020 8566 1546
2a The Grove, W5 5LH
1-5yrs. Full time.

Happy Child Day Nursery   020 8567 2244
283-287 Windmill Road, W5 4DP
3mths-5yrs. Full day

Happy Child Montessori School   020 8840 9936
Welsh Chapel, Ealing Green, W5 5EN
2-5yrs. Full day

s Harvington School   020 8997 1583
20 Castlebar Road, W5 2DS
Girls 3-16; Boys 3-5yrs

Jumpers Nursery   020 8799 4871
YMCA, 25 St Mary's Road, W5 5RE
6mths-5yrs. 8am-6pm. 51wks.

Maria Montessori Nursery   07850 509 415
Church of the Ascension Hall, Beaufort Road,
Ealing, W5 3EB
2½-5yrs. 9am-12pm. Termtime.

Mount Park Montessori   07946 624 370
Methodist Church Hall, Pitshanger Lane, W5 1QP
2-5yrs. 9am-3.30pm. Termtime.

New World Montessori   020 8810 4411
Nursery School
St Barnabus Millenium Church Hall, Pitshanger
Lane, W5
2-5yrs

New World Montessori School   020 8566 9507
38a Meadvale Road, Ealing, W5 1NP
9.15am-12.30pm. Termtime.

Nursery Land Daycare Centre   020 8566 5962
9th Ealing Scouts Hut, Northfield Avenue, W5 4UA
2-4yrs

Resurrection Day Nursery   020 8810 6241
18 Carlton Road, Ealing, W5 2AW
2-5yrs. 8am-5pm. 51wks.

Resurrection Day Nursery   020 8998 8954
84 Gordon Road, W5 2AR
2-5yrs. Full day

s St Augustine's Priory   020 8997 2022
Hillcrest Road, Ealing, W5 2JL
An ideal school environment fostering academic curiosity,
independence and kindness

St Barnabas Playgroup   020 8991 7653
St. Barnabas Millennium Hall, Pitshanger Lane,
Ealing, W5 1QG
9.30am-12pm. Termtime.

s St Benedict's Junior School   020 8862 2050
5 Montpelier Avenue, W5 2XP
Boys 4-18yrs, Girls 16-18yrs

St Matthew's Montessori School   020 8579 2304
St Matthew's Church Hall, North Common Road, W5
2-5yrs

St Peter's Playgroup   020 8998 5439
Mount Park Road, Ealing, W5 2RU
2-5yrs. 9.15-11.45am. Termtime.

Tulip Pre-School   020 8998 4236
St. Barnabas Millennium Hall, Pitshanger Lane,
Ealing, W5 1QG
2-5yrs. 12.30-3.15pm. Termtime.

W6
Bringing Up Baby: 020 8746 1015
Richford Street Day Nursery
50 Richford Gate, 61-69 Richford Street, W6 7HZ
www.bringingupbaby.co.uk
A day nursery for 58 children aged 3mths-5yrs. Open
8.15am-6.15pm. 50wks.

Happy Times   0800 652 2424
Ravenscourt Park, W6 0TN
www.happytimes.co.uk
3mths-5yrs. 7am-7pm

Bayonne Nursery School   020 7385 5366
50 Paynes Walk, W6
3-5yrs. 8am-5.30pm. Termtime.

s Bute House School   020 7603 7381
Luxembourg Gardens, W6 7EA
Girls 4-11yrs

Howard House Nursery School   020 8741 5147
58 Ravenscourt Road, Ravenscourt Park, W6 0UG
2½-5yrs. 9am-4pm. Termtime.

S = SCHOOL

Jigsaw Day Nursery 020 8563 7982
Centre West, Hammersmith Broadway, W6 9YD
3mths-5yrs. Come and see for yourself why we are the best

Jordans Nursery School 020 8741 3230
Lower Hall, Holy Innocents Church, Paddenswick
Road, W6 0UB

**S Larmenier & Sacred Heart Catholic Primary
School** 020 8748 9444
Great Church Lane, W6
Co-ed 3-7yrs.

S Latymer Preparatory School 020 8748 0303
36 Upper Mall, W6 9TA
Co-ed 7-18yrs.

S Ravenscourt Park Prep School 020 8846 9153
16 Ravenscourt Avenue, W6 0SL
Co-ed 4-11yrs

S St Paul's Girls' School 020 7603 2288
Brook Green, W6 7BS
Girls 11-18yrs

Step By Step Day Nursery 020 8748 1319
1 Bridge Avenue, Hammersmith, W6 9JA
2-5yrs

The Beanstalk Montessori 020 8723 2200
Nursery School
St Peter's Church, Black Lion Lane, W6 9BG
2¹/₂-5yrs. Sessional 9.30am-12.30pm and 1-3.30pm.
Termtime.

W7
Bunny Park Day Nursery 020 8567 6142
37 Manor Court Road, Hanwell Village, W7 3EJ
2-5yrs.

Buttons Nursery School 020 8840 3355
99 Oaklands Road, W7 2DT
3mths-5yrs. 8am-6pm. 51wks.

Playhouse Day Nursery 020 8840 2851
Leighton Hall, Elthorne Park Road, W7 2JJ
2-5yrs. 8am-6pm. 51wks.

Sticky Fingers Day Nursery 020 8566 4606
Bernard Sunley Hall, Greenford Avenue, W7 1AA
2-5yrs. Full day

W8
S Thomas's Kensington 020 7937 0583
(Lower School)
39-41 Victoria Road, W8 5RJ
www.thomas-s.co.uk
Co-ed 4-8yrs. Admissions criteria: registration at birth - as
well as an interview at 4yrs. This is the junior department of
Thomas's Prep-School in Cottesmore Gardens.

S Thomas's Kensington 020 7361 6500
(Prep School)
17-19 Cottesmore Gardens, W8 5PR
www.thomas-s.co.uk
Co-ed 7-11yrs. Termtime. A lively co-educational day school
in the heart of Kensington.

S Hawkesdown House School 020 7727 9090
27 Edge Street, W8 7PN
www.hawkesdown.co.uk
Boys 3-8yrs. First class education in a kind and caring
school.

Holland Park Pre-School 020 7603 2838
Stable Yard, Holland Park, W8 6LU
2¹/₂-5yrs. 9.30am-3.30pm. Termtime

Iverna Gardens 020 7937 0794
Montessori Nursery School
Armenian Church Hall, Iverna Gardens, W8 6TP
2¹/₂-5yrs

Little Cherubs Nursery School 07810 712 241
16a Abingdon Road, W8 6AF
2-5yrs. 9am-3.15pm. Termtime.

W9
Ashmore Pre-School 020 8968 6225
St. Lukes Church Centre, Fernhead Road, W9 3EH
2-4yrs. 9am-12pm. Termtime.

Buffer Bear St Stephens Nursery 020 7641 4346
The Annexe, Essendine Road, W9 2LR
6mths-5yrs. 8am-6pm. 51wks.

Elgin Pre-School 020 7289 7895
Elgin Community Centre, Harrow Road, W9 3RS
2¹/₂-5yrs. 9.30am-12pm and 12.45-3.15pm. Termtime.

Kiddicare Nursery 020 8964 3656
389 Harrow Road, W9 3NA
2-5yrs. 8am-6pm.

Little Sweethearts Montessori 020 7266 1616
St Saviour's Church Hall, Warwick Avenue, W9 2PT
2-7yrs. 8.55am-4.15pm and sessional care: mornings
8.55am-12pm and afternoon 1.15-3.45pm. Termtime.

St Stephen's Day Nursery 020 7641 4346
Essendine Road, W9 2LR
8am-6pm. 50wks.

Windmill Montessori 020 7289 3410
Nursery School
Former Caretaker's Cottage, Oakington Road, W9 2EB
2-5yrs

W10
S Bassett House School 020 8969 0313
60 Bassett Road, W10 6JP
Co-ed 3-8yrs. Girls 8-11yrs. 9am-3.30pm. Termtime.

Dalgarno Pre-School 020 8969 1463
1 Webb Close, W10 5QB
2¹/₂-5yrs. Sessional 9.30am-2.30pm. Termtime only. Also
stay and play drop-in sessions from 12.30-2.30pm.

Katharine Bruce Day Nursery 020 7641 5835
Queens Park Court, Ilbert Street, W10 4QA
1-4yrs. 8am-6pm. 51wks.

Maxilla Nursery Centre 020 8969 6494
4 Maxilla Walk, W10 6NQ

New Studio Pre-School 020 8960 6661
Kelfield Mews, Kelfield Gardens, W10 6LS
2¹/₂-5yrs. 9.25am-1.25pm. Termtime

Spanish Day Nursery 111 020 8960 6661
317a Portobello Road, W10 5SY
2-5yrs. 9am-4.30pm. 43wks.

Sunrise Pre-School 020 8968 2921
The Moberly Centre, 101 Kilburn Lane, W10 4AH
2-5yrs

Swinbrook Nursery 020 8968 5833
39-41 Acklam Road, W10 5YU
2-8yrs. 8am-6pm. 51wks.

Venture Pre-School 020 8960 3234
103a Wornington Road, W10 5YB
2¹/₂-5yrs. 9.30am-12pm. Termtime

W11
Cherry Tree Pre-Nursery School 020 8961 2081
St Francis of Assisi Community Centre, Pottery Lane
18mths-3¹/₂yrs

Delaney's Nursery School 020 7603 6095
St James, Norland Church, St James's Gardens,
W11 4RB
2-5yrs old

Dr Rolfe's Montessori School 020 7727 8300
154 Holland Park Avenue, W11 1NR
2¹/₂-5yrs. Full day 9am-3.15pm. Termtime

Kidsunlimited Nurseries 0845 850 0222
Ladbroke Grove
34 Ladbroke Grove, W11 3BQ
3mths-5yrs. 7.30am-6pm. 51 wks.

Ladbroke Square Montessori 020 7229 0125
School
43 Ladbroke Square, W11 3ND
2¹/₂-5yrs

Maria Montessori Children's House 020 7221 4141
All Saints Church, 28 Powis Gardens, W11 1JG
2¹/₂-5yrs

Miss Delaney's Nursery 020 7603 6095
St James, Norland Church, St James's Gardens
2¹/₂-5yrs. 9am-12pm or 1-4pm. Termtime.

Miss Delaney's Too 020 7727 0010
St Clement's Church, 95 Sirdar Road, W11 4EQ
2¹/₂-5yrs. 9am-12pm or 1-4pm. Termtime. Call 020 7603
8181 for registration details.

S Norland Place School 020 7603 9103
162 166 Holland Park Av, W11 4UH
Co-ed 4-8yrs. Boys 8-11yrs.

S Notting Hill Prep School 020 7221 0727
95 Lancaster Road, W11 1QQ
Co-ed 5-13yrs.

Rolfe's Nursery School 020 7727 8300
206-208 Kensington Park Road, W11 1NR
2¹/₂-5yrs. 9am-3.15pm. Termtime.

S Southbank Intl School 020 7229 8230
36-38 Kensington Park Road, W11 3BU
Co-ed 4-18yrs

St Peters Nursery School 020 7243 2617
59a Portobello Road, W11 3BD
2¹/₂-5yrs

Strawberry Fields Nursery School 020 7727 8363
5 Pembridge Villas, W11 3EN
2-5yrs. 9am-3pm. Termtime.

The Square Montessori School   020 7221 6004
18 Holland Park Avenue, W11 3QU
A small and cosy home from home environment with
excellent teaching standards

Villas Nursery School   020 7602 6232
32 St Ann's Villas, Holland Park Avenue, W11 4RS
2-5yrs. Full day

W12
Acorn Pre-School   020 8740 5522
76 Braybrook Street, W12 0AP
2½-5yrs. 9.30am-3pm. 51wks..

Harmony Neighbourhood Nursery   020 8743 2089
Australia Road, W12 7PT
1-5yrs. 8am-6pm. 50wks.

Ladybird Day Nursery   020 8741 3399
277 & 287 Goldhawk Road, W12 8EU
6mths-5yrs. 8am-6pm. 51wks.

Little People Day Nurseries   020 8749 5080
61 Hadyn Park Road, W12 9AQ
3mths-3yrs. 8am-6pm. 51wks.

Little People of Willow Vale   020 8749 2877
9 Willow Vale, W12 0PA
4mths-5yrs. 8am-6pm. 51wks.

Stepping Stones Nursery School   020 8742 9103
St Saviour's Church, Cobbold Road, W12 9LN
2-5yrs. 9.30am-12.30pm. Termtime.

Vanessa Nursery School   020 8743 8196
14 Cathnor Road, W12 9JA
3-5yrs. 9.15-11.45am and 1-3.30pm. Termtime.

Wendell Park Pre-School   020 8749 2108
Wendell Park School Annex, Cobbold Road,
Shepherds Bush, W12
2-5yrs. 9.30am-1.30pm. Termtime.

W13
Corner House Day Nursery   020 8567 2806
82 Lavington Road, W13 9LR
3mths-5yrs. 8am-6pm. 51wks. Expert care and education
provided by only qualified staff.

s Avenue House School   020 8998 9981
70 The Avenue, W13 8LS
3-11yrs. 8.45-11.45am and 12.45-3.30pm. Termtime.

Children's Corner Day Nursery   020 8840 5591
29 Hastings Road, W13 8QH
18mths-5yrs. 8am-6pm. 51wks.

Children's House Nursery School   07976 273 896
W13 Youth Centre, Churchfield Road, W13 9NF
2-5yrs. 8.30am-12.30pm. Termtime.

Cybertots on the Green   020 8997 3990
2a Drayton Green, West Ealing, W13 0JF
3mths-5yrs. 8am-6pm. 51wks.

Happy Child Baby Nursery   020 8566 5515
Green Man Passage, W13 0TG
3mths-2½yrs

Happy Child Day Nursery   020 8566 5515
Green Man Passage (off Bayham Road), W13 0TG
1-5yrs. 8am-6pm. 51wks.

Home from Home Day Nursery   020 8566 7706
St Luke's Hall, Drayton Grove, W13 0LA
2-5yrs. 8am-6pm. 51wks.

Jigsaw Nursery & Montessori School   020 8997 8330
1 Courtfield Gardens, W13 0EY
18mths-5yrs. 8am-6pm. 51wks.

Little Angels Day Nursery   020 8566 3349
1a Dudley Gardens, W13 9LU
6mths-4yrs. 8am-6pm. 51wks.

s Notting Hill and Ealing   020 8799 8400
High School
2 Cleveland Road, W13 8AX
Girls 5-18yrs.

Playways Day Nursery   020 8998 2723
2 Amhert Road, W13 8ND
3mths-5yrs. Full day

Splash and Dash Pre-School   020 8566 2182
Kingsdown Avenue, Ealing, W13 9PR
2-5yrs. 9am-12pm. Termtime.

W14
Playdays   020 7386 9083
13 Barton Road, W14 9HB
3mths-5yrs. 8am-6pm. 51wks.

Playdays   020 7385 1955
45 Comeragh Road, W14 9HT
3mths-5yrs. 8am-6pm. 51wks.

s Holland Park Prep School   020 7602 9266
5 Holland Road, W14 8HJ
www.hpps.co.uk
2-8yrs. 9am-3pm. Termtime. Developing confident and
contented children from birth to 8 years. See our website on
www.hpps.co.uk or ring 020 7602 9266 for a prospectus.

Bright Sparks Montessori School   020 7371 4697
25 Minford Gardens, W14 0AP
2½-5yrs. 9.15am-4.15pm. Termtime.

Busy Bee Nursery   020 7602 8905
45 Redan Street, W14 0AB
3-5yrs

Holland Park Day Nursery   020 7602 9066
9 Holland Road, W14 8HJ
3mths-2yrs. 7.30am-6.30pm or 9am-3pm. Termtime (but the
school is open during the holidays for flexible wrap-around care).

Corner House Day Nursery
Established 1989
Specialised, professional care and education from fully qualified staff.
For children aged 3 months to 5 years
Tel: 020 8567 2806

Montessori at Brook Green   07803 984 639
St.Simon's Church Hall, Minford Gardens, West
Kensington, W14
2¹/₂-5yrs. 9am-12pm. Termtime.

Ripples Montessori School   020 7602 7433
The Crypt, St John the Baptist Church, Holland
Road, W14 8AH
2¹/₂-5yrs

School House Nursery   020 7602 9066
5 Holland Road, W14 8HJ
2-8yrs. Full day

Sinclair Montessori   020 7602 3745
Nursery School
Garden flat, 142 Sinclair Road, W14 0NL
2¹/₂-5yrs

s St James Independent School   020 7348 1777
Earsby Street, W14 8SH
Boys and Girls 4-10yrs, separate schools

Under 5's Pre-School   020 7603 3728
Minford Gardens
56 Minford Gardens, W14 0AW
2-5yrs. 9.30am-2.30pm. Termtime.

Warwick Pre-School   020 7602 3080
78 Warwick Gardens, W14 8PR
2¹/₂-5yrs. 9.15am-1.15pm and 1.15-3pm. Termtime

WC1

Collingham Gardens Nursery   020 7837 3423
Henrietta Mews, Wakefield Street, WC1N 1PH
2¹/₂-5yrs. 9am-5pm. 51wks.

Coram Fields Nursery   020 7833 0198
93 Guildford Street, WC1N 1DN
3-5yrs. 9.30am-4pm. 51wks.

Great Ormond Street Hospital   020 7829 7824
Staff Nursery
40-41 Queen Square, WC1N 3BB
3mths-5yrs. 7.30am-6.30pm. 51wks.

VICTORIA PAGE

Est.1982

07050
246 810

020 7381
9911

Fulham

Mace Montessori Nursery School 020 7242 5842
38-42 Millman Street, WC1N 3EW
2-5yrs. 8am-6pm. 50wks.

Thomas Coram Early 020 7520 0385
Childhood Centre
49 Mecklenburgh Square, WC1N 2NY
6mths-5yrs. 8.30am-5.30pm. 52wks.

University College London 020 7679 7461
Day Nursery
20 Taviton Street, WC1H 0BW
3mths-5yrs. 9am-5.30pm. 52wks.

Westminster Kingsway 020 7278 0541
College Nursery
Sidmouth Street, WC1H 8JB
2-4yrs. 9am-5pm. Termtime.

WC2
Macklin Street Nursery 020 7831 9776
25 Macklin Street, WC2B 5NN
0-5yrs. 8am-6pm. 51wks.

Chandos Day Nursery 020 7836 6574
47 Dudley Court, 36 Endell Street, WC2H 9RF
3mths-5yrs. 8.30am-6pm. 51wks.

spanish nursery schools

SW4
Anglo Spanish Nursery 020 7622 5599
152 Clapham Manor Street
18mths-5yrs. Full day

SW6
Peques Nursery School 020 7385 0055
St John's Church, Walham Green,
North End Road, Fulham
www.peques-nursery.co.uk
3mnths-5yrs. Open 8am-6pm. 50wks. For a safe, happy
secure learning and developing environment with qualified
staff (see ad pg 130).

W10
Spanish Day Nursery 020 8960 6661
317 Portobello Road
2-5yrs. Full day

gifted children

Gifted Monthly
28 Wallis Close, SW11
www.giftedmonthly.com
online newsletter for parents with gifted children

National Association for 0870 770 3217
Gifted Children

learning difficulties

Willoughby Hall Dyslexia Centre 020 7794 3538
1 Willoughby Road, NW3
6-12yrs

David Mulhall Centre 020 7223 4321
31 Webbs Road, SW11

left-handedness

Anything Lefthanded 020 8770 3722

www.RU-lefthanded.co.uk 0800 781 5338
Small range of products and advice on how to help left
handed children start to write correctly

speech therapists

Speech, Language 020 7383 3834
and Hearing Centre
1-5 Christopher Place, Chalton Street, NW11.
www.speech-lang.org.uk
Specialist centre for babies/toddlers with hearing or speech
impairment

tuition

Victoria Page Private Tuition 020 7381 9911
Fulham, SW6
3-11yrs scholarship, maths, english, reasoning, remedial
reading, common entrance. Also reached on 07050 246 810.

Fleet Tutors 020 8580 3911
One-to-one tuition at home

As every mother will know, idle little hands and minds need channelling. A mix of physical and creative activities will help develop confidence, co-ordination, concentration, creativity and individual skills. Our listings will give you loads of inspiration and guide you to the multifarious classes, clubs and centres that abound. For active kids, we list gym clubs, dance classes, swimming classes, football and more; for creative youngsters there are arts and crafts clubs, drama classes, musical activity groups and ceramic cafes. Add a soupçon of French language here and a shot of mini-tennis there, and your toddler will be the most accomplished in town

Age range	Activity ideas and when to introduce them
First **6** weeks	Lots of **physical contact**, **gentle voices**, **faces** to look at.
6 weeks to **3** months	Put toys within **touching** distance; use **bouncing** chairs; **massage**; **stretching** exercises and kicking; holding **rattles** (soft so they don't bash themselves); and **rolling** over onto tummy. Encourage baby **babble** by repeating the sounds they make/peek-a-boo.
3 months to **6** months	Looking at picture **books**, **sitting** and **bouncing** on your knee, introduce an **activity mat** with dangling toys with interesting textures/colours; if good head control introduce **baby bouncers**. Start socialising within **music** groups (see pg 168) and **baby swimming** (see pg 173).
6 months to **10** months	Encourage **sitting** up with support and getting more **active** (see gym groups on page 162). Provide interestingly shaped **objects** (ie keys that rattle) and encourage **passing** from one hand to another. Introduce **signing actions** with songs.
10 months to **1** year	Practise **waving bye-bye** and **clapping hands**; encourage use of **finger** and **thumb** to pick up small objects (such as string attached to a toy); encourage **standing up** with your support; **dropping** things and seeing where they go; **filling** and **emptying** containers.
1 year to **18** months	First real **words** appear at this stage so continue with nursery rhymes; play with **sand** and **water**; **copying** games (such as making faces in a mirror); introduce push-along toys, **ball** throwing, **stacking** bricks and shape **sorting**; begin to **stand** and **walk** or **cruise** between furniture.
18 months to **2** years	Provide **ride**-on toys; go **climbing** and **sliding** in the playground or in indoor activity playcentres (see pg 165); jigsaws (lift-out and inset); introduce **playdough** (see our recipe opposite); encourage **colouring** and continue going to **music** clubs.
2 years to **3** years	Introduce ball games such as **football** or **skittles** (and emphasise **taking turns**); help with **construction** toys; encourage **sentences** and **remembering songs**; develop **turning** one page at a time whilst **reading books**. Practise **cutting** out with scissors.
3 years to **5** years	Hold a **crayon** between **first two fingers and thumb** and draw **shapes** not scribble; encourage **dressing up** (see pg 48) and **make believe**. Introduce **numbers** and **letters** (particularly in their name); try **listening games** or **cooking** (eg decorating biscuits); encourage **swimming** without aids; start **dance**, **drama** classes, football groups or **foreign** language clubs.

adventure playgrounds

For that Robinson Crusoe experience these adverture playgrounds offer a selection of wooden structures creating imaginative outside space for energetic 2-5yr olds. There will be climbing nets and platforms linked by a series of wooden walkways. They are usually set amongst mature trees which make for great hide and seek games. Open between 10am–6pm weekends and holidays, and 3.30pm–7pm termtime.

NORTH LONDON

Timbuktu   020 7272 2183
Grenville Road, N19

EAST

Apples & Pears   020 7729 6062
28 Pearson Street, E2

Brooks Farm   020 8539 4278
Skeltons Lane Park, Leyton, E10

Discover Story Garden   020 8536 5555
1 Bridge Terrace, Stratford, E15
Designed to inspire 2-7yrs olds to create their own stories - sliding down a monster's tongue, dressing up and an interactive sound and light installation.

SOUTH LONDON
Home Park   020 8659 2329
Winchfield Road, SE23

Loughborough   020 7926 1049
Moorland Road, SW9

Battersea Park   020 8871 7539
Sun Gate Entrance, Albert Bridge Road, SW11

York Gardens   020 7223 3269
Lavender Road, SW11

Kimber BMX   020 8870 2168
Kimber Road, SW18

Tiger's Eye   020 8543 1655
42 Station Road, SW19

WEST LONDON
White City   020 8749 0909
Canada Way, W12

Log Cabin   020 8840 1506
259 Northfield Avenue, W5 4UA

Distillery Lane Children's Centre 020 8748 9224
Distillery Lane, W6
Book in advance.

Playdough

The texture of playdough is fascinating for toddlers of about 18mths. But if your shop bought playdough has hardened you can rustle up your own from our recipe below. Initially kids will need to be shown how to squeeze and squash it into recognisable shapes – and later you can provide implements for cutting. It's also a useful activity if you are in the kitchen cooking and they want to copy you.

Recipe
- **2 x teaspoons cream of tartar**
- **1 x cup plain flour**
- **1 x tablespoon oil**
- **1 x cup water**

Mix to form a smooth paste. Put in a saucepan and cook slowly, until the dough comes away from the side of the pan and forms a ball. When cool enough knead the dough for 3-4 minutes. When not in use keep in an airtight container in the fridge. Food colouring can be added to the water or the dough for colour variety.

art & crafts

These classes are where young children can go to experience all types of art media, materials and craft projects with something to take home at the end of the day

Art 4 Fun
212 Fortis Green Road, N10   020 8444 4333
172 West End Lane, NW6   020 7794 0800
444 Chiswick High Road, W4   020 8994 4100
www.Art4Fun.com
Make, design, decorate ceramics, wood, glass, mosaic, etc. Great for parties. Under 4s can get really messy with clay, dough, plaster and papier mâché.

Blue Kangaroo **020 7371 7622**
555 Kings Road, SW6
www.thebluekangaroo.co.uk
Regular creative classes held on weekday mornings including painting, sticking, playdough along with storytelling.

Chaos Art Club **020 8693 4621**
Fantastic art workshops for children aged 2-4yrs in St Peter & St Clements Church (off Barry Road) in East Dulwich. Classes take place on Wednesday mornings during termtime - as well as an after-school club from 4pm for children 5yrs+ . The groups are run by Stephanie Newell-Price, who has a MA in fine art and ran a foundation course in art and design prior to setting up this group. There are 4-

5 different types of activity per session (some themed to seasonal activities such as Easter). Older children are able to experiment with watercolours, printing processes as well as looking at artists' work and examining their techniques.

Creative Wiz Kids **020 7794 6797**
www.creativewizkids.com
As seen on ITV! Art, music and movement classes for children aged 1-3 (mother and toddlers) as well as holiday clubs for children aged 3-7yrs. Classes take place in Notting Hill and Hampstead. Celebrating creativity since 1990. Also see "tweens to teens" parties.

Gymboree Play & Music	**0800 092 0911**
Business Design Centre, N1	020 7288 6657
Bickerton House, N19	020 7272 0979
The O2 Centre, NW3	020 7794 8719
Exchange Shopping Ctr, SW15	020 8780 3831
Whiteleys Shopping Centre, W2	020 7229 9294
Holmes Place, Wimbledon, SW19	020 7258 1415
St George's Leisure Centre, HA1	020 8863 5191

www.gymboreeplayuk.com

Little Brushes **07812 501 395**
www.littlebrushes.com **07886 119 355**
Get messy with our paint and create classes and allow your little ones the freedom to explore with many different mediums, materials and techniques. Our classes run to a variety of exciting themes, from Under the Sea to Lost in Space. Free trial classes offered. Classes run in Battersea, Earlsfield, Putney and Clapham/Brixton - but check the website for new venues.

Paint Pots Creative Classes **020 7352 1660**
St Mary's Church Hall, The Boltons, SW10 9TB
www.paint-pots.co.uk

18m-2yrs	Toddler Art
2-3yrs	Arts, Crafts, Music & Movement
3-5yrs	Arts, Crafts, Music & Drama
3-5yrs	Cookery Club
5-8yrs	Art Club
5-8yrs:	Cookery Club

Creative Classes to help children explore their creativity and learn about the world around them through music, movement, drama and a variety of art media. Also children's parties.

ceramic cafés

Ceramic cafés are definitely one of London's great offerings. Children can have great fun decorating some pottery, or you can get a memento plate of your baby's hand or foot print. Great creative party venues too

NORTH & WEST LONDON

Art 4 Fun
172 West End Lane, NW6   020 7794 0800
444 Chiswick High Road, W4   020 8994 4100
www.Art4Fun.com
Make, design, decorate ceramics, wood, glass, mosaic, etc.

Ceramic Coffee House   020 8444 6886
452 Muswell Hill Broadway, N10

The Ceramics Café   020 8810 4422
6 Argyle Road, W13

SOUTH LONDON

All Fired Up   020 7732 6688
34 East Dulwich Road, SE22

Brush and Bisque-it   020 8772 8702
85 Nightingale Lane, SW12

Crawley Studios   020 8516 0002
39 Wood Vale, Forest Hill, SE23

Pottery Café
735 Fulham Road, SW6   020 7736 2157
323 Richmond Road, TW1   020 8744 3000
www.pottery-café.com
Decorate your own English pottery - parties, baby's footprints, children's activities.

dance

Most ballet classes are for children from 2¹/₂ yrs-3yrs or 'out of nappies' and are great for posture, co-ordination and for graceful confidence. Some children will progress to professional ballet schools, but many more will experience dance as a pleasure and a cherished childhood memory. It will also encourage an apprecation of dance throughout adult life

Royal Academy of Dance   020 7326 8000
36 Battersea Square, SW11
www.rad.org.uk
The RAD is an internationally recognised body for teaching, training and setting an exam syllabus for classical dance. Teachers who qualify can apply for membership, and parents can send an SAE or request an email of local teachers. At this location they offer ballet, jazz and contemporary dance from 2 1/2yrs.

Imperial Society of   020 7377 1577
Teachers of Dancing
www.istd.org.uk
Find out about modern, jazz or tap dancing available to you locally.

International Dance   01273 685 652
Teachers' Association
www.idta.co.uk
You can ring for a list of local ballet teachers in your area.

Arts Education School   020 8987 6666
14 Bath Road, Chiswick, W4
Dance classes for children aged 3yrs+ on Sat am in this purpose-built dance studio. These are ballet groups based on the RAD syllabus. Children learn how to carry themselves, where to put their hands, what to do with their feet etc. Parents can see their children on the end of term open day, but do not attend. Located in Chiswick (Turnham Green tube is 2 mins walk).

Baby Ballet Song &   0870 1430 063
Dance Academy
www.babyballet.co.uk
Baby Ballet is a wonderfully exciting educational movement to music program for pre-school boys and girls. Designed to encourage babies and young children to enjoy the benefits and joys of song and dance, Baby Ballet has built up a fantastic reputation for providing children with the opportunity to express themselves within a fun, safe and caring environment.

Biodanza   020 7485 2369
www.biodanzauk.com
South American dance classes from 1yr+ in Camden.

Boogie Tots   020 8898 5622
www.childrensparties-london.co.uk
Stimulating dance, movement and music classes for the under 5s. These classes incorporate exciting visuals and props. Classes are held in Twickenham Green.

Chalk Farm School of Dance   020 8348 0262
Ballet classes for 3-5yrs on Thurs pm and Sat am. Term-time only. Locations in Primrose Hill and Hampstead.

Chantraine School of Dance   020 7435 4247
This well established (1978) dance school was founded on the French dance method developed by Alan and Francoise Chantraine. The syllabus covers all aspects of dance from rhythm and movement (jumping kangaroos or stretching giraffes), inner awareness (relaxing), technique, creativity, songs and choreography, incorporating different styles of dance, not just ballet. The classes are from 4yrs+ and take place in 6 locations across West Hampstead, NW6 and in Wanstead, E11

Chelsea Ballet School   020 7351 4117
www.chelseaballet.co.uk
All classes are taken by a RAD trained dancer, assistant and pianist. Classes are from 21/2yrs (or out of nappies) and are great for posture, graceful physical development and the confidence to walk elegantly across a room. There are a few watching sessions for parents or nannies and an end-of-term show. Lesson are held at St Barnabas Church Hall, Ranelagh Grove, SW1 and St Barnabas Church Hall, Dulwich Village, SE24. Scottish dancing course during Christmas holidays.

Crazee Kids   020 8444 5333
Jackson Lane Com Ctr, 269a Archway Rd, N6
From 2-10yrs. Creative movement, dance, drama and music through a wide range of exciting and magical adventures, building confidence and self-awareness. Themed holiday workshops also.

Dance Attic Studios   020 7610 2055
368 North End Road, Fulham, , SW6
www.danceattic.com
Baby ballet classes are held for children aged 3yrs+ on Mon and Fri at 4pm at the Dance Attic Studios, 368 North End Road, SW6 by Laura Snowball.

Ealing YMCA   020 8799 4800
25 St Mary's Road, W5 5RE
www.westlondonymca.org
Ballet classes from 3-4yrs are held at this popular Ealing location. They also offer gym and music groups so check out the website for class times.

Fancy Footwork   0845 094 1774
www.fancyfootwork.co.uk
Lucy Clay runs very popular parent and toddler music and movement classes for 2-3yr olds and Baby Ballet for 3-5yrs during termtime. Classes are a lead up to proper ballet at 4yrs+ where they gain huge self-confidence through expressing themselves to music, as well as working together in a group. Lucy takes all the classes and is RAD trained. Classes are held in St Luke's Community Hall, Ramsden Road, and in Endlesham Road, both SW12 and Chatham Hall, Northcote Road, SW11.

Finchley Ballet School   020 8449 3921
Established in 1959, Helen offers ballet classes from 3yrs+ in the Finchley and Totteridge area.

First Steps School of Dance   020 7381 5224
and Drama
234 Lillie Road, Fulham, SW6 7QA
Ballet from 21/2yrs+, tap and jazz from 4yrs+ and drama from 5yrs+ at 234 Lillie Road, Fulham, SW6.

Footsteps School of   020 8540 3090
Dance and Drama
Dance classes take place in West Wimbledon from 21/2yrs+.

Frances Lundy School of Dance   020 8675 0433
Ballet classes from 2yrs+ taking place in several locations in Chiswick.

Grafton Regal Dance Centre   020 7978 8624
7 Village Way, Dulwich, SE21 7AW
Ballet classes are held weekly at this central Dulwich location from 3yrs+.

Greenwich Dance Agency   020 8293 9741
The Borough Hall, Royal Hill, SE10
www.greenwichdance.org.uk
Classes for 0-2yrs play and dance, and 3-5yrs First Steps. Term-time only. Pay per class. Also offers holiday summer school.

Islington Arts Factory   020 7607 0561

2 Parkhurst Road, N7 0SF
www.islingtonartsfactory.org.uk
Ballet classes from 5yrs+ at £20 per term. Also art classes for 4-6yrs on Mondays 4-5pm where children learn technical drawing and painting skills.

Islington Ballet School   01992 813 572
Ballet classes and creative dance for children from 3yrs+ at Unity Church, 49 Florence Street, N1.

**June Carlyle School of   020 8992 4122
Educational Dance**
June Carlyle runs a well-established dance school in the magnificent Ascension Church Hall, Beaufort Road, Ealing, W5 which is a large and bright space with polished floor for little ones aged 3yrs+ to run around without fear of knocking something over. Mother's and nanny attend every class, seeing a mixture of exercises such as clapping in rhythm to the pianist, galloping with a partner, plies etc.

Jump Up   07946 581 933
www.jumpup.co.uk
Located in the heart of Hampstead, we offer dance classes for boys and girls (3yrs+) during the week and Saturday mornings.

Kensington Ballet School   07957 650 042
Ballet classes for children aged 18mths-7yrs with mum's participating alongside toddlers up to 2½yrs. The school's aim is to enable young children to discover the magic and joy of dance, and forever remember their first ballet setps in a fun but structured environment. Venues held in Kensington, Chelsea, Westbourne Park and Putney.

**La Sylvaine and Wendy   020 8964 0561
Bell School of Dance**
Classes start from 2½yrs+ and take place at Bousfield School in the Boltons, SW10 and The Mission Hall, Parsons Green Lane, SW6.

Laban Centre   020 8691 8600
Deptford Creekside, SE8 3DZ
www.laban.org
Laban is a world-leading school offering degree-level training in contemporary dance. Facilities open to the general public include London's largest Pilates studio, a café open daily from Mon-Sat, and a lively programme of dance and movement classes for toddlers through to adults. Call to find out more information.

Lauderdale House   020 8348 8716
Highgate Hill, Waterlow Park, N6 5HG
www.lauderdalehouse.co.uk
Lauderdale House is an arts and education centre offering fun and creative term-time classes for pre-school children to explore dance, movement and co-ordination. Their experienced and friendly tutor runs sessions for everyone from "tiddly toddlers" of 6 months to lively 5 year olds. And their beautiful parkland location and handy café are an extra bonus! See the website for full details (also, children's shows and after school classes).

Little Magic Train   01865 739 048
www.littlemagictrain.com
The Little Magic Train runs dance and drama sessions at
Holmes Place, Cannons, David Lloyd Health Clubs and
church halls across London, Herts, Bucks, Essex and
Oxfordshire. There are Hi-5 dance classes for 3-7yrs and
RAD ballet classes from 4yrs. They have recently introduced
official Angelina Ballerina classes from 3yrs+.

London Dance Academy   07851 636 020
www.thelondondanceacademy.co.uk
This ballet school has been founded by Kate Stober and Alex
Foley, former English National Ballet dancers and qualified
Royal Academy of Dance teachers. They offer classes for
boys and girls aged 2^1/$_2$+ in a new studio at the Wilberforce
Centre, Holy Trinity Church on Clapham Common. Street
dance and adult classes also available.

London Dance School   020 8940 3793
www.londondanceschool.com
They offer ballet, tap and jazz classes for children from
2^1/$_2$yrs+ at locations across Chiswick, Hammersmith and
Twickenham.

McAlpine Dance Studio   020 8673 4992
Longfield Hall, 50 Knatchbull Road, SE5 9QU
Term-time classes from 3yrs+ for ballet, jazz, Spanish dance
and drama. Also an Easter holiday course.

North London Performing   020 8444 4544
Arts Centre
76 St James Lane, N10 3DF
www.nlpac.co.uk
Ballet for 3-5yrs term-time. Also Drama Fun for 3-5yrs and
holiday workshops.

NW3 Dance Academy   01689 606 751
www.nw3danceacademy.com
Formerly the Stella Mann School of Dancing established in
1946. These ballet classes are for boys and girls aged 3yrs+
and are held at the O2 Shopping Centre, 255 Finchley Road,
NW3.

Paint Pots Creative Classes   020 7352 1660
St Mary's Church Hall, The Boltons, SW10 9TB
www.paint-pots.co.uk
Ballet classes 2-3yrs; creative dance 3-5yrs and 5-8yrs.

Pineapple Performing Arts Centre   020 8351 8839
www.pineapplearts.com
Pineapple Chunks is a dance, drama and singing class for
children aged 3-5yrs held on Sundays from 11am-12pm.
The classes are a gentle introduction to the full three hour
session provided to the 5yrs+ group. The emphasis here is
on performance, and the school has well developed links with
TV, film and theatres. They advise booking a trial day before
enrolment to allow children to sample a class. The classes
are held at 7 Langley Street, London, WC2H 9JA.

Pleasing Dance School of Ballet   020 7722 1829
Classes from 2^1/$_2$yrs+ held in Hammersmith, Ravenscourt
Park and Hampstead.

Rainbow School of Ballet   020 8877 0703
Ballet classes in Battersea/Earlsfield area from 2^1/$_2$yrs, small
classes with pianist. Termtime only.

Southfields School of Ballet   020 8835 0939
Classes start from 2^1/$_2$yrs+ and are held on weekday pm and Sat
ams. The baby classes are imaginative and creative journeys,
where children are encouraged to develop good posture, point
their toes and move like "butterflies" in time to the music. Parents
are invited to observe a class at the end of each term. Boys
welcome too. They also hold fairy ballet parties (boys are pirates)
bringing a mixture of costumes, face painting and dancing games.
Locations are: Lavenham Road, SW18 and Lingfield Road, SW19.

Stagecoach   01923 254 333
www.stagecoach.co.uk
Stagecoach is Britain's largest theatre school for children,
offering drama, dance and singing tuition at weekends and in
workshops during the school holidays and half-terms. They
have venues all across London and are highly regarded by
parents who enjoy watching their children gain confidence in
the fun, and informal performances produced.

St John's Wood Ballet School   01992 813 572
Ballet classes and creative dance for children from 3 years in
NW8.

Streatham School of Dance   020 8857 4206
St Leonard's Church Hall, 8 Tooting Bec
Gds,SW16
Classes on Wed and Sat from 3yrs+ termtime only. Ballet
until 5yrs then tap and modern available.

Southwest School of Ballet   020 8392 9565
The Garage Studio, 26 Priests Bridge, SW14 8TA
Ballet classes held on Wed and Sat for pre-school children.

Vacani School of Dancing   020 7592 9255
www.vacani.co.uk
General dancing classes from 2yrs+ and classical ballet from
4yrs. Classes are held in Bayswater, Chelsea, Belgravia, East
Sheen, Fulham, Swiss Cottage, Richmond and Clapham.

West London School of Dance   020 8743 3856
www.wlsd.org
Ballet classes for boys and girls from 2^1/$_2$-5yrs Mon-Fri in the
afternoons held in Notting Hill, Gloucester Road, Bond Street and
Ladbroke Grove. Term-time only. Classes last 45 mins and are
accompanied by a pianist. Café for parents to use whilst waiting.

Woolborough Academy   020 8351 7713
Woolborough House, 39 Lonsdale Road, SW13
www.woolborough.com
Dance classes are held at the beautifully restored dance
studios at the headquarters of the British Ballet Organisation
after school and on Sat ams. The classes introduce children
aged 3yrs+ to ballet in a more creative and imaginative style,
bringing energy to this unique dance school. They also give
performances at locations around Barnes and Hammersmith.

Music, Movement & Make-believe

Channel your child's natural creative instincts with **Mini Ps**!

Specially formulated for children aged 6 months to 4 years, these lively parent-present sessions use catchy original songs, fun games and colourful props to stimulate physical, cognitive and social development as well as being a great chance to make new friends. It's **Mini Ps** but Maxi Fun!

We offer a **Free Trial Session*** so that you and your child can experience the fun and benefits of **Mini Ps** firsthand. For more info or to book, call **0845 400 4000** or visit **perform.org.uk**.

everything is possible

BARNES | DULWICH | HAMPSTEAD
ST JOHN'S WOOD | WEST EALING

*Free Trial Session subject to availability.
One Free Trial per child. Terms and Conditions apply.

0845 400 4000   **perform.org.uk**

drama

If you already have a drama queen (or king) in the family, you might as well capitalise on any natural talents. These drama groups offer a small range of activities for the 3yrs+ which are fun, confidence-building, and increase co-ordination and concentration

NATIONAL
Stagecoach   **01923 254 333**
The Courthouse, Elm Grove,
Walton-on-Thames, KT12 1LZ
www.stagecoach.co.uk
60 venues across London but with no more than 15 in a group. Holiday workshops and termtime weekend sessions are always popular so book early.

Helen O'Grady Drama Academy   **01481 200 250**
Garenne House, Rue de la Cache,
St Sampsons, GY2 4AF
www.helenogrady.co.uk
With 8 groups across London, starting 5yrs+.

Paint Pots Creative Classes   **020 7352 1660**
St Mary's Church Hall, The Boltons, SW10 9TB
www.paint-pots.co.uk
3-5yrs: Arts, Crafts, Music & Drama and 5-8yrs: Film Making Club.

Perform's Mini Ps   **020 7209 3805**
66 Church Way, NW1 1LT
www.perform.org.uk
Specially formulated for children aged 6 months to 4 years, these are lively parent-present sessions helping to stimulate physical, cognitive and social development.

NORTH LONDON

Allsorts Drama   **020 8969 3249**
www.allsortsdrama.com
Allsorts drama for children provide after school, Saturday and holiday courses covering all aspects of drama in a fun and friendly environment. Ages 4-6 in Hampstead, Kensington, Notting Hill and Fulham.

Club Dramatika   **020 8883 7110**
Drama club for 4-6yrs on Saturday mornings and summer holiday workshops at King Alfred's School, 149 North End Road, NW11.

Crazee Kids   **020 8444 5333**
Jackson's Lane Community Centre, 269 Archway Road, Highgate, N6
From 2-10yrs. Creative movement, dance, drama and music through a wide range of exciting and magical adventures, building confidence and self-awareness. Themed holiday workshops also.

Dramarama 020 8446 0891
www.dramarama.co.uk
Drama, games, stories fill these action-packed workshops for 3-4yrs during termtime, half-terms and the holidays. Fantastic for building self-confidence. Classes are held in South Hampstead High School, NW3. Their half-term workshops last five days and parents see their children in a performance at the end of the week. They also organise theatrical parties at specified venues.

Tricycle Theatre 020 7328 1000
269 Kilburn High Road, Kilburn, NW6 7JR
www.tricycle.co.uk
Drama workshops run throughout termtime from 18mths-16yrs. There are also one-off themed workshops from 3yrs+. They also have theatre shows every Sat at 11.30am and 2pm for 2-12yr olds and family films shown every Sat.

EAST LONDON

Allsorts Theatre School 020 8555 0099
Three Mills Film Studios, 1 Sugar House Business Centre, 24 Sugar House Lane, E15 2QS
www.allsortsagency.com
Allsorts theatre offer professional training, singing and dance tuition for children aged 3-18yrs. There are also sister schools in Chafford Hundred, Slough, Waltham Abbey, Romford and Stratford.

SOUTH LONDON

Blackheath Conservatoire of 020 8852 0234
Music and the Arts
19-21 Lee Road, SE3 9RQ
www.conservatoire.org.uk

New Peckham Varieties 020 7708 5401
Magic Eye Theatre, Havil Street, SE5 7SD
www.npvarts.co.uk
From 18mths+ workshop on Saturdays and including baby signing, musical theatre, drama, tap dance and ballet. For 4yrs+ on Mon pm as well as sessions at weekends. Older children can try jazz, steel bands and break dancing.

Polka Theatre 020 8543 488
240 The Broadway, Wimbledon, SW19
www.polkatheatre.com
Drama workshops during termtime and during the holidays from 3yrs+.

Big Foot Theatre Company 0870 011 4307
www.bigfoot-theatre.co.uk
Drama courses running through the year in SW2 and SW18.

WEST LONDON

Centrestage 020 7328 0788
www.centrestageschool.co.uk
Branches in Holland Park, Harley Street and Hampstead offer a range of theatrical activities for 4-15yrs. Workshops take place on Saturdays during termtime and also during the holidays, culminating in a performance - including the youngest. The little ones will be able to have a go at simple magic and mime - whilst the older children will have plays and musicals.

Barbara Speake Stage School 020 8743 1306
East Acton Lane, W3 7EG
This is both a school (with excellent academic results) as well as a weekend and holiday theatre school. Their ethos is to bring out the best in every child and allow natural talent to flourish. Every child will dance (rather than do sports), sing, act and generally have a unique schooling. Great for children who are shy or "too clever for their own good" as it challenges them in a completely different way.

football

Football in the Community guarantees that all clubs organise coaching courses, fun trial days and skills workshops for children around 5yrs+. These take place at the clubs with FA qualified coaches

Little Kickers 01829 271 751
www.littlekickers.co.uk
The UK's most popular pre-school football classes. Our qualified coaches run weekly classes throughout London and beyond for children aged 2 to rising 5. In addition to learning valuable ball skills, children also develop a variety of early learning skills. For more information please see our website.

Kick It Soccer 01895 435 571
Football for 3-12yrs – venues across London.

Socatots 0113 244 2005
Socatots is the first soccer-specific play programme for pre-school children. They have 60 venues across the UK so call now to find your nearest class.

Soccer Tots
Soccer Tots, different from that above, offer pre-school football coaching in a number of leisure centres throughout London. The syllabus has been developed by an FA coach and all sessions are taken by fully-qualified FA coaches. Classes seem to come and go - but do enquire at your local leisure centre or primary school.

Super Soccer Saturdays (Fit4Kidz) 07903 148 274
Wandsworth Common, Trinity Road, SW18
Football for boys & girls aged 4-12 from 10.30am-12.00pm every Saturday morning. Newcomers arrive at 10.15am for registration purposes. Professional coaching and skills

training, supported and run by coaches from clubs such as Chelsea, Fulham, West Ham & Wimbledon.

Sports Galore   **01285 656 098**
Sunday morning, 2-hour football sessions for 4-14 yrs in Battersea Park (10am-12pm), and Paddington Recreation Ground (9am-11am). Price £132 for 11-week classes. Fully qualified FA coaches.

foreign language classes & clubs

CHINESE
Easy Mandarin   **020 7828 2998**
www.easymandarinuk.com
Termly Mandarin classes held in Belgravia, London SW1 for four age groups, 3-5yrs, 6-8yrs, 9-12yrs and 13-18yrs on weekdays and weekends.

Chinese Learning Centre   **07730 987 030**
www.chineselearningcentre.com
Learn to speak and write Mandarin Chinese from age 3-13 on Fri afternoons, Sat & Sun mornings at St. Peter's Church at Eaton Square, Belgravia.

FRENCH
Bonjour French Fun   **020 8670 7134**
After-school French classes from 4yrs+ in East Dulwich, Herne Hill and Clapham (termtime).

Club Petit Pierrot   **020 7385 5565**
www.clubpetitpierrot.uk.com
Fun French lessons from 8mths-9yrs old. Clubs in Chelsea, Pimlico, South Kensington, Fulham, Putney, Notting Hill, Hampstead and St John's Wood. Parent and toddler groups, after-school, Saturday and holiday clubs. Small groups, excellent results, native French teachers. Highly recommended by BBC and Daily Express.

The Bi-Lingual Belgravia   **020 7259 2151**
Nursery School
77-79 Kinnerton Street, SW1X 0ED
Bilingual nursery school. 2-5yrs plus a toddler group from 1-2yrs. Session from 9am-12pm. Termtime and an afternoon club (French or Spanish) all year round.

French à la carte   **020 8946 4777**
97 Revelstoke Road, Wimbledon Park, SW18 5NL
www.frenchandspanishalacarte.co.uk
Termtime and holiday classes from 2yrs+ and Saturday morning classes from 5yrs in Wimbledon.

French Ecole   **020 8856 5131**
www.frenchecole.com
French language classes for children aged 3-11yrs plus holiday clubs in centres across London.

French Nursery School   **020 7259 2151**
65-67 Queen's Gate, SW7 5JS
Nursery school and toddler group from 1-2yrs.

Le Club Français   **01962 714 036**
www.leclubfrancais.com
Fun clubs for children from 3yrs+ to learn French.

Le Club Tricolore   **020 7924 4649**
www.leclubtricolore.co.uk
French activites for the under 5s in South London where learning the language is all part of the fun.

Le Club Frere Jacques   **020 7354 0589**
Founded in 1989 Le Club Frere Jacques now teaches over 3000 children across London's nursery and pre-prep schools, and also runs a number of after-school French clubs for the 3-5yrs age group. Venues include: Islington, West Hampstead, Ealing, Chiswick, Barnes, Muswell Hill and Eastcote. The lessons are 1hr and consist of pure listening and speaking with native French speaking tutors. Via this process young children pick up an authentic accent. They also produce 10 cassettes of French nursery rhymes and sketches of commonly used vocabulary.

Les Petites Marionnettes   **020 7637 5698**
24 Weymouth Street, W1 3FA
Les Petites Marionnettes offer private French tuition in your own home from 2yrs+ after school and during termtime only.

Les Petits Lapins   **07947 823 067**
www.lespetitslapins.com
French from 12mths to 8yrs. Classes also held in W8, SW4, SW6 and SW15; also holiday courses/after-school clubs.

ITALIAN
Italiano nelle Docklands   **07788 427 301**
Italian from 1yr+ every Sat at 10.30am in the Docklands, E14.

The Italian Nursery School 020 7259 2151
65-67 Queen's Gate, SW7
Toddler groups run during termtimes morning and
afternoons.

GERMAN
German Saturday School 020 7370 1278
Between 10am-12pm during school terms starting from
3yrs+ in W2.

German School 020 8940 2510
Douglas House, Petersham Road, Richmond, TW10
www.dslondon.org.uk
German Kindergratens from 3yrs+.

Hansel & Gretel 020 8693 4152
From 0-5yrs this is a German playgroup attending on Mon
pms and Wed ams at St Faith's Community Centre, Red Post
Hill, SE24. Singing and play activities as well as making
things for all the German festivals. They also produce a
quarterly newspaper and contact sheet to help German
families to keep in touch.

SPANISH
Peques Nursery School 020 7385 0055
St John's Church, Waltham Green, North End
Road, Fulham, SW6 1PB
www.peques-nursery.co.uk
3mths-5yrs. 8am-6pm. 50wks and a Saturday club. Enquire
for further details.

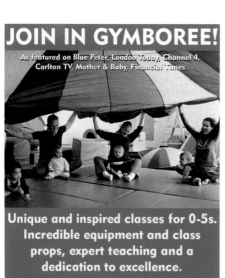
gyms : mini

ACROSS LONDON
Tumble Tots
- St John's Wood, Muswell Hill 020 8381 6585
  Finchley Central and Hendon
- Fulham, Wimbledon, 020 8944 8818
  Barnes, Victoria
- Chiswick, Kew, Twickenham, 01932 865 100
  Kingston, Hampton
- Battersea, Dulwich, Clapham, 020 8464 4433
  Blackheath
www.tumbletots.com
The leading national active physical play programme for pre-
school children.

Gymboree Play & Music 0800 092 0911
- Business Design Centre, N1 020 7288 6657
- The O2 Centre, NW3 020 7794 8719
- Exchange Shopping Ctr, SW15 020 8780 3831
- Whiteleys Shopping Centre, W2 020 7229 9294
- Holmes Place, Wimbledon, SW19 020 7258 1415
- St George's Leisure Centre, HA1 020 8863 5191
www.gymboreeplayuk.com
Well structured gym groups from 0-5yrs throughout the week
and at the weekends.

Crêchendo Playgyms 020 8772 8120
www.crechendo.com
Classes held throughout London.

- **Battersea**
  Battersea Arts Centre, Lwr Hall, Town Hall Rd,
  SW11
  Wednesday, Thursday
- **Chiswick**
  Chiswick Christian Centre, Fraser Street, W4
  Tuesday, Wednesday
- **Fulham**
  West Lndn Family Church, 230 Lillie Road,
  SW6
  Tuesday
- **Kensington**
  St Barnabas Church Hall, 23 Addison Road,
  W14
  Friday
- **South Kensington**
  Baden Powell House, Queen's Gate, SW7
  Monday, Tuesday, Wednesday, Thursday, Friday
- **Sheen**
  Baden Powell House, Queen's Gate, SW7
  Friday
- **Wimbledon**
  Trinity Church Hall, Mansel Road, SW19
  Thursday

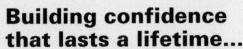
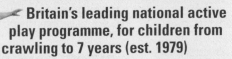
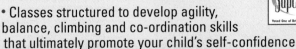
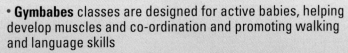
NORTH LONDON

Little Steps Gym (Muswell Hill)   020 8883 1608
Middlesex Cricket Club, Finchley
www.stepsgym.com

Active Kids   020 7281 2604
Fortismere School, North Gym, N10
Multi-sport classes for 3-7yr olds during weekdays,
weekends and school holidays.

Fit Start   020 8374 7680
Sobell Leisure Centre, Hornsey Road, N7
Mornington Sports Centre, NW1
Activity sessions for children aged 6mths-3yrs.

Hornsey YMCA   020 8340 6088
184 Tottenham Lane, N8 8SG

EAST LONDON

Redbridge School of Gymnastics   020 8530 3810
Pulteney Road, E18
Drop-in sessions for under 5s to encourage balancing,
running, jumping.

SOUTH LONDON

Ladywell Gym Club   020 8690 7002
The Playtower, Ladywell Road, SE13 7UW

TJ's Mini-Gym   020 8659 4561
Crystal Palace National Sports Centre, SE19
Babies' gym classes from 10mths-2yrs in soft play area, ball
pit and mini trampolines. Toddler gym sessions are
termtime only.

Budokwai Toddlers   020 7370 1000
4 Gilston Road, SW10 9SL
3-16yrs.

The Little Gym   020 8874 6567
Compass House, Riverside West, SW18 1DB
www.thelittlegym.co.uk
Developing your child's skills and confidence.

TJ's Mini Gym Club Wimbledon   020 8640 2678
Church Hall, Kohat Road, SW19
Mother and toddler mini-gym sessions from 1-7yrs.
Termtime only.

Tiny Tumblers   020 8542 1330
Wimbledon Leisure Centre, Latimer Road, SW19
Gym classes from 18mths+ in soft play area. Baby bounce
classes from 12mths. Also at: Newham Leisure Centre, E13;
Atherton Leisure Centre, E15; St Mark's Church, Becton, E6;
and Froud Centre, Manor Park, E12.

WEST LONDON

Tiny Tots Gym   020 7727 9747
Kensington Sports Centre, Walmer Road, W11

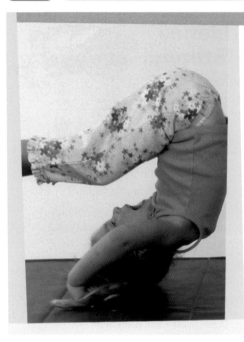

'Your kids will be head over heels at The Little Gym'

The Little Gym is dedicated to developing your child's skills and confidence while they just have FUN. Our curriculum based motor skill development programme for children aged 4 months to 12 years uses gymnastics, sports, music and games to promote co-ordination, balance and flexibility while also enhancing their intellectual and social skills.

We offer:
- Weekly classes (Monday - Saturday)
- Fantastic Birthday Parties for all ages
- Holiday and summer camps

Book your FREE TRIAL Class now
......and see how much FUN your kids can have at The Little Gym

Wandsworth	Hampton Hill
Riverside West	94 - 102 High Street
Smugglers Way	Hampton Hill
SW18 1DB	TW12 1NY
020 8874 6567	**020 8977 0099**

www.thelittlegym.co.uk

Tippitoes, W5	020 8566 1449

Ealing YMCA Health   020 8799 4800
& Fitness Centre
25 St Mary's Road, W5 5RE
www.estlondonymca.org
Activity sessions for "Crawlers 8mths-12yrs" and "Tiny Tumbles 1-2yrs".

Crackerjack   020 8840 3355
W7
1yr+.

holiday activities

(see also drama, gyms:mini and health clubs)

Camp Beaumont   0845 608 1234
www.daycamps.co.uk
From 3yrs+ multi-activity day camps from 8.30am to 5.30pm.

Creative Wiz Kids   020 7794 6797
Notting Hill and Hampstead
www.creativewizkids.com
Fun, action packed holiday clubs for 1-6yrs.

Paint Pots Creative Classes   020 7352 1660
St Mary's Church Hall, The Boltons, SW10 9TB
St John's Hyde Park, St John's Parish Hall, Hyde

Park Crescent, W2 2QD
www.paint-pots.co.uk
2-8yrs: Arts, Crafts, Music & Drama in our Christmas, Easter & Summer Holiday programmes

Pippa Pop-ins Holiday Activities   020 7731 1445
430 Fulham Road, SW6 1DU
Summer holiday activites at this popular London nursery school for children aged 2-10yrs.

Sports Galore Activity Weeks   01285 656 098
Easter and summer holiday sports and activity weeks from 10am-4pm daily including minibus transport and an out-of-hours club. For 4-5yr olds activities are interspersed with art, storytime and party games.

The Little Gym   020 8874 6567
Riverside West, Smugglers Way, SW18
Hampton Hill, 94-102 High Street, TW12
www.thelittlegym.co.uk
Great holiday activities developing your child's skills and.

indoor playcentres

Perfect for rainy days or as party venues. Supervision not provided so you have to expect a few knocks. Equipment includes ball pits, climbing ropes, slides and tunnels

Space Zone 020 8650 0233
Beckenham Leisure Centre, 24 Beckenham Road, BR3 4PF

NORTH LONDON

Clown Town 020 8361 6600
Coppetts Centre, Colney Hatch Lane, N12 0AQ

Fantasy Island 020 8904 9044
Vale Farm, Watford Road, Wembley, HA0

Highgate Newtown Community 020 7272 7201
Centre Skate and Bounce
25 Bertram Street, N19

Pirates Playhouse 020 8800 1771
271 Green Lane, N4 2HA
10am-6pm Mon-Thurs.

Playstation 020 8889 0001
2a Brabant Road, Wood Green, N22

Pyramid Soft Play 020 7226 5982
Highbury Roundhouse, 71 Ronalds Road, N5

Adventure Centre 020 7625 6260
Under 5s Soft Room
150 Brassey Road, NW6

The Play House 020 7704 9424
The Old Gymnasium, Highbury Grove School, Highbury New Park, N5

Tropical Adventure Trail 020 8345 6666
Lee Valley Leisure Centre, Picketts Lock Lane, Edmonton, N9

Zoomaround 020 7254 2220
46 Milton Grove, N16

EAST LONDON

Discover 020 8536 5540
1 Bridge Terrace, Stratford, E15
www.discover.org.uk
Outside there is a wooden pirate ship (about 10ft high) where you can walk up a chain, jump from a gang plank, and peep through portholes. The spaceship (which brought the baby space monster, Hootah, from planet Squiggly Diggly to the storygarden) allows children to climb to the top and descend via a fireman's pole. Open between 10am-5pm except Mon during termtime. Entry is £3.50 for children aged 2yrs+ - under 2s are free. It's a 5-10min walk from Stratford underground (Jubilee/Central).

BRAMLEY'S BIG ADVENTURE
INDOOR ACTIVITY PLAYGROUND & FAMILY CAFÉ

OPENING TIMES
Monday - Friday: 10am - 6pm
Weekends/Holidays: 10am - 6.30pm

OUR FACILITIES
• Play sessions - from £2 per child
• 3 levels of play equipment
• Separate under 2's & under 5's areas
• Children's Parties - from £8 per child
• Private Hire available
• Group & School bookings
• Bramley's Parent Membership
• Healthy food in our Family Café
• Toys and Gift Shop
• WiFi access • High Chairs • Lockers

136 Bramley Road, London, W10 6TJ
Tel/Fax: 020 8960 1515
www.bramleysbig.co.uk enquiries@bramleysbig.co.uk

Soft Play Activity Sessions 020 8539 8343
Cathall Leisure Centre, Cathall Road, E11 4LA

Atherton Leisure Centre 020 8536 5500
189 Romford Road, E15 4JF

Kids Mania 020 8533 5556
28 Powell Road, Clapton, E5 8DJ

SOUTH LONDON

The Blue Kangaroo 020 7371 7622
555 King's Road, SW6
www.thebluekangaroo.co.uk
Family restaurant and playcentre plus a great party venue.

Camberwell Leisure Centre 020 7703 3024
Artichoke Place, Camberwell Church Street, SE5 8TS

Discovery Planet 020 7237 2388
Surrey Quays Shopping Centre, Redriff Road, Surrey Quays, SE16 7LL

It's a Kid's Thing 020 8739 0909
279 Magdalen Road, SW18 3NZ
www.itsakidsthing.co.uk
Award-winning indoor playcentre and cafe, which offers a full kid's menu of healthy options. The centre is also a location for termtime classes both sporting and arty. Great party venue too.

Kid's Korner 020 8852 3322
232 Hither Green Lane, SE13 6RT

Peckham Pulse 020 7525 4990
Melon Road, SE15 5QN

Rascals 020 8317 5000
Greenwich Leisure, High Street, Woolwich, SE18 6DL

Spike's Madhouse 020 8778 9876
Crystal Palace National Sports Centre, SE19 2BB

Tiger's Eye 020 8543 1655
42 Station Road, Merton Abbey Mills, SW19 2LP
www.tigerseye.co.uk
A very popular and large indoor playcentre with ball ponds, soft play areas, slides and nets. Also includes a jungle-themed party area.

SOUTH WEST LONDON

Eddie Catz 0845 201 1268
1st Floor, 68-70 Putney High Street, SW15
www.eddiecatz.com
Playframe, games, kiddie rides, padded toddler area. TV lounge, internet access, café restaurant. Daily morning classes for under 5s. Holiday camps and workshops. Children's parties. Open 7 days a week.

Gambado! Chelsea 08700 273 705
7 Station Court, Townmead Road, Chelsea, SW6
www.gambado.com/chelsea
Gambado is the fastest growing children's indoor play company in the UK and has a unique offering featuring state-of-the-art adventure play, fairground rides, parties, programmable creative zones, high-quality food and beverage facilities and relaxation areas for adult companions. Open 9.30am-6pm daily.

The Little Gym 020 8874 6567
Riverside Way, Smugglers Way, SW18
Hampton Hill, 94-102 High Street, TW12
www.thelittlegym.co.uk

Lollipop Club 020 8332 7436
Old Deer Park, 187 Kew Road, TW9 2AZ

Snakes and Ladders 020 8847 0946
Syon Park, Brentford, TW8 8JF

WEST LONDON

Bramley's Big Adventure 020 8960 1515
136 Bramley Road, W10 6TJ
www.bramleysbig.co.uk
London's most central indoor playground with a gift shop and family café. Play sessions from £2 and children's parties from £8 per child. Also available for private hire and group bookings.

THE PATTER OF 200,000 TINY FEET AND WE'RE STILL WALKING TALL!

15 years and 100,000 children later - Crêchendo are still providing young lives with the very best preparation for all that lies ahead.

We cherish our enduring reputation for high standards as much as a continuing ability to enhance your child's personality, mobility, balance, knowledge and confidence.

And who takes the credit for this success?

Well that's almost entirely due to our carefully selected, highly skilled playleaders whose daily energy and professional dedication will, through interactive play, enthuse, inspire and enliven growing characters from 6 months to 5 years.

But don't take our word for it - **BOOK A FREE TRIAL CLASS** and decide for yourself! Crêchendo has centres throughout central and west London. To discover more, call our office team on 020 8772 8124 or email us at playgyms@crechendo.com

www.crechendo.com

Crêchendo

PLAYGYMS

Fun is a serious business

Bumper's Backyard   **020 7727 9747**
Kensington Sports Centre, Walmer Road, W11 4PQ

Jungle Gym   **020 7723 8019**
Seymour Place, W1H 5TJ

Rainbow Playhouse   **020 8995 4648**
Homefield Recreation Ground, Chiswick Lane, W4

model agencies

Elisabeth Smith   **020 8863 2331**
(Model Agency) Ltd
www.elisabethsmith.com
Established in1960 specializing in babies up to teenagers, plus families. Elisabeth has also recently published a book about baby and child modelling so parents know what is required from both the child and the parents.

music groups

Most young children will be able to sing all the verses of "Old MacDonald" before they decide to talk. These classes and workshops are great for boosting physical, musical and emotional development, in addition to the CDs and tapes you might play at home. The list is not exhaustive, and locations are either by postcode or area due to the increasing number of classes available, so ring for details

Applegarth Studios   **020 7603 3602**
Augustine Road, London, W14
For all ages, babies and toddlers 0-90 tues/weds 9.30-10.30 10.30-11.30 from 12th september. Inspirational classes successfully running for 22years. Its a spring board to learning cildren enjoying rythme, memory and movement. Offering singing, voice coaching and percussion for all ages.

Bea's Baby Music School   **020 8670 9378**
www.babymusic.co.uk
Groups 6mths to 6yrs. Stimulating, fun, educational. Live professional musicians. Classes in SE27, SW3, SW6, SW12, SW15.

Blueberry Playsongs   **020 8677 6871**
www.blueberry.clara.co.uk
Fun with music for 9mths-4yr olds. Clapham, Putney, Chelsea, Hammersmith, Notting Hill, Barnes and Wimbledon.

Boogie Tots   **020 8898 5622**
www.boogietots.co.uk
Stimulating dance, movement and music classes for the under 5s. These classes incorporate exciting visuals and props. Classes are held in Twickenham Green.

Creative Wiz Kids   **020 7794 6797**
www.creativewizkids.co.uk
As seen on ITV! Art, music and movement classes for children aged 1-3 (mother and toddlers) as well as holiday clubs for children aged 3-7yrs. Classes take place in Notting Hill and Hampstead.

Gymboree Play and Music 0800 092 0911
Business Design Centre, N1 020 7288 6657
The O2 Centre, NW3 020 7794 8719
The Exchange Shopping Centre, SW15 020 8780 3831
Whiteleys Shopping Centre, W2 020 7229 9294
Holmes Place Wimbledon, SW19 020 7258 1415
St Georges Leisure Centre, HA1 020 8863 5191
www.gymboreePlayUK.com
Interactive play and music classes for newborns to under 5s
in six centres across London.

Hickory Jig Music 07966 454098
www.hickoryjigmusic.co.uk
6mths-7yrs. Imaginatively planned and presented classes. Live
instruments and fabulous props. New class just opened in Dulwich.

Jazz-Mataz 01962 717 181
www.jazz-mataz.com
Fun clubs for under 5s to enjoy music, games

Jo Jingles 01494 719 360
www.jojingles.com
Jo Jingles is the leading pre-school music and movement
experience from 6mths-7yrs (see ad right).

Little Acorns 020 8408 0322
www.thelittleacorns.com
Nursery music workshops for babies and young children in
Putney and Wimbledon(see ad right).

British Suzuki 020 7471 6780
www.britishsuzuki.net
Teaching young children to play muscial instruments from a
very young age with lots of parental participation. Highly
regarded from 2yrs+

Mini Crotchets 020 8675 1052
www.minicrotchets.co.uk
Wonderful music classes for toddlers aged 9mths-3yrs.

Monkey Music 01582 766 464
www.monkeymusic.co.uk
Music classes for the under 5s throughout London.

• **Jayne Harris** 020 8767 9827
Chelsea & Westminster

• **Louise Krupski** 020 8699 0977
Clapham & Battersea, Forest Hill & Crystal
Palace and Sydenham

• **Helen Beach** 020 8451 7626
Hampstead & Notting Hil,l Primrose Hill, Queens
Park, Holland Park and Kensington.

• **Genevieve West** 020 8889 0114
Muswell Hill, Crouch End & Highgate

• **Jeni Eastlake** 020 8480 6064
Putney, Barnes & Fulham

• **Carmel Grovestock** 01582 766 464
South Woodford & Chingford, Kingston &
Surbiton

• **Katy Miller** 020 8449 4025
Southgate, Winchmore Hill & East Barnet, High
Barnet, Mill Hill & Whetstone

• **Bronwen Jones** 020 8764 5185
Wandsworth, Tooting & Streatham, Wimbledon
& Merton Park

Musical Bumps 01732 321 217
www.musicalbumps.com
Groups in London (East and North) Richmond and Kent.

Music for the Young 020 8765 0310
St Luke's Church, Sydney Street, SW3
Music classes on Tues pm for 3-5yrs. Term-time.

Music House for Children   020 8932 2652
Bush Hall, 310 Uxbridge Road, W12 7LJ
www.musichouseforchildren.co.uk
Instrumental tuition at home. Quality dedicated teachers
since 1994.

Music Makers   020 7207 5501
www.desatge.com/musicmakers
Music groups in central Pimlico for babies and toddlers aged
0-3yrs. The classes are run by Jeremy de Satge, a
professional and classically trained baritone. So alongside
the nursery rhymes, action songs, bell shaking and other
percussion instruments, children will have direct access to a
first-class musician.

Muzsika   020 7794 4848
Creative and lively music classes for babies and young
children (6mths-6yrs) in St John's Wood.

Paint Pots Creative Classes   020 7352 1660
St Mary's Church Hall, The Boltons, SW10 9TB
www.paint-pots.co.uk
6-12mths   Baby Moves & Music
12-18mths: Baby on the Move & Music
18mths – 2yrs: Music & Fun

Rucksack Music Inc   020 8806 9335
www.rucksackmusic.co.uk
Relaxed musical sessions for babies and toddlers in and
around London including North Finchley, Stoke Newington,
Crouch End, Highgate, East Finchley, Southgate, Muswell hill,
Upper Clapton, Islington, Hoxton, Hampstead and St John's
Wood.

Sing and Sign   01273 550 587
www.singandsign.com
Help your baby communicate before speech. Fewer
tantrums, more fun!

Whippersnappers   020 7738 6633
Brockwell Lido, Dulwich Road, SE24
Zany and zestful interactive musical workshops for the under
5s.

one o'clock clubs

One of the UK's best inventions! These free
weekday clubs set within parks have outdoor and
indoor play facilities for children under 5. They
open between 12.30pm – 4pm, but do check as
some close one day in the week. Activities
include painting, sticking, playdough, water, sand,
trikes, balls and toys (no need to book)

NORTH LONDON
Barnard Park   020 7278 9494
Copenhagen Street, N1

Finsbury Park   020 8802 1301
Jamboree Playhuts, Seven Sisters Road, N4

Highbury Fields   020 7704 9337
The Bandstand, N5

Clissold Park   020 8809 6700
Stoke Newington Church Street, N16

Whittington Park   020 7263 6896
Yerbury Road , N19

Parliament Hill Fields   020 7485 6907
Peggy Jay Centre, Gospel Oak Road, NW3

EAST LONDON
Wapping Park   020 7481 9321
High Street, E1

Haggerston Park   020 7729 6662
Queensbridge Road, E2

Victoria Park   020 8986 6150
Cadogan Terrace, E9

Millwall Park   020 7515 6807
Stebondale Street, E14

SOUTH EAST LONDON
Geraldine Harmsworth Park   020 7820 9724
St George's Road, SE1

Ruskin Park   020 7733 6659
Denmark Hill, SE5

Leyton Square   020 7639 1812
Peckham Park Road. SE15

Peckham Rye   020 8693 0481
Peckham Rye Road, SE15

Southwark Park   020 7231 3755
Hawkstone Road, SE16

Norwood Park   020 8761 1752
Salters Hill, SE19

Crystal Palace Park   020 8659 6554
Crystal Palace Park Road, SE26

SOUTH WEST LONDON
Brockwell Park   020 8671 4883
Arlingford Road, SW2

Clapham Common   020 8673 5736
Windmill Drive, SW4

Bishop's Park   020 7731 4572
Rainbow Playroom, Stevenage Road, SW6

Heathbrook Park   020 8871 7827
St Rule Street, SW8

Vauxhall Park   020 7582 3209
Fentiman Road, SW8

Loughborough Park   020 7926 1049
Moorland Road, SW9

Max Roach Park   020 7274 6693
Wiltshire Road, SW9

Slade Gardens   020 7733 3630
Robsart Street, SW9

Battersea Park   020 8871 7541
Prince of Wales Drive, SW11

Triangle   020 8673 4106
Tooting Bec Common, off Emmanuel Road, SW12

Streatham Vale Park   020 8764 3688
Abercairn Road, SW16

Bolingbroke Grove   020 7228 6674
Chivalry Road, Wandsworth Common, SW18

Colliers Wood
Clarendon Road, SW19

Marble Hill Park   020 8891 0641
Richmond Road, Twickenham, TW1

WEST LONDON
Kensington Memorial Park
St Marks Road, W10

Meanwhile Gardens   020 8960 7894
Elkstone Road, W10

Randolph Beresford   020 8741 8400
Australia Way, W12

Llamas Park   020 8810 0240
Elers Road, W13

Pitshanger Park   020 8998 1918
Meadowvale Road, W13

Acton Park, W3   020 8743 6133
East Acton Lane, W3

Rainbow Play House   020 8995 4648
Homefields, Chiswick Lane, W4

Ravenscourt Park, W6   020 8748 3180

swimming classes

Born to Swim   020 8452 0606
www.borntoswim.co.uk
Born to Swim offer classes from 8wks-4yrs at a number of
locations throughout London and Middlesex. The classes are
offered in 5-week terms and run throughout the year. They
also organise underwater photography sessions with the
world-renowned photographer Zena Holloway.

Swimming Nature   0870 900 8002
www.swimmingnature.co.uk
Classes held in Brondesbury Park, Chelsea, Hallam Street,
Marylebone, Notting Hill, Queen's Park, Regent's Park, South
Kensington and Victoria.

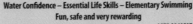
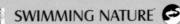

Born To Swim

BABY AND TODDLER SWIMMING ORGANISATION FROM 8 WEEKS TO 4 YEARS

Research documents the stimulating effect early swimming lessons have on small children. It increases regular eating and sleeping patterns, concentration, alertness and perceptual abilities. It also increases strength endurance, lung efficiency and much, much more. After only 5 weeks your little one will be swimming underwater from teacher to parent, kicking, floating on their backs and more...

BORN TO SWIM now run courses in a pool near you
Tel 0208 452 0606 office hours
Mon-Fri 10am - 5pm
Or visit our website www.borntoswim.co.uk

swimming pools - outdoor

Park Road Pools 020 8341 3567
Park Road, N8

Finchley Lido 020 8343 9830
Great North Leisure Park, High Road, Finchley

Parliament Hill Lido 020 7485 3873
Parliament Hill Fields, Gordon House Road, NW5

Charlton Lido 020 8856 7180
Hornfair Park, Woolwich, SE18

Brockwell Park Lido 020 7274 3088
Brockwell Park, Dulwich Road, SE24

Tooting Bec Lido 020 8871 7198
Tooting Bec Common, Tooting Bec Road, SW16

Richmond Pools on the Park 020 8940 0561
Old Deer Park, Twickenham Road, SW16

Serpentine Lido 020 7298 2100
Hyde Park, W2

Oasis Sports Centre Outdoor Pool 020 7831 1804
32 Endell Street, Holborn, WC2

tennis - mini

The LTA (Lawn Tennis Association) launched mini-tennis for children aged 4yrs+ in 2000. The game consists of 3 colour-coded stages: red, orange and green (akin to traffic lights). At the first stage children play on small courts with low nets, small rackets (17") and large, foam balls. The balls bounce low and slower giving children a good chance of hitting it. There are over 770 clubs offering mini-tennis in the UK and they can be found on www.arielminitennis.co.uk.

riding

Many stables do not recommend riding for under 3s and keep children on the leading rein until 5yrs old. But pony parties really are fantastic at about 6yrs

London Equestrian Centre 020 8349 1345
Lulington Garth, Woodside Park, N12
Café. 2yrs+.

Trent Park Equestrian Centre 020 8363 9005
Bramley Road, N14

Newham Riding School, E6 020 7511 3917
Docklands Equestrian Centre, 2 Claps Gate Lane

Dulwich Riding School 020 8693 2944
Dulwich Common, SE21

Stag Lodge Stables 020 8974 6066
Robin Hood Gate, Richmond Park, SW15

Deen City Farm 020 8543 5858
39 Windsor Avenue, Merton Abbey, SW19
4yrs+

Ridgeway Stables 020 8946 7400
93 Ridgeway, Wimbledon Village, SW19
3$^{1}/_{2}$yrs+

Wimbledon Village Stables 020 8946 8579
24 High Street, SW19

Ross Nye's 020 7262 3791
8 Bathurst Mews, W2
6yrs+

Hyde Park & Kensington Stables 020 7723 2813
63 Bathurst Mews, W2

Ealing Riding School 020 8992 3808
17-19 Gunnersbury Avenue, W5
5yrs+

Westways Riding Stables 020 8964 2140
20 Stable Way, W10

Wormwood Scrubs Pony Centre 020 8740 0573
Woodmans Mews, Scrubs Lane, W12

parties

Birthdays, for children, are synonymous with parties. And so, whether you like it or not, you will be throwing one for at least the first five years of your child's life. Fear not: here we offer enough tips, ideas and resources to make it a breeze, with listings of party entertainers, cake-makers and sources of party-bag fillers, bouncy castles and themed tableware. And if it all gets too much, you can always call in a party organiser, who will take care of the whole event

parties

First Birthdays

The first birthday party is a baptism by fire for most first-time parents. Plan to hold it at home with family, a few friends, and not too many competing babies - this is an excuse for grown-ups to shower or angel or urchin with adoration and gorgeous baby gifts (see pg X). NB Presents should be targeted to delight mum rather than baby, who will invariably find the wrapping paper more interesting. The key to making the party flow is to provide lots of Champagne and food for the grown-ups.

Second and Third Birthdays

A tea party at home with small tables and chairs will ensure that the catering aspect of the party contains itself to one room and not your carpet. A ball pond or a few tunnels will provide plenty of excitement for 2yr olds – but remember to put away toys that you don't want to be played with (especially the favourites or new presents). Party games like "pass the parcel" don't really work at 2yrs – so you can leave that one for another year.

Things begin to get serious by the age of 3. The party needs orchestrating and guests corralling, to avoid tears and tantrums before your party fairy or Spiderman has got as far as cutting the cake. We highly recommend a musical party (see music groups on page X).

You must plan to cater for parents as well – and make it clear whether siblings can come. We recommend that you just invite children from your child's age group otherwise you will find you have older children getting bored and running riot.

Fourth and Fifth Birthdays

If your child attends a nursery or playgroup, then you will find that this becomes a whole class event.

Parents are not expected to stay and you can let them know what time to pick the children up afterwards. You also need space if you want to hold the party at home – so many opt for an indoor activity centre (see toddler activities), or a party venue that has a party programme pre-prepared (see party venues). Themed parties with dressing up are very popular. You can also play traditional party games or try making things (see arts and crafts pg X or cooking pg X).

Party entertainers are in their element with 4-5yr olds. Magic, silly songs, puppets, balloon modelling, bubble machines, face painting, white rabbits, doves, snakes – all delight and entrance; and such is their popularity you need to book around 6 weeks ahead, particularly during festive seasons such as Christmas. Entertainers normally attend for around 2 hrs with a 45 minute session whilst you are getting the food ready, then another 45 minutes after the meal. What makes a good entertainer? Getting all the children to remain seated, fully engaged and responsive for the whole session – and they're worth every penny.

Tips from the experts

• Book your entertainer well ahead. If you haven't found a venue locally then many party organisers, such as Twizzle, have a whole range at their fingertips for every postcode. Let them know how many children they are entertaining and what the age range will be.

• Try and orientate parties around your child's natural mealtimes so that everyone has a good appetite. For 2-3yrs they recommend 11-1pm or 12-2pm rather than afternoons, and for 3-5yrs 12.30-2.30pm or 3.30-5.30pm.

• Liaise with other parents if children's birthdays in the same class clash across one weekend.

• Make sure the sweet things aren't on the table before the savoury – and decide whether to put the cake in the party bag or serve it at the table. Ask parents to mention allergies before the day so you can cater accordingly.

• Party bags are becoming ever more sophisticated, but stick to your budget and you'll be surprised how much you can find that delights the under 5s (see party supplies online).

For additional entertainers in other areas of the UK check the www.babydirectory.com website for our recommendations.

party entertainers

Action Station   **0870 770 2705**
www.theactionstation.co.uk
Interactive storytelling parties for 4-7 yrs. Fairies, mermaids, wizards, witches, spacemen, action heroes, pirates, cowboys.

Albert & Friends Instant Circus   **020 8237 1170**
www.albertandfriendsinstantcircus.co.uk
Albert the Clown does two styles of parties. For the 2-5yr age group he does games, magic, silly songs and balloons.

Boogie Tots   **020 8898 5622**
www.childrensparties-london.co.uk
Dazzling full disco, pop & party dance tuition, games, magic, parachute fun, balloon modelling, & more. Various packages for boys and girls 4 yrs upwards, to teens. Boogie Tots parties for little people 2-5 years. BoogieTots dancing, music, bubbles, games, parachute fun, magic & more!

Christopher the Magician 020 7993 4544
www.christopherhowell.net/magic_for_kids.htm
Christopher's magic is woven with storytelling to transport
little imaginations through an unforgettable magical
adventure. For ages 4-6.

Clarity The Clown 020 8690 4453
Puppets, silly songs, games, balloons, magic and bubbles.

Clown Violly & Fairies 0800 458 2866
www.enchantingparties.com
Magic, music, puppets, balloons.

Clozo The Clown 020 8907 3790
Mime, magic, music and dance with balloons, games and
silly tricks. Circus-trained clown who gets up to lots of tricks.

Diane's Puppets 020 7820 9466
1yr+. Gentle puppet parties for the very young.

Rainbow Fairyland Parties 020 8877 0703
Fairyland parties for girls and boys under 5. 1-2hrs of
treasure hunt, traditional party games, shake the parachute,
music, cat and mouse games. Also little dances with fairies,
mice and other small animals. All over London.

Jenty the Gentle Clown 07957 121 764
Singing, balloon modelling, puppets, face painting and
dancing. From 1-11yrs.

Jolly Roger 020 8546 7985
From 4yrs+ join pirate Jolly Roger and his ship the Dirty Rat
for a hilarious afternoon of entertainment.

Julie's Gymjive Parties 020 8932 4123
For 1-4yrs. Parties with music and dance, bubbles, finger
puppets, tunnels and climbing equipment.

Jugglers etc 0870 644 6659
www.jugglingjohn.com
From 3yrs+. One of the artists from this agency will delight
children with storytelling, juggling, comedy jokes.

Katie Rainbow 020 8675 3380
Fantastic storytelling with puppets (enormous giant puppets,
"it's behind you" pantomime style). Exotic magic, games and
dancing. Delightful rainbow costume. From 3-6yrs.

Laurie Temple 020 8951 9469
The Party Wizard
www.thepartywizard.co.uk
Highly recommended. Fun-filled parties for all ages plus
themed parties and organising services.

Lydie's Parties 020 7622 2540
Magical storytelling for Peter Pans, Batmans or in fairyland.
Lydie has 10yrs experience as a dancer and jazz musician.

Marvellous Productions 020 7736 0616
www.marvellousproductions.co.uk
Mrs Marvel will take you on a magic carpet ride with singing,
dancing and then make a puppet or mask in the theme of the
event. Within M25.

Mr Boo Boo 020 7727 3817
www.mr-booboo.co.uk
Music, games, puppets, silly songs, juggling, balloon modelling, bubble machines and much more (highly recommended).

Mr Lolly's Parties 020 8540 2994
www.mrlolly.com
Mr Lolly has been a full-time professional children's entertainer for 14 years during which time he has established himself as one of the finest (and funniest!) party magicians in the South. He offers a wide range of party options from Fantastic Majic Shows through to a variety of Themed Parties.

Mystical Fairies 020 7431 1888
www.mysticalfairies.co.uk
Specialising in unique parties featuring fairies, princesses, Wizmo the Wizard, Peter Pan and many more magical characters.

Patchy Peter & Snowy 01442 261 767
Magic, balloons, ventrilloquism, puppets and a live rabbit.

Pekko's Puppets 020 8575 2311
www.pekkospuppets.co.uk
Delightful and unique puppet show from 3-12yrs. Both traditional and original stories and action rhymes. "Skilful, poetic, inspired"; "completely captivating" say mums.

Pippa Reid Musical Parties 020 8866 4232
Interactive fun for 3-8s. Imaginative themes, singing, dancing, stories, music. Equity and CRB approved. Parties, after-school clubs and folk festivals.

Pippin Puppets 020 8348 4055
www.pippinpuppets.co.uk
Choose from one of 12 popular puppet shows with magic and games from 2-8yrs.

Pop Group Dance Parties 0208 898 5622
Disco, lights and atmospheric "smoke", teaching pop moves for the under 8s.

Potters Parties 07779 271 655
www.pottersparties.co.uk
Games, drama, dancing and magic for children aged 3-8yrs.

Seahorse Parties 020 8997 3355
Hundreds of fancy dress costumes for princes/princesses, medieval knights, animals and witches/wizards.

Silly Milly the Clown 07939 239 397
Funny magic shoes, puppets, party games, silly songs and balloon animals from 3-12yrs.

Splodge 020 7350 1477
www.planetsplodge.com
Themed parties at Battersea Zoo or Holland Park Ecology Centre for children aged 2-12yrs. Puppets and interactive treasure hunts are all part of the show.

Tony Macaroni 020 8442 0122
Magic, puppet shows, games, storytelling from 3-13yrs.

Twizzle Parties & Events 020 8789 3232
www.twizzle.co.uk
Organisers of children's parties from 2yrs+, offering a range of different activities and themes for small children.

Vicky's Pop Star Parties 020 8446 7641
Makeover, dance routine, rehearsal and performance. Children's dreams come true.

Walligog The Wizard 0118 973 0737
Games, magic and animal fun with live rabbits and doves.

Yogabananas 020 8874 3858
www.yogabananas.com
An inspiring, original and fun approach to a party that will introduce your child to the many benefits of yoga.

YogaBugs 020 8772 1800
www.yogabugs.com
Yoga parties for the under 5s.

party equipment

B Bounced 01895 905949
www.bbounced.co.uk
Hire and sale of bouncy castles, tables & chairs, balloons and party bags.

Cool Quads 0844 450 0045
Electric cars, bouncy castles, slides and soft play equipment for hire.

Great Jumps 020 7609 4325
www.greatjumps.co.uk
Bouncy castles with free delivery in North and Central London. No cancellation fee.

Mexicolore 020 7622 9577
www.pinata.co.uk
Handmade traditional papier mâché Mexican party piñatas in a wide range of colours and sizes.

party food

Amato's Patisserie 020 7734 5733
14 Old Compton Street, W1
Seriously delicious cakes in all ranges (sponge, chocolate, fruit) in classic or themed styles.

Cake Dreams 020 8889 2376
www.cakedreams.co.uk
Delicious hand-crafted fantasy cakes.

Canapes Gastronomiques 020 7794 2017
www.canapes-gastronomiques.co.uk
Catering on an imaginative miniature scale for children and their parents .Specialisig in mini decorated cakes.

Choccywoccydoodah 020 7724 5465
47 Harrowby Street, W1
www.choccywoccydoodah.com
Chocolate cakes that can be layered with fresh Belgian truffles for a really indulgent mouthful.

Mini Munchies   020 7237 6691
Established since 1994 we cater for nursery school lunches, providing a healthy balanced diet. We can also provide catering for special occasions including children's parties,christening and weddings.

Jane Asher Party Cakes   020 7584 6177
22-24 Cale Street, SW3
Select an off-the-shelf design, buy a cake kit and DIY, or design your own.

La Cuisiniere   020 7223 4487
81-83, Northcote Road, SW11
Hire cake tins, birthday cakes, etc. Children's cutlery.

Mallard Catering   020 7642 5495
84 Bellenden Road, SE15 4RQ

Sweet Sensation   020 8838 1047
39 Goodhall Street, NW10

The Cake Store   0800 052 0058
www.thecakestore.com
Highly recommended online cake store with delivery to all London postcodes.

party ideas

AQUARIUMS
Aquatic Experience   020 8847 4730
Syon Park, Brentford, North Middlesex, TW8 8JF
www.aquatic-experience.org

London Aquarium   020 7967 8000
www.londonaquarium.co.uk

ARTS & CRAFTS
Art 4 Fun
172 West End Lane, NW6   020 7794 0800
444 Chiswick High Road, W4   020 8994 4100
www.Art4Fun.com
Make, design and decorate ceramics, wood, glass, mosaic. Great for parties.

Creative Wiz Kids   020 7794 6797
www.creativewizkids.com
Established 1990 - as seen on ITV! Art and music parties for children aged 1-12yrs. Fun and stimulating. Every "Wiz Kid" takes home something they have created. NEW NEW NEW tweens to teens parties. 'Be the star of your own show - painter, actor, karaoke king or queen'.

Messy Play Parties   020 8959 9045
From 2yrs+ experiment with finger art, collage, playdough, decorating biscuits, painting, water-play, stampers, glass painting and beadwork for 5yrs+.

Paint Pots   020 7352 1660
St Mary's Church Hall, The Boltons, SW10 9TB
creative classes@paint-pots.co.uk
Children's birthday parties as a complete package.

Splat Cooking Parties

Parties
Workshops
Cookie cutters
Cooking kits
Cake cases
Chef's hats
Aprons
Sprinkles
Cake stands
Gifts

www.splatcooking.net
0870 766 8290

Party Creations   020 7738 8495

Create an all-in-one party and going home present - how smart is that? Paint your own apron, photo frame or decorate a flower pot. From 2-8yrs.

Petit Artisan   020 8931 3687
www.petitartisan.com
Creative and fun craft activities for children.

Pottery Café   020 7736 2157
735 Fulham Road, SW6
www.pottery-café.com
Includes invitations, clay items & paints, sandwiches and drinks.

COOKERY
Splat Cooking Parties   0870 766 8290
www.splatcooking.com
Splat's philosophy is that cooking should be fun. They have put together a fabulous range of cooking equipment especially for children and grown ups who like to have fun, and get to eat the results. Everything from fantasy cookie cutters to complete cooking parties.

Cookie Crumbles   020 8876 9912
www.cookiecrumbles.net
Arrange a cookery party for up to 15 kids.

Gill's Cookery Workshop   020 8458 2608
7 North Square,Golders Green, NW11
Saturday cookery parties at this location.

Cake Dreams

come to life –
as a delicious
hand-made cake!

Birthdays, Christenings,
all special occasions – adults too

Tracey Bush 020 8889 2376

www.cakedreams.co.uk

minimunchies

Established since 1994 we cater
for Nursery school lunches,
providing a healthy balanced diet.

We can also provide catering
for special occasions including
children's parties, christenings
and weddings.

Unit 16G Tower Workshops,
Riley Road, London SE1 3DG.
Tel: 0207 237 6691

FACE PAINTING

Fantastic Faces   020 8677 4193
Call Caragh for face painting parties and other occasions.

Mini Makeovers   020 8398 0107
www.minimakeovers.com
Witness the metamorphis of your child into a glittering,
sparkling fairy.

Creative Faces   07885 966 336
www.creativefaces.co.uk
A company supplying face painters to entertainers and direct
to parents. Over 10 years' experience.

David Jackson   020 7723 2913
Face Painting by Lynn   020 8749 0067
Face painting with   020 7794 8032
Sandra Wiseman
Fancy Faces   020 7372 1045
Magic Mirror   020 8764 8986

MUSIC

Amanda's Action Kids   020 8578 0234
www.amandasactionkids.co.uk

Blueberry Playsongs   020 8677 6871
Clapham, Putney, Chelsea, Hammersmith
www.blueberry.clara.co.uk
Fun, interactive musical parties for 1-6yr olds. One of our
talented entertainers will play guitar and sing songs with
actions, jumping and dancing. Puppet appearance, shaky
eggs and parachute games. Perfect for your party.

Gymboree Play and Music   0800 092 0911
Bayswater, Islington, Putney, Swiss Cottage, Wimbledon
www.gymboreeplayuk.com
Great venues for children's parties, including arts & crafts,
music and games.

Monkey Music   01582 766 464
www.monkeymusic.co.uk
Music parties held throughout London.

Whippersnappers   020 7738 6633
Brockwell Lido, Dulwich Road, SE24
Including tables, chairs, helium balloons as well as songs,
puppets, disco, bubble machine.

Vicky's Pop Star Parties   020 8446 7641
Makeover, dance routine, rehearsal and performance.
Children's dreams come true.

Story Fun   020 8444 0244
Specialising in birthdays for under 6s, acting out stories with
percussion instruments, drums and music.

SPORT

Active Kids   020 7281 2604
Unique, high energy, health-promoting parties. Tailor-made
to incorporate your child's favourite sport or activity. Call the
number above or 07939 277 943

Big Parties for
Little People

From Tots
to Teens

"Party of the Year" - Harpers & Queen

T: 020 8789 3232
W: www.twizzle.co.uk
E: party@twizzle.co.uk

Twizzle
Parties & Events

Goals Wembley 020 8997 4040
www.goalsfootball.co.uk
You have 1hr on the all-weather five-a-side pitch with a
trophy given to the birthday boy/girl. Hot dogs, drinks and a
chocolate bar to fill up the kids afterwards.

ZOOS
Battersea Park Zoo 020 7924 5826
North Carriage Drive, SW11
Excellent children's parties held at this venue. The children
are given a special tour around the animals, and asked to put
together little fruit treats for the monkeys. Also includes t-
shirt painting, pass-the-parcel and a healthy tea.

London Zoo 020 7722 3333
Regents Park, NW1 4RY
www.londonzoo.co.uk

party organisers

Boo Productions 020 7287 9090
www.booproductions.com
Themed parties for all ages from babies to teens! Visit our
website or call us for a chat on 020 7287 9090 and find out
why Boo! are the best.

Children's Party Company 020 7938 3239
Emily Astor and Marie-Eve Jenkins offer a complete party
service including the catering, selecting an entertainer, table
decorations, face painting, the birthday cake, balloons and
party bags - either in your own home or at a local venue.

Happy Times 020 8746 4222
www.happytimes.com
Themed children's party planners and tailor-made parties.

Jugglers Etc 020 8672 8468
www.jugglersetc.com
Juggling John was such a success with parents that he has
set up Jugglers Etc and can arrange everything from
selecting an entertainer to a complete party service.
Juggling, clowning, magic, face painting, games from 3-5yrs.

Laurie Temple & 020 8951 9469
The Party Wizard Company
www.thepartywizard.co.uk
Highly recommended. Fun-filled parties for all ages plus
themed parties and organising services. Call on the number
above or on 07951 596 240.

Mini Minors Birthday Parties 020 8371 9686
The cosiest, friendliest day and residential camps for children
and personalised birthday organisers. Branches: Christ
College School, East End Road, N2.

Paint Pots 020 7352 1660
St Mary's Church Hall, The Boltons, SW10 9TB
creative classes@paint-pots.co.uk
Children's birthday parties as a complete package.

Parties to Remember 020 7249 3242
A well thought-through party service where children play lots
of traditional party games.

Raspberry Productions 020 8952 6777
www.raspberryproductions.co.uk
Hand-picked items to create your child's favourite birthday.
Entertainers, balloons, cakes, face painters, party bags.

Twizzle Parties & Events 020 8789 3232
www.twizzle.co.uk
Organisers of children's parties from 2yrs+, offering a range
of different activities and themes for small children.

party shops

Balloonland 020 8906 3302
12 Hale Lane, NW7
www.balloonland.co.uk

Bouncing Kids 020 8840 0110
127 Northfield Avenue, Ealing, W13

Carnival 020 8567 3210
129 Little Ealing Lane, W5

Circus Circus 020 7731 4128
176 Wandsworth Bridge Road, SW6

Just Balloons 020 7434 3039
127 Wilton Road, SW1

It's My Party 020 7350 2763
23 Webbs Road, SW11

Oscar's Den 020 7328 6683
127-129 Abbey Road, St John's Wood, NW6

Partyworks 0870 240 2103
www.partybypost.co.uk

Party Party 020 7267 9084
11 Southampton Road, Gospel Oak, NW5

Party Plus 020 8987 8404
4 Acton Lane, Chiswick, W4

Party Superstore 020 7924 3210
268 Lavender Hill, Clapham, SW11

Non Stop Party Shop
214-216 Kensington High Street, W8 020 7937 7200
694 Fulham Road, SW6 020 7384 1491

Surprises 020 8343 4200
82 Ballards Lane, N3

The Party Shop 020 8676 7900
67 High Street, Penge, SE20

party supplies (online)

Flutterby   020 7751 3172
www.flutterbycards.com
Personalised party invitations, party bags, chocolate bars and unique gifts themed for any occasion. Extensive range of stationery for adults and children.

Great Little Parties   01908 266 080
www.greatlittleparties.co.uk
Great Little Parties is a specialist supplier of children's party products. Great website, well laid out and quick and easy to use.

Monster Parties   07092 262 837
www.monsterparties.co.uk
Pre-filled party bags available to purchase online from 99p.

Party Directory 4 Kids   01252 851 601
www.partydirectory4kids.co.uk
A-Z kids' party supplies by post. Over 700 great party products and ideas. Free catalogue. Nationwide delivery.

party venues

Aquatic Experience (Syon Park)   020 8847 4730
www.aquatic-experience.org
Tour the rainforest and meet snakes, lizards, frogs and baby crocs. From 4yrs+.

Music House for Children

- baby music sessions
- music appreciation for 3 - 6 years
- dance for little ones
- early years musical instruments
- birthday party venue & entertainment
- music, drama & art workshops

All classes take place at The Music House,
based in West London

020 8932 2652

notes@musichouseforchildren.co.uk
www.musichouseforchildren.co.uk

Blue Kangaroo   020 7371 7622
555 King's Road, SW6
www.thebluekangaroo.co.uk
Family-friendly restaurant and an excellent party venue

Bramley's Big Adventure   020 8960 1515
136 Bramley Road, W10
www.bramleysbig.co.uk
All inclusive children's parties from £8 per child, 75 minutes
play and 45 minutes in the private party room. Three party
packages available. Also available for private hire.

Eddie Catz   0845 201 1268
68-70 Putney High Street, Putney, SW15 1SF
www.eddiecatz.com
Playframe, games, kiddie rides, padded toddler area. TV
lounge, internet access, café restaurant. Daily morning
classes for under 5s. Holiday camps and workshops.
Children's parties. Open 7 days a week.

Gymboree Play & Music   0800 092 0911
Business Design Centre, N1   020 7288 6657
The O2 Centre, NW3   020 7794 8719
Exchange Shopping Ctr, SW15   020 8780 3831
Whiteleys Shopping Centre, W2   020 7229 9294
Holmes Place, Wimbledon, SW19   020 7258 1415
St George's Leisure Centre, HA1   020 8863 5191
www.gymboreeplayuk.com

Golden Hinde   08700 118700
Pirate fun for 4-11yrs aboard Sir Francis Drake's 16th century
galleon. Includes treasure hunt, hoisting the anchor and
adventure tales.

Lazy Daisy Cafe   020 7221 8416
59a Portobello Road, Notting Hill, W11
www.lazydaisycafe.co.uk
Spacious facilities for children's parties including balcony for
parents. Party food for kids and adults catered for too.

Highgate Newtown   020 7272 7201
Community Centre Skate and Bounce, 25 Bertram
Street, London, N19 5DQ
Wonderful indoor and outdoor space for birthday parties.

The Little Gym   020 8874 6567
Compass House, Riverside West, SW18
www.thelittlegym.co.uk
Fully supervised private party with music, games and
obstacle courses that kids love. And they can take care of
everything from invitations to clean-up. Parties are held on
Saturday and Sunday afternoons (see ad pg 162).

Music House for Children 020 8932 2652
310 Uxbridge Road, W12 7LJ
www.musichouseforchildren.co.uk
Birthday parties in the fabulous Music House studio complete
with beautiful garden. Great party bags, music entertainment
and delightful staff. Contact 020 8932 2652 or email
notes@musichouseforchildren.co.uk.

The Party Bus   07836 605 032
Up to 24 children accommodated for games, jokes and
magic tricks. Includes drinks and snacks.

Puppet Theatre Barge   020 7249 6876
35 Blomfield Road, Little Venice, W9
In addition to a puppet show you can hire the barge for
private parties.

Science Museum Sleepover 020 7942 4747
www.sciencemuseum.org.uk
Book well in advance for these spectacular sleepovers.

Wetlands Centre   020 8409 4407
www.wwt.org.uk
This Wetlands centre in Barnes can host a "pond-dipping"
party - great for nature enthusiasts.

days out

Londoners are spoilt for choice when it comes to outings.
We have art galleries and museums of world standing, all with
excellent activities and attractions for children. We have castles
and farms, aquariums and adventure playgrounds, nature
reserves and zoos, both in and out of town. Add to that our
great children's theatres, cinema clubs and parks and little
Londoners are highly privileged. If you can't decide what to do
or where to go, take a look overleaf for inspiration.

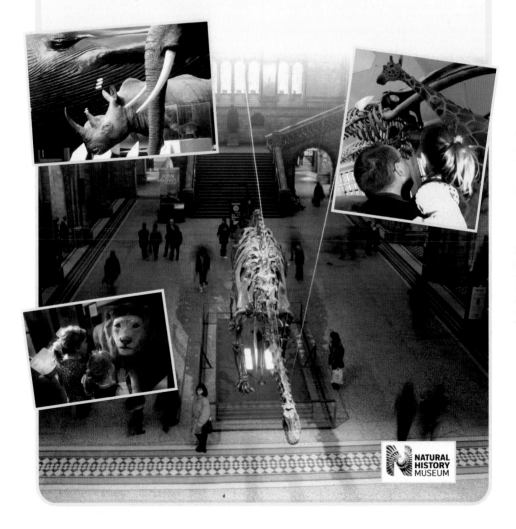

NATURAL
HISTORY
MUSEUM

Before you head out for any of these excursions please do ring and check that the venues are open before you visit. Also you may find changes to planned programmes and activities, which do change seasonally.

aquariums

Tropical Forest   020 8847 4730
Syon Park, Brentford, North Middlesex, TW8 8JF
www.aquatic-experience.org
This is a collection of endangered species which have been kept as pets and subsequently rescued and re-housed in a rainforest themed tropical forest. You will see piranhas, snakes, crocodiles, monkeys, toads and poisonous frogs all housed in a wonderful tropical environment complete with waterfalls and lush vegetation. They also host animal birthday parties. Open daily 10am-5.30pm.

London Aquarium   020 7967 8000
County Hall, Westminster Bridge Road, SE1 7PB
www.londonaquarium.co.uk
This is one of Europe's largest and most impressive aquariums, displaying marine life from over 14 different climatic zones. Young children are mesmerised by the shoals of mackeral and, with noses pressed to the glass, watch in awe as sharks tuck-in during feeding time. Open daily 10am-6pm. Highly recommended to pre-book tickets online to fast-track queues or better still go during termtime mid-week. Children can do craft activities such as making badges, hats and mobiles - no need to book. Birthday parties also available. Open daily 10am-6pm.

art centres & galleries

You can no longer claim that having children has impacted on your enjoyment of London's top galleries and art centres. There is a better reason for going to visit galleries now than ever before. You will not be disappointed by the well structured workshops, tours, facilities and goodie bags on offer. More importantly, they provide an interesting insight for parents as to how to open their children's eyes to the world of art

Barbican Centre   020 7382 2333
Silk Street, EC2Y 8DS
www.barbican.org.uk
The arts education programme has original and hands-on workshops which embrace the arts, music and film. Try making papier mâché masks during the London Children's Film Festival.

Camden Arts Centre   020 77472 5500
Arkwright Road, NW3 6DG
www.camdenartscentre.org
New galleries recently opened, landscaped gardens and a well-organised programme of workshops and creative activities. Open Tues-Sun 10am-6pm.

Somerset House   020 7845 4600
The Strand, WC2R 0RN
www.somerset-house.org.uk
Family activites on the first Saturday of the month from 11.30am are a delight for parents and children. Tours focus on a particular theme and conclude in a practical workshop. The Family Free Time festival during July has lots of activities. Wonderful winter skating and summer fountains in the 18th century courtyard bring delight to young children and parents alike. Open 10am-6pm.

Dulwich Picture Gallery   020 8693 5254
Gallery Road, SE21 1AD
www.dulwichpicturegallery.org.uk
Set in the heart of leafy Dulwich this gallery offers a quick fix for parents needing visual refreshment, and your children can spill into Dulwich Park afterwards to let off steam. Good café with highchairs. There are also family activity workshops at the weekend and during the holidays, and evening courses for adults both for art appreciation as well as bringing on artistic skills. Open 10am-5pm Tues-Fri; 11am-5pm Sat, Sun.

London International   020 7435 0903?
Gallery of Children's Art
02 Centre, 255 Finchley Road, NW3 6LU
www.ligca.org
The LIGCA hosts exhibitions of children's art from all over the world including artwork by local children. They also run a schools education programme relating to these exhibitions, including exhibition tours and workshops in the gallery. Out of school hours, they offer an exciting range of art workshops and courses catering for 2-12 year olds. They can also host children's birthday parties. Open from 4-6pm Tues-Thurs and 12-6pm Fri-Sun. Closed Mondays. Admission free.

Jackson's Lane Centre   020 8340 5226
269A Archway Road, N6
www.jacksonslane.org.uk
North London's busiest art centre hosts shows and art workshops for young children from 18mths+ as well as parent and toddler groups. Workshops during the holidays and half-terms for dance and art, either drop-in or courses. Most are oversubscribed so book in advance.

National Gallery   020 7747 2870
Trafalgar Square, WC2N 5DN
www.nationalgallery.co.uk
Have you been on the Magic Carpet? Starting at 11.30am Tues–Fri, under 5s are taken on a 1/2hr journey by the enthusiastic staff who tell spellbinding stories about a selection of paintings. 'Spot the Difference' with visiting artists (Sat & Sun 11.30am and 2.30pm). Check the website for details. Open 10am-6pm daily.

National Portrait Gallery   020 7306 0055
2 St Martin's Place, WC2H 0HE
www.npg.org.uk
Grab a Family Activity Rucksack from the information desk, full of artistic little goodies such as jigsaws, fuzzy felt, dressing up items, and a discussion guide for parents to get the most out of the activities. "Are you sitting comfortably?" storytelling sessions take place on Saturdays. Workshops and holiday activities take place in the Clore Gallery for 4yrs+ (booking essential). Open 10am-6pm daily.

families

Have great days out at Tate

BRITAIN

TATE

A visit to Tate is child's play...

There's loads to do for **FREE** at Tate Britain – from terrific trails and imaginative activities on the *Art Trolley*, sponsored by Tate & Lyle, to creative workshops and special holiday events. Visit the free BP British Art Displays and also enjoy reduced price family admission to one of the major exhibitions.

Sign up for free families email bulletins to find out more:
www.tate.org.uk/bulletins

Tate Britain
Millbank
London SW1P 4RG
⊖ Pimlico or Vauxhall
⇌ Vauxhall
🚢 Millbank Pier

Open daily 10.00–17.50
Open first Friday of every month until 22.00
Closed 24–26 December

Call 020 7887 8888
www.tate.org.uk/families

BP British Art Displays 1500–2006

Supported by BP   bp

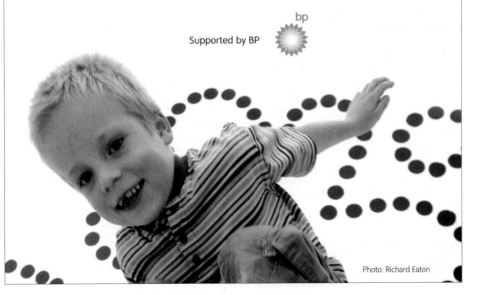

Photo: Richard Eaton

Royal Academy 020 7300 8000
Burlington House, Piccadilly, W1J 0BD
www.royalacademy.org.uk
The Art Tray (akin to a Pony Club grooming box) stacked full
of paper, crayons, scissors, glue, crêpe paper and glitter, is
provided to all children who want to create their own works of
art. The Summer Exhibition is a real favourite. If you go on a
hot day, be prepared with a change of clothes, to let little
ones play in the fountain jets in the main courtyard. Good
selection of cafes inside and out.

South Bank Centre 020 7960 4201
Belvedere Road, SE1
www.rfh.org.uk
A lot of time has been invested in choosing a fun programme
for younger audiences with a good selection of festivals
orientated towards families and young children, including face
painting, circus performances, drumming, etc. Events are
seasonal so check out the website for current events.

Tate Britain 020 7887 8888
Millbank, SW1P 4RG
www.tate.org.uk/families
At Tate Britain, families can explore with the free Spot the
Circle discovery trail. At weekends and during the school
holidays, discover new and unusual materials on the new Art
Trolley, then head off to the galleries to imagine,draw, snip
and stick. Get creative at workshop sessions or during BP
Ssaturdays, when the gallery hosts a day of fantastic events.

Family friendly facilities include buggy parking, baby changing
and tasty, healthy treats in the café and restaurant.

Tate Modern 020 7887 8888
Holland Street, SE1 9TG
www.tate.org.uk/families
At Tate Modern prepare your eyes for an adventure with Tate
Teasers, a series of free trails, or the interactive multimedia
guide for children. Visit the Learning Zone which is packed
with inventive activities or play games and puzzles based
around the Collection displays. UBS Openings: Family Zone
has imaginative ways of introducing children to modern art
and at the weekends and during holidays, Start offers free
games that encourage children to match images, sort clues
and make connections. There are great facilities for families,
including tasty, healthy treats in the café and restaurant.

Tricycle Theatre 020 7328 1000
269 Kilburn High Road, NW6 7JR
www.tricycle.co.uk
An amazing range of art workshops and tours offered for
children by the Tricycle, including events for 18mth+. A new
Creative Space studio offers dance and poetry classes or
music lessons for 5yrs+. Saturday theatre productions are
also scheduled (11.30am, 2pm). Enquire online and book
early for holiday events or termtime classes. Open ????

baby shows

The Baby Show 0870 122 1313
www.thebabyshow.co.uk/bd
These are the UK's biggest baby shows for mums, dads,
babies and toddlers. Taking place three times a year in
London's Excel Centre (March), at the NEC in Birmingham
(May), and London's Earls Court (October). There are
hundreds of exhibitors displaying everything from cloth
nappies and pushchairs, to hand and foot casting companies
as well as fashion shows, advice workshops and creche
facilities if you have little ones in tow. You can make huge
savings on lots of nursery products and clothing as many
exhibitors offer special Baby Show discounts. You'll also be
able to check out the products of many mail order and
catalogue brands. Tickets cost £10.95 online/advance
telephone order or £12.95 on the door, with a special £2
grandparent discount.

castles & palaces

There's nothing like a few ancient battles to get
imaginations going. And this selection has a few
that are outside London but are within easy reach
and access from London, making them a perfect
day out

Buckingham Palace 020 7766 7300
Buckingham Palace Road, SW1A 1AA
www.royalcollection.org.uk
See the nature trail for children in the gardens and visit the
family activity room during August. In the Royal Mews you
can watch horses being groomed and take a peek at the
Gold State Coach. Open Mar-Oct 11am-3.15pm.

Changing the Guard
Buckingham Palace, The Mall, SW1
www.changing-the-guard.com
The soldiers seen changing the guard at Buckingham Palace (daily 11.30am from April to end of July - alternate days in winter) are from the Household Division, namely the Life Guards, the Blues and Royals and the Household Cavalry - as well as foot soldiers from the Grenadiers, Coldstream, Scots, Welsh and Irish Guards. To get a good view they recommend the following spots: Wellington Barracks, St James's Palace or on the Mall (good for the mounted guards). You can get a picture with the guard on Pall Mall (past St James' Palace). You can also visit the Guards Museum and try on a bearskin.

Eltham Palace   020 8294 2548
Court Yard, SE9 5QE
www.elthampalace.org.uk
Once a ruin, Eltham Palace's makeover in the 1930s by Stephen and Victoria Courtauld, including a special room for their pet lemur, provides a grand backdrop for picnics and an annual theatre and dance festival each summer. Good tearoom and shop as well as a programme of family-focused events. Check the website for details.

Tower of London   0870 756 6060
Tower Hill, EC3N 4AB
www.hrp.org.uk
Despite the pricey entrance fees this really is one of London's great days out. Family trail booklets and pencils are given at the Sentry Box and costumed actors get visitors in the mood with singing, dancing and playing musical instruments. Crown Jewels, Torture at the Tower and the Armoury are all worth visiting. Open daily Mar-Oct 9am-5pm Tues-Sat, 10am-5pm Mon, Sun. Nov-Feb 10am-4pm Mon, Sun and 9am-4pm Tues-Sat. Beefeater tours half-hourly (outside only). Free for under 5s.

Windsor Castle   020 7766 7304
Windsor, Berkshire, SL4 1NJ
www.windsor.gov.uk/attractions/castle
Visit the Castle, the State Apartments and St George's Chapel or watch Changing of the Guard which takes place on alternate days at 11am (call 01753 831 118 to double check). Open March-Oct from 9.45am-5.15pm daily, and Nov-Feb 9.45am-4.15pm.

Bodiam Castle   01580 830 436
Robertsbridge, East Sussex TN32
www.nationaltrust.org.uk
A favourite venue for family picnics on fine days or budding knights wanting to tear around in lots of space. Their Bat Pack includes a tabard to wear, adventure trail and a good range of exciting activities. During half-terms and holidays there are additional events and activities. Café/tearoom with nappy changing facilities and shop. Open Mid-Feb to Oct 10am-6pm/dusk daily and mid-Nov-Feb 10am-4pm/dusk on Sat and Sun. Last entry is 1hr before closing. Admission £4 adults, £2 5s-16yrs and free for under 5s.

Groombridge Place Gardens   01892 863 999
Tunbridge Wells, Kent, TN3
www.groombridge.co.uk
Wonderful gardens and an enchanted forest make this a great place to come with young children. They have many special events throughout the year such as Easter Eggstravaganzas in March, Adventures of Robin Hood in May so check their website for the dates. The gardens are open 9.30am-6pm (or dusk if earlier).

Hampton Court Palace   020 8781 9500
East Molesey, Surrey, KT8
www.hrp.org.uk
Set within 60 acres of riverside gardens Hampton Court Palace is a great day out. Not least the new permanent Gardens Exhibition and the maze. For the house there are special family trails and audio guides. There are seasonal festivals running throughout the year, as well as the Christmas ice-rink. Open 9.30-6pm Tues-Sun and 10.15am-6pm Mon during the summer, and closes at 4.30pm during the winter.

Hever Castle   01732 865 224
Edenbridge, Kent, TN8
www.hevercastle.co.uk
This was the childhood home of Anne Boleyn and where she first courted Henry VIII - and the castle, garden and lakes were restored in the early 20th century. The gardens are extensive, and there's a maze, adventure playground, secret grottos and a water maze which is perfect for hot sunny days (bring a change of clothes)! Castle open Mar-Oct 12-6pm daily and Nov 12-4pm daily. Free for under 5s.

Leeds Castle   0870 600 888
Broomfield, Maidstone, Kent ME17
www.leeds-castle.com
Built soon after 1066 Leeds Castle is a fantastic day out with many family and children's events throughout the holidays and weekends. A maze, aviary, secret grottos and also children's classical concerts and open-air summer theatre to give you an excuse to visit. Castle open Apr-Oct 11am-5.30pm daily and Nov-Mar 10am-3.30pm daily. Last entry 1hr before closing. Admission for castle, gardens and museum is £11 adults, £7.50 5-16yrs and free for under 5s.

Mountfitchet Castle   01279 813237
& Norman Village
Stansted, Essex, CM24 8SP
This castle and village take you back almost 900 years to witness a picture of medieval life. There are animals to feed as you wander around the village (goats, guinea fowl, chickens, peacocks) and plenty of places to picnic. Also café with nappy changing facilities and a shop. Open 10am-5pm daily. Admission £3.80 or £3 for 2-14yrs, free for under 2s.

> **Don't forget to check our monthly e-newsletter with special things to do a see throughout the year**

cinema clubs

We are continually impressed by what the cinemas below have lined up for movie-mad kids. And for movie-mad mums with under 1s, there are separate screenings for blockbusters. It's usually free seating and nobody minds children wandering around a bit or having the odd tantrum. The workshop activities that accompany the screenings really extend children's whole experience of the film and make it even more memorable. Perfect for a wet weekend morning

E8
Rio Cinema　　　　　**020 7241 9410**
103-7 Kingsland High Street, E8
www.riocinema.co.uk
Kids Club on Sat 11am. Membership cards are stamped, with a free movie and poster given after collecting 10 stamps.

E15
Stratford Picturehouse　　　**020 8522 0043**
Theatre Square, Stratford, E15 1BX
www.picturehouses.co.uk
Well-organised programme of films and activities for young children including a film club, quarterly newsletter. Mother with babes on Tues at 10.30am.

EC2
Barbican Centre　　　　**020 7382 7000**
Silk Street, EC2
Family Fun Film Club on Sat 11am with themed workshops starting at 10am.

SE1
Movie Magic at the NFT　　　**020 7928 3232**
National Film Theatre, South Bank, SE1
www.bfi.org.uk/moviemagic
Films for younger audiences are screened Sat & Sun 3pm including themed workshops (eg making Dickensian glowing lanterns and short animation films for older children). Additional holiday activites/screenings midweek at 2pm.

SE10
Greenwich Picturehouse　　　**020 8853 0484**
180 Greenwich High Road, SE10 8NN
www.picturehouses.co.uk
Children's club on Sat at 11am and mothers with babes on Fri 11.30am.

SW2
Ritzy Cinema　　　　**020 7733 2229**
Brixton Oval, Coldharbour Lane, Brixton, SW2 1JG
www.ritzycinema.co.uk
Kids Club movies on Sat at 10.30am (£1 children and £2 accompanying adult). Free newspapers, tea & coffee. During holidays themed workshops held on Tues & Thurs 10.30am. Mothers with babes on Fri at 11am.

SW4
Clapham Picture House　　**020 7498 3323**
76 Venn Street, SW4 0AT　　0870 755 0061
www.picturehouses.co.uk
The Clapham Kids Club screens movies on Sat 11.45am as well as workshops and quizzes starting at 11.15am. Also Thurs 10.30am screenings for mothers with babes in arms (under 12mths)

W11
Electric Cinema　　　　**020 7908 9696**
191 Portobello Road, W11 2ED
www.electrichouse.com
Kids Club screenings on Sat 11am and 1pm with themed workshops. Also kids' activities most afternoons during holidays. Tues 3pm screening for mothers with under 1s.

Gate Cinema　　　　**0870 755 0063**
87 Notting Hill Gate, W11 3JZ
www.picturehouses.co.uk
Saturday Kid's club with pre-screening activities from 11am.

circus

From about 2 yrs+ children will be amazed, amused and sometimes bemused by the amazing acrobatics performed by the visiting circus troupes. These days it's less about elephants and tigers, more palaminos and canaries, but it doesn't dampen the enthusiasm for the unique spectacle of clowns, candy floss and the big band sound. Check websites for locations and timing

Zippo's
www.zippocircus.co.uk

Chinese State Circus
www.chinesestatecircus.co.uk

Cirque du Soleil
www.cirquedusoleil.com

Moscow State Circus
www.moscowstatecircus.co.uk

CIRCUS SCHOOLS
The Circus Space　　　**020 7613 4141**
Coronet Street, N1 6HD
www.thecircusspace.co.uk

Albert and Friends Instant Circus　**020 8237 1170**
www.albertandfriendsinstantcircus.co.uk

farms: city

Brooks Farm　　　　**020 8539 4278**
Skeltons Lane Park, Leyton, E10 5BS
Shetland ponies (no riding), llamas and Monty the pig are firm favourites. There is also an aviary, rabbit warren and a children's petting zone. Open 10.30-5.30pm (closed Mon and between **12.30-1.30pm daily**) except Bank Holidays.

Coram's Fields   020 7837 6138
93 Guilford Street, WC1N 1DN
This seven acre site sits in the middle of London WC1 and in its pets corner offers pigs and guinea pigs, goats, sheep and ducks. Highly recommended by one of our readers.

Deen City Farm   020 8543 5300
39 Windsor Avenue, Merton Abbey, SW19 2RR
Good selection of farm animals, including rheas (small ostrich) and pets. There's a farm tour, club, own-a-pony days, mother and toddler groups as well as birthdays and holiday activities. Snakes and lizards also on show seasonally. Watch eggs hatch or gaze at the fish in the café. For pony rides (daily) enquire about times. Open 10am-5pm daily except closed on Mon.

Freightliners Farm   020 7609 0467
Sheringham Road, Islington, N7 8PF
www.freightlinersfarm.co.uk
Mixture of rare-breed chickens, goats, sheep, rabbits, guinea pigs. Craft-based activity workshops for under 4s during the summer holidays. Open Tues-Sun 10–5pm.

Hackney City Farm   020 7729 6381
1a Goldsmiths Row, off Hackney Road, E2 8QA
www.hackneycityfarm.co.uk
Hackney City Farm offers lots for young children including a great family café, music and movement classes and pottery sessions. Open Tues-Sun 10am-5pm (closed on Mon).

Hounslow Urban Farm   020 8751 0850
Fagg's Road, Feltham
www.hounslow.info/urbanfarm
Rare breed farm featuring Highland cattle, Middle White pigs, donkeys including Eeyore, but no small animals. Entrance £3 adults, £1.50 children 2-16yrs. Animal feeding at 3.30pm. Open 10-5pm Tues-Sun (closed Mon).

Kentish Town City Farm   020 7916 5421
1 Cressfield Close, NW5 4BN
Cows, sheep, horses, pigs, chickens, ducks, rabbits and plenty of opportunities to touch. You can ride the ponies for £1 Sat & Sun at 1.30pm. Wed playgroup during termtime from 10.30am (closed on Mon).

Mudchute Farm   020 7515 5901
Pier Street, Isle of Dogs, E14 9HP
www.mudchute.org
Cow, chickens, sheep, pigs, rabbits, donkeys etc. Farm tours available for 10 or more children, and holiday play activities during the summer holidays. Book in advance.

Newham City Farm   020 7474 4960
King George Avenue, E16 3HR
This is essentially a traditional livestock farm with a Shire horse which gives cart rides on special event days. Rare breeds are a specialty with Golden Guernsey goats and Portland sheep, as well as llamas, wallabies and birds of prey. They have recently expanded into providing a visitor centre where you can buy farm duck or chicken eggs, honey and herbs. Open Tues-Sun 10am-5pm. Closed Mon.

Spitalfields City Farm   020 7247 8762
Weaver Street, E1
www.spitalfieldscityfarm.org
Sited on a former railway goods depot, the farm was started in 1978 in response to local people's wishes to convert wasteland into allotments. There is now a large range of farm animals, with lots of volunteer groups, drop-in clubs and donkey rides. Festivals throughout the year. Open daily 10am-4pm. Closed Mon.

Stepping Stones Farm   020 7790 8204
Stepney Way/Stepney High Street, E1 3DG
This is a working farm in the middle of an East End housing estate. There is a shop selling home-made jams and chutneys. There is a wildlife pond and play area which makes a good picnic spot. Open Tues-Sun 9.30am - 6pm. Closed Mon.

Surrey Docks City Farm   020 7231 1010
Rotherhithe Street, SE16 1EY
Complete range of animals including donkeys, pigs, sheep, goats, rabbits and ponies. They have recently added a bee room with inspection hive, a forge and new activity rooms. Open 10am-5pm. Closed Mon and Fri.

Vauxhall City Farm   020 7582 4204
24 St Oswalds Place, SE11 5JE
Positioned in the shadow of the MI6 building this little farm has donkeys, ponies and other farm animals. Also holiday activity classes. Open 10.30am-4pm. Closed Mon and Fri.

farms: out of town

Aldenham Country Park   020 8953 9602
Elstree, Herts WD6
Wide range of rare breed farm animals. Their Winnie the Pooh nature trail includes Eeyore, Piglet and Pooh's houses, Pooh sticks bridge and the honey tree. £3 per car. Open 9am-6pm closing earlier during winter.

Bocketts Farm Park   01372 363 764
Young Street, Fetcham, Leatherhead, KT22
www.bockettsfarm.co.uk
Bocketts Farm has created a winning formula. All sorts of animals, accessible to feed and touch; horse rides around the orchard, and pig races which are highly competitive events and get the adults quite steamed up. But for the budding mechanics there are plenty of ride-on tractors.

Burpham Court Farm Park   01483 576089
Clay Lane, Jacobs Well, Guildford, GU4 7NA
www.burphamcourtfarm.org
Some of the rarest farm animal breeds that are on the survival trust's list can be found at Burpham; such as Middle White pigs, Leicester Longwool sheep, white-faced Caspian Horse. All set out in little paddocks with a central walkway. Outdoor play area with sandpit, swings and ride-on tractors. The tearooms offer light refreshments and there is a souvenir shop. Birthday parties can be held in one of the tea-rooms or the picnic barn in the summer. Open 10am-6pm/dusk all year round. Entry is £4.75 adults, £3.95 children and Under 2s are free.

Godstone Farm　　　　01883 742 546
Tilburstow Hill Road, Godstone, RH9 8LX
www.godstonefarm.co.uk
For children who need space, this is an ideal environment. An adventure playground, and ball pit adjoins the animal enclosures. Hatching eggs are mesmerising for the little ones, as are the other baby animals. Open 10-6pm, £4.30 child 2yrs+, adults free.

The Hop Farm Country Park　01622 872 068
Paddock Wood, Kent, TN12 6TY
www.thehopfarm.co.uk
Based amid the largest collection of oast houses, this former working hop farm is now bustling with family-focused activities. There's a large children's play area set amongst pens of farm animals as well as enormous shire horses and tiny shetland ponies. Visit the website to find out about holiday activities and family events. Open daily 10am-5pm.

Horton Park Children's Farm　　01372 743984
Horton Lane, Epsom, Surrey KT19 8PT
www.hortonpark.co.uk
Open 10am-6pm daily. Very suitable for younger children with small enclosures of rabbits, chicks, hamsters to touch, with lizards and snakes for the very brave. Café and picnic areas with soft toy barn if it's pouring with rain.

Lockwood Donkey Sanctuary　　01428 682 409
Farm Cottage, Sanhills, Wormley, Godalming, GU8
Lockwood is the retirement home of old and sick donkeys, which are delighted to meet children bearing carrots. Open daily 9am-5.30pm.

Odds Farm Park　　　　01628 520 188
Woburn Common, High Wycombe, Bucks, HP10
www.oddsfarm.co.uk
Wide range of large and small animals, with small enclosures for feeding and touching. Easter Egg and Halloween workshops during holidays. Café and picnic areas around sand and playgrounds. Open daily 10am-5.30pm.

Rare Breeds Centre　　　01233 861 493
Highlands Farm, Woodchurch, Ashford
www.rarebreeds.org.uk
Take a big picnic on a fine day and hang out with some of the most odd-looking rare breeds. Indoor play areas and particularly good for parties.

Willows Farm Village　　　01727 822 106
Coursers Road, London Colney, St Albans, AL2
www.willowsfarmvillage.com
Huge variety of things for the under 5s with a programme of events daily. Most popular are the pet handling areas, guinea pig village, indoor and outdoor play areas specifically built for the under 5s (small trampolines and sand pits), tractor rides and arena events (such as dogs herding ducks). Farm shop, restaurants plus picnic areas. Open from March to end October. Prices are £8.95 adults, £7.95 children at weekends and during holidays. £6.95 adults, £5.95 children weekdays and termtime.

Wimpole Hall Home Farm　　01223 207 257
Arrington, Royston, SG8 0BW
www.wimpole.org
Rare breeds farm and working estate attached to National Trust-owned Wimpole Hall. Animal activites include Shire horses pulling wagons; sheep and goat feeding. Also adventure playground and barn during winter. Open 10.30am-5pm (closed Mon & Fri).

museums

British Museum　　　　020 7323 8000
Great Russell Street, WC1B 3DG
www.thebritishmuseum.ac.uk
You can't expect to do this museum in a morning, unless you do the 90 minute tour which concentrate on specific areas of the collection. But the family activities are plentiful during the holidays, and the family backpack with games and puzzles will help bring the ancient arts alive. Open 10am-5.30pm daily and to 8.30pm Thurs and Fri. Admission free.

Geffrye Museum　　　　020 7739 9893
136 Kingsland Road, E2
www.geffrye-museum.org.uk
The Geffrye was converted into a furniture and interior design museum in 1914 and features room sets of different periods

from Elizabethan to the present day. They organise activities during holidays and weekends with family Sundays offering model-making, cooking and decorative activities. The restaurant overlooks the gardens where you can picnic. Open Tues-Sat 10am-5pm, 12pm-5pm Sun. Admission free.

Horniman Museum 020 8699 1872
100 London Road, Forest Hill, SE23 3PQ
www.horniman.ac.uk
Picnic area in fantastic gardens and animal enclosures are two of the many reasons to visit the Horniman. Music and musical instruments from around the world and a grass-roofed house get the little ones thinking. Great children's activites arranged for the holidays. Weekends and under 5s storytelling sessions, with Auntie Dee and Nzinga Dance journeying through the stories, games, dances and songs of Africa and the Caribbean. The new revamped aquarium is open after a £15m overhaul. Café/restaurant with highchairs, changing facilities and shop. Open 10.30am-5.30pm daily. Admission free.

Imperial War Museum 020 7416 5000
Lambeth Road, SE1 6HZ
www.iwm.org.uk
The IWM displays the realities of 20th century warfare. From tanks, rockets and fighter planes in the main lobby to a walk-in trench and secret war gallery. There are termtime programmes as well as holiday activities from 5yrs+ such as model-making. Café, restaurant and shop. Open 10-6pm daily. Admission free.

Livesey Museum for Children 020 7635 5829
682 Old Kent Road, Peckham, SE15 1JF
www.liveseymuseum.org.uk
Hands-on exhibition exploring numbers and maths. Free.

London Transport Museum 020 7565 7299
The Piazza, Covent Garden, WC2E 7BB
www.ltmuseum.co.uk
Closed for refurbishment until September 2007.

Museum of Childhood 020 8980 2415
Cambridge Heath Road, Bethnal Green E2
www.museumofchildhood.org.uk
This museum has been closed for refurbishment over the last year, but is re-opening in November 2006. They will display the largest collection of toys and games in the UK dating back as early as the 1600s. Also planned are a great range of children's activities and a shop selling pocket-money priced items. Café and gardens. Open 10am-5.30pm Mon-Sun. Admission free.

Museum of London 020 7600 3699
150 London Wall, EC2Y 5HN
www.museumoflondon.org.uk
Colourful workshops and puppet shows, mask making on Grandparents' day are some of the features lined up this year. Check the website for family events in 2006/07. Open Mon-Sat 10am-5.50pm: Sun 12-5.50pm. Admission free.

© Estate of E H Shepard 2006
Licensed by ©pyrights Group

The Wind in the Willows
Based on the famous EH Shepard drawings this fantastic permanent exhibition brings the classic story of Mole, Ratty, Badger and the irrepressible Mr Toad to life.

The River & Rowing Museum, a great day out

Mill Meadows
Henley on Thames
RG9 1BF
01491 415600
www.rrm.co.uk

THE
WIND
IN THE
WILLOWS
at the River & Rowing Museum

River & Rowing Museum 01491 415 610
Mill Meadows, Henley-on-Thames, Oxfordshire
www.rrm.co.uk
The much-loved tale of Wind in the Willows has been lovingly brought to life in this enchanting walk-through exhibition at the River and Rowing Museum. Minute models of Ratty and Mole's picnic boat, a full-scale walk-in model of Toad's gypsy caravan, and scenes of poor mole getting lost in the wild woods have been lovingly brought to life with wonderful models and theatrical sets, sound tracks and windy tunnels to accompany you on the trail. Other fun holidays activities and events are listed on their website. We can't recommend a visit more highly.

parks and gardens
Hampton Court Palace 020 8781 9500
East Molesey, Surrey, KT8
www.hrp.org.uk
Set within 60 acres of riverside gardens Hampton Court Palace is a great day out. Not least the new permanent Gardens exhibition and the maze, plus family craft workshops which are run on a drop-in basis. There are seasonal festivals running throughout the year, as well as the Christmas ice-rink. Open 9.30am-6pm Tues-Sun and 10.15am-6pm Mon during the summer, and closes at 4.30pm during the winter.

London Wildlife Trust Centre   **020 7252 9186**
28 Marden Road, East Dulwich, SE15 4EE
www.wildlondon.org.uk
Created on a disused bus depot, visit this herb garden, woodland and pond areas as well as a plant nursery. The project has an award-winning visitors' centre demonstrating innovative environmental building techniques, which provides a base for school parties and an 'Acorns' parent and toddler group. Outside young children will make a beeline for the sandpit. During spring children can go pond-dipping or bat walking as well as participate in craft-based activities. Open 10.30am-4.30pm Tues, Wed, Thurs, Sun.

Royal Botanic Gardens at Kew   **020 8332 5000**
www.kew.org.uk
This is a 300-acre garden with giant Victorian greenhouses which contain some of the world's most tropical plants. The Climbers and Creepers exhibition offers some fantastic interactive features (such as a giant flower which your toddler can climb into). There are also plenty of cafes dotted about to keep everyone refreshed and a special picnic place. Open from 9.30am-4.30pm or later during the summer (7.30pm). Admission £7.50 adults and free for under 16s. Take the rail or tube to Kew, or the river boat to Kew Pier.

RHS Gardens, Wisley   **01483 224 234**
Working, Surrey
www.rhs.org.uk
Free for under 6s and a stunning garden for summer picnics.

restaurants

NORTH

Maremma   **020 7226 9400**
11-13 Theburton Street, N1 0QY
www.metrogusto.co.uk
Very child-orientated with kids' menus, highchairs, baby changing and no smoking.

Yellow River Café   **0207 354 8833**
206 Upper Street, Islington,N1 1RQ
www.yellowrivercafes.co.uk
Kids' menu, highchairs, baby changing facilities. Also colouring in and baby chopsticks provided.

Giraffe   **020 7359 5999**
29-31 Essex Road, N1 2SA
www.giraffe.net

Tiger Lil's   **020 7226 1118**
270 Upper Street, N1 2UQ
Kids' menu, highchairs and baby changing facilities.

Giraffe   **020 8883 4463**
348 Muswell Hill Broadway, N10
Kids' menu, highchairs, baby changing facilities. Great place for families.

Banners   **0871 075 8638**
21 Park Road, N8 8TE

Highchairs, toys, space for buggies, agreement with shop nearby to use baby changing facilities.

NORTH WEST

Benihana   **020 7586 9508**
100 Avenue Road, NW3
Clown on Sunday lunchtime and a special children's menu. Highchairs. Also in SW3, W1.

Maxwell's Restaurant   **020 7794 5450**
76 Heath Street, NW3 1DN
www.maxwells.co.uk
Kids menu, highchairs and colouring activities.

Giraffe   **020 7435 0343**
46 Rosslyn Hill, NW3 1NH
www.giraffe.net
Great families' meals and facilities. Branches also at 7 Kensington High Street (020 7938 1221); 30 Hill Street, Richmond (020 8332 2646); Royal Festival Hall (020 7928 2004); 21 Wimbledon High Street (020 8946 0544); 270 Chiswick High Road (020 8995 2100); 27 Battersea Rise (020 7223 0993).

SOUTH EAST

Pizzeria Castello   **020 7703 2556**
20 Walworth Road, Elephant & Castle,SE1 6SP
www.pizzeriacastello.co.uk
Highchairs and baby changing facilities. A new branch has also opened on the Jamaica Road, SE16.

Gourmet Pizza Company   **020 7928 3188**
Gabriels Wharf, 56 Upper Ground, SE1 9PP
Children's portions of pasta and pizza, highchairs but no baby changing facilities.

Joanna's   **020 8670 4052**
56 Westow Hill, SE19
Kids' menu, highchairs but no baby changing facilities.

Blue Mountain Café   **020 8299 6953**
18 North Cross Road, SE22 9EU
Kids' menu, highchairs and baby changing facilities.

Café Provencal   **020 7978 9228**
2-6 Half Moon Lane, Herne Hill, SE24
Kids' portions, highchairs, toys/play area. No baby changing facilities. Next door to the fab Brockwell Park where you can go afterwards to let off steam.

SOUTH WEST

La Famiglia   **020 7351 0761**
7 Langton Street, SW10 0JL
No specific children's menu but kids' are always welcome. Highchairs and baby changing facilities.

Ransome's Dock   **020 7223 1611**
35-37 Parkgate Road, SW11
Kids' menus, highchairs and baby changing facilities, colouring activities, children's cups and cutlery provided.

Tootsies   020 7924 4935
1 Battersea Rise, SW11
www.tootsiesrestaurants.co.uk
Organic kids' menu, £5.50, including drink and dessert.
Highchairs, colouring, goodie bags, balloons and free baby food
as well as a great party venue. Other venues include: Jubilee
Place, 45 Bank Street, Canary Wharf (020 7516 9110); 148
Chiswick High Road (020 8747 1869). 196-198 Haverstock Hill,
Belsize Park (020 7431 3812); 35 St James Street, W1 (020
7486 1611); 107 Old Brompton Road, SW7 (020 7581 8942)
and 30 Brewhouse Street, Putney Wharf (020 8788 8488)
which has a huge soda fountain full of ice cream and sweets.

Le Bouchon Bordelais   020 7738 0307
5-9 Battersea Rise, SW11 1HG
www.lebouchon.co.uk
Free crèche on Saturdays 12.30-3.30pm and on Sundays
12.30-4pm with videos, toys and colouring-in activities.

The Boiled Egg & Soldiers   020 7223 4894
63 Northcote Road, SW11 1NP
Kids' menu, highchairs but no baby changing facilities.

The Castlenau   020 8748 4486
201 Castlenau Road, SW13 9ER
Baby changing facilities and highchairs.

The Naked Turtle   020 8878 1995
505 Upper Richmond Road, SW14
www.naked-turtle.com
Kids' menu, highchairs and baby changing facilities. Kids eat
for free on Sat and Sun lunch and there's face painting on Sun.

Moomba   020 8785 9151
5 Lacy Road, SW15 1NH
No kids' menu but highchairs, games and colouring activities
provided.

Outback Steakhouse   020 8877 1599
Smugglers Way, Wandsworth, SW18 1EG
www.outbackpom.com
Activity comic and crayons, freshly-prepared kids' food,
highchairs and boosters, baby changing facilities.

San Lorenzo   020 8946 8463
38 Wimbledon Hill Road, Wimbledon, SW19
Child-friendly with kids' play area. Kids' menus, highchairs
and baby changing facilities.

Est Est Est   020 8947 7700
38 High Street, Wimbledon, SW19
Kids' menu, highchairs, colouring/crayons provided but no
baby changing facilities.

Henry J Beans   020 7352 9255
195-7 King's Road, SW3
Children's menu, highchairs and baby changing facilities.

> Let us know about your favourite
> restaurants and cafes and we'll
> include them in the next edition.

Big Easy   020 7352 4071
332-334 King's Road, SW3 5UR
Children's menu, highchairs, baby changing facilities and
balloons on Sat & Sun. "Baby Easy" t-shirts also available.

Newton's   020 8673 0977
33 Abbeville Road, Clapham Common South Side,
SW4 9LA
www.newtonsrestaurants.co.uk
Kids' menu, highchairs, baby changing facilities as well as
colouring activities and kids' packs.

Blue Elephant   020 7385 6595
4-6 Fulham Broadway, SW6
No specific children's menu, but they have highchairs, baby
changing facilities and a cloakroom for buggies.

Blue Kangaroo   020 7371 7622
555 King's Road, SW6 2EB
www.thebluekangaroo.co.uk
Family restaurant and play centre plus a great party venue.
There is a specific kids' menu, highchairs, baby changing
facilities, and a basement coffee area with a special soft play
area for the under 3s. Open 9.30am-7.30pm, 7 days a week.

Pizza Organic   020 7589 9613
20 Old Brompton Road, SW7 3DL
Kids' menus, highchairs and baby changing facilities.

Le Bouchon Lyonnais   020 7622 2618
36-40 Queenstown Road, SW8 3RY
Kids' menu and highchairs.

WEST & CENTRAL
Browns   020 7491 4565
47 Maddox Street, W1
Children's menu, highchairs, and baby changing facilities.

Lazy Daisy Café   020 7221 8416
59a Portobello Road, W11 3DB
This café is a haven for parents and children. Great kids'
food, toys, books, colouring, highchairs and space for
buggies.

Julie's Restaurant   020 7229 8331
135 Portland Road, W11 4LW
www.juliesrestaurant.com
Crèche during Sunday lunch at 12.30pm for 2-12yr olds.
Kids' menu, highchairs, but no baby changing facilities.

Cafe Cibo   0870 830 7700
Mamas & Papas, 256-258 Regent Street, W1
Cafe Cibo is the result of a collaboration between the talent
behind the famous restaurant at Harvey Nichols and the
founder of Mamas & Papas, Luisa Scacchetti. Reflecting the
Italian heritage of Mamas and Papas, each dish is freshly
prepared to include timeless classics or modern favourites
with a twist. With a focus on nutrition for mum and baby,
Cibo is the perfect rendezvous for breakfast brunches, ligh
luncheons and early suppers. The organic children's menu
features failsafe favourites without compromising on quality.
There is also a private feeding and changing room as well as
a bottle warming service.

Giraffe 020 7935 2333
36-38 Blandford Street, W1H 3HA
www.giraffe.net
Kids' menu, highchairs, baby changing facilities,
colouring/crayons provided (£4.95 for main course, ice cream
and a juice). Also great for parties.

Yo! Sushi 020 7287 0443
52 Poland Street, W1R 1TA
Also at Harvey Nichols, Selfridges, 02 Centre, Farringdon
Road, Finchley Road. Baby chopsticks, crayons, kids' club.

Carluccio's 020 7935 5927
St Christopher's Place, W1U 1AY
www.carluccios.co.uk
Winner of the Best Family Restaurant in 2002. This Italian
café serves inexpensive dishes with a particularly hospitable
welcome to bambini. Highchairs, baby changing facilities.
Also has branches in St John's Wood, South Kensington,
Putney, Islington, Hampstead, Fulham, Fenwicks of Bond
Street, Canary Wharf, Neal Street and Ealing.

Planet Hollywood 020 7287 1000
13 Coventry Street, W1V
www.planethollywood.com
Kids' menus, highchairs and baby changing facilities, live DJ
and movie clips.

Amalfi 020 7437 7284
29-31 Old Compton Street, W1V 5PL
Children's menu, no baby changing facilities.

Rainforest Café 020 7434 3111
20 Shaftesbury Avenue, W1V 7EU
Kids' menus, highchairs and baby changing facilities. Great
for parties with branded goody bags. They are looking to
introduce a baby food menu in 2006.

Mandarin Kitchen 020 7727 9468
14-16 Queensway, W2 3RX
No specific kids' menu, but Sunday is their family day;
highchairs provided but no baby changing facilities.

Texas Lone Star 020 8747 0001
50-54 Turnham Green Terrace, W4 1QP
Kids' menu, highchairs but no baby changing facilities. Also
colouring activities and balloons.

Pizza Organic 020 8998 6878
100 Pitshanger Lane, W5 1QX
Kids' menu, highchairs, baby changing facilities, colouring-in
sheets and crayons, plus balloons to take home.

Old Orleans 020 8579 7413
26-42 Bond Street, W5 5AA
www.oldorleans.com
Kids' menu, highchairs, baby changing facilities, kids' packs
stuffed with colouring-in activities.

Wagamama's 020 7376 1717
26 Kensington High Street, W8 4BF
Kids menu, highchairs and baby changing facilities.

Haagen-Dazs on the Square 020 7287 9577
14 Leicester Square, WC2
www.haagen-dazs.co.uk
Ice creams and pastries, highchairs and baby changing
facilities. Other branches in Camden, Hampstead, Odeon
Kensington, Odeon South Woodford, Queensway,

Rock Garden 020 7240 3961
6 The Piazza, Covent Garden,WC2
www.rockgarden.co.uk
Kids' menus, highchairs and baby changing facilities.

Smollensky's Balloon 020 7240 0766
105 Strand, WC2R 0AA
www.smollenskys.co.uk
The place for children (and parents) to see and be seen any
weekend lunchtime is Smollensky's famous American-style bar
and grill on the Strand. There are five family-friendly
Smollensky's restaurants in London and one in Oxford, but the
original Smollensky's on the Strand is the one where, on
Saturdays and Sundays, between 12 noon and 3pm, young
diners can enjoy clowns, magicians, a teeny tots' disco, party
packs, and face painting, plus there's even some PS2 action
for those who think they're too old for 'kid's stuff'. So, while
they're off enjoying themselves, you can have a great meal too.

Porters 020 7836 6466
17 Henrietta Street, WC2E 8QH
www.porters-restaurant.com
Kids' menus, highchairs and baby changing facilities and
balloons to take home.

TGI Friday   **020 7379 0585**
6 Bedford Street, WC2E 9HZ
www.tgifridays.co.uk
Kids' menu, highchairs and baby changing facilities. Face painter comes between 12-5pm on Sat and Sun. And there's a Sat pm magician from 6.30-9.30pm. Great kids' packs with colouring activities. Free baby food (Organix range). Other branches are at 96/98 Bishopsbridge Road, W2 (020 7229 8600); Fulham Broadway Retail Centre, 472 Fulham Road, SW6 (020 7385 0470) and 25-29 Coventry Street, W1 (020 7839 6262).

Café Pacifico   **020 7379 7728**
5 Langley Street, WC2H 9JA
Kids' menu, highchairs, colouring/crayons provided. No baby changing facilities.

Brown's Restaurant   **020 7497 5050**
82-84 St Martin's Lane, WC2N 4AF
Family restaurant with kids' menu, highchairs and baby changing facilities.

theatres

Arts Depot   **020 8369 5454**
Nether Street, North Finchley, N12
www.artsdepot.co.uk
There is an amazing line up of children's shows at this new North London theatre and art venue. Do visit the website or ring for their brochure of events.

Broadway Theatre   **020 8690 0002**
Catford Broadway, Catford, SE6
www.broadwaytheatre.org.uk
Great Sat am shows for children aged 3yrs+. Classic and riotous pantomimes at Christmas. Highly recommended and book up early.

Chicken Shed Theatre   **020 8292 9222**
Chase Side, Southgate, N14
www.chickenshed.org.uk
Fantastic theatre shows for pre-school children on Fri and Sat ams. Each week the topic changes and with audience participation you could be watching two different shows. They also have an outdoor amphitheatre for the summer months. Also great Christmas season of festive productions.

Colour House Theatre   **020 8640 5111**
Merton Abbey Mills, Watermill Way, Merton, SW19
www.wheelhouse.org.uk
Great musical shows for children aged 3yrs+. With the Three Little Pigs and Rumpelstiltskin currently showing they have a great line up of shows for the 2005-06 season. The shows are held every weekend at 2pm and 4pm and last for just 1hr and are based on original adaptations of classic international fairy tales. This is a great first theatre experience for children and shouldn't be missed.

Edware Alleyn Theatre   **020 8299 9232**
Dulwich College, SE21 7LD
www.dulwich.org.uk/drama
250 seat theatre which hosts family-friendly shows throughout the year. Theatre workshops during the holidays from 7yrs+.

Little Angel Theatre   **020 7226 1787**
14 Dagmar Passage, Cross Street, Islington, N1
www.littleangeltheatre.com
Established in 1961 this is London's first and only permanent puppet theatre. The variety of shows throughout the year is enormous, and there is a good range of shows for the 2-5yrs age group. There is a Sat am puppet club run in conjunction with the shows – where children can have fun learning how to make puppets and perform with them.

London Bubble Theatr Co   **020 7237 4434**
5 Elephant Lane, Rotherhithe, SE16 4JD
www.londonbubble.org.uk
Theatre shows from 3yrs as well as workshops from 5ys+.

Lauderdale House   **020 8348 8716**
Highgate Hill, Waterlow Park, Highgate, N6
www.lauderdale.org.uk
Children's theatre every Saturday morning at 10am and 11.30am from 2-6yrs. Clowns, puppet shows, magic and storytelling. Also termtime workshops from 18mths-3yrs and seasonal workshops such as mask-making at Halloween, making Christmas decorations and Chinese dragons. See website for workshop dates and times.

Lyric Theatre   **020 8741 2311**
King Street, Hammersmith, W6
www.lyric.co.uk
This is more a great theatre with children's shows than a children's theatre. But they have a comprehensive programme of events and shows for pre-school children. Their website includes a section "Lyric Children" with shows highlighted in blue for the under 5s. There's also a café, nappy changing facilities and a great picnic place round the corner on the riverbank.

Nettlefold Theatre   **020 7926 8070**
West Norwood Library, Norwood High treet, SE27
Childe-friendly shows run monthly. Also home to the Bigfoot Theatre Company which runs drama, music and movement classes from 5ys+.

New Wimbledon Theatre   **0870 060 6646**
The Broadway, Wimbledon, SW19 1QG
www.theambassadors.com/newwimbledon
This theatr regularly stages shows for children. Check the website diary for performance details.

Open Air Theatre   **020 7486 2431**
Inner Circle, Regent's Park, NW1
www.open-air-theatre.org.uk
August is when the children's play is held in a 1,200 seat theatre. Book early.

Polka Theatre for Children   **020 8543 4888**
240 The Broadway, SW19
www.polkatheatre.com
A dedicated and comprehensive children's theatre. Daily shows are held at 10.30am and 2pm. There is also an opportunity to see the costumes and props from previous shows in the exhibition centre, run around the adventure playground or take refreshments in the cafe. Other activites take place at the weekends and during the school holidays.

Puppet Theatre Barge   020 7249 6876
Opposite 35-40 Blomfield Road, Little Venice, London
www.puppetbarge.com
This is one of London's most enchanting treasures - in a unique location and with wonderful marionettes and rod puppets combined into theatrical shows. There are just 50 seats, so the theatre is small and cosy with a variety of performances held on Saturday and Sunday afternoons. Between Nov-June the barge is moored in Little Venice, and then heads off up the Thames to Henley, Marlow and Richmond for summer performances. Check the website for holiday and half-term shows.

Unicorn Theatre   0870 053 4534
147 Tooley Street, SE1 2HZ
www.unicorntheatre.com
Theatre shows from 3yrs+ as well as family fun days with themed workshops.

Bekonscot Model Village   01494 672 919
& Railway
Warwick Road, Beaconsfield, Buckinghamshire,
www.bekonscot.com
An unforgettable experience for everyone, this unique miniature world of make-believe is just waiting to be explored by children and adults alike. Depicting rural England in the 1930's the village also boasts the ultimate train set - an historic Gauge 1 famous since 1929 as one of the largest, most exciting and complex in Great Britain. Refreshments, picnic areas, play area. Open daily 10am-5pm mid Feb-end Oct.

theme parks

Alton Towers   0870 520 4060
www.altontowers.com
For white-knuckle water rides head to this theme park and model farm. Using the Parent-Q-Share pass you can help minimise waiting in long queues with young children. Price £21, 4-11yrs.

Chessington World of Adventures   0870 444 7777
www.chessington.co.uk
You pay a one-off fee to enter Chessington which allows you to go on as many rides as many times as you like. For little ones (free for under 4s) there are roundabouts, carousels, Toytown, Professor Burp's Bubble Works and a small circus with trapeze artists and clowns. There is also a zoo which you can see on a monorail and a creepy crawly cave of spiders and insects. Open March-Nov, 10am-5.15pm.

Diggerland   0870 034 4437
Whitewall Road, Strood, Kent, ME2
www.diggerland.com
Open 10am-5pm holidays, this theme park is a must for Bob the Builder enthusiasts. Includes diggers, fork-lift trucks, dumpers and tractors.

Legoland   0870 504 0404
Winkfield Road, Windsor, Berkshire
www.legoland.co.uk
Young ones will be amazed to see what they can build with the basic lego brick. Go outside school holidays to avoid the queues which can be colossal.

Paulton's Park   023 8081 4455
Ower, Nr Romsey, SO51 6AL
A smaller version of Chessington that caters well for younger children. It has around 40 attractions including exciting rides and a selection of exotic birds and animals. Adventure playground, Tiny Tots Town and petting zoo. Restaurant, café, picnic areas. Open daily Mar-Oct, 10am-6.30pm.

Thorpe Park   0870 444 4466
Staines Road, Chertsey, KT16 8PN
www.thorpepark.couk
Under 5s can visit Thorpe Farm or Model World, which features miniature versions of the Eiffel Tower, whilst older brothers and sisters can have their stomachs churned on the Nemesis Inferno... Open Mar-Oct, 9.30am-5pm (later in summer).

trains

Didcot Railway   01235 817 222
Didcot, Oxfordshire
www.didcotrailwaycentre.org.uk
Price £4.50, 3-15yrs. Take a ride on the old steam engine line. For seasonal family events check the website.

Miniature Steam Railway
Brockwell Park, Brixton
Price £1 return. The line runs along the east side of the park (Herne Hill side) and trains run on Wed, Sat & Sun when dry.

zoos

Battersea Park Zoo   020 7924 5826
North Carriage Drive, SW11
www.batterseaparkzoo.co.uk
Now under new management little ones will love meeting the animals at Battersea Zoo. Designed so even the youngest can meet the monkeys, pop-up inside the Meer cat enclosure and watch busy little mice in the Mouse House. They also have farm animals with set times for petting sessions. They host excellent birthday parties here with a chance for the children to make the monkeys a snack, as well as T-shirt painting, a nutricious tea and pass-the-parcel. Shop, café and toilets with baby changing facilities. Open 10am-5.30pm daily (closed Christmas and Boxing Day).

London Zoo   020 7722 3333
Regents Park, NW1 4RY
www.londonzoo.co.uk
Lions and tigers, giraffes, monkeys (all types and sizes), penguins and exotic birds. The renowned reptile house is only for those who can keep calm. Huge amount to see - as well as a fairground carousel to keep the little ones going. Shop, cafe, toilets and baby changing facilities.

> If you've got a drama queen or king in the family - then check our toddler activities section which has local dance and drama classes from 3yrs+ or visit us online at www.babydirectory.com

travel

Some parents swear that travel abroad and babies do not mix. They may well be right. Or they may be missing out. Here we offer ideas for both the adventurous and the stay-at-homes, featuring family-orientated travel companies and websites, camping and ski companies and homeswap agencies, as well as child-friendly hotels and holiday centres in the UK. Bon voyage!

hotels and holidays

The following hotels offer special facilities for children and babies, ranging from crèches and child-listening to playgrounds and pools

Avon

The Bath Spa Hotel   01225 444 424
Sydney Road, Bath
www.bathspa-hotel.co.uk

Channel Islands

Stocks Island Hotel   01481 832 001
Manor Valley, Sark
www.stockshotel.com

Fowey Hotel   01726 833 866
Hanson Drive, Fowey
www.luxuryfamilyhotels.com
One of the group of four excellent country-house hotels aimed at families, with all-day crèches, babysitting, etc, to allow parents a luxury break.

Bedruthan Steps Hotel   01637 860 555
Mawgan Porth
www.bedruthan.com

Sands Family Resort   01637 872 864
Watergate Road, Porth
www.sandsresorts.co.uk

Tredethy House Country Hotel   01208 841 262
Helland Bridge, Bodmin
www.tredethyhouse.co.uk

Watergate Bay Hotel   01637 860 543
Watergate Bay, Newquay
www.watergate.co.uk

Wringford Down Hotel   01752 822 287
Cawsand
www.cornwallholidays.co.uk

Cumbria

Cumbria Allerdale Court Hotel   01900 823 654
Market Place, Cockermouth
www.allerdalecourthotel.co.uk

Armathwaite Hall Hotel   0176 877 6551
Nr. Keswick
www.armathwaite-hall.com

Castle Inn Hotel   01768 776 401
Bassenthwaite, Keswick
www.corushotels.com/castleinn

www.babydirectory.com

Hilton Keswick Lodore   01768 777 285
Borrowdale Road, Keswick

Devon

Langstone Cliff Hotel   01626 868 000
Mount Pleasant Road, Dawlish Warren, Dawlish
www.langstone-hotel.co.uk
19 acres of woodland, children's suppers, indoor and outdoor pools, tennis, therapy rooms, go-karts.

The Bulstone Hotel   01297 680 446
Higher Bulstone, Branscombe, Sidmouth
www.childfriendlyhotels.com

Thurlestone Hotel   01548 560 382
Thurlestone
www.thurlestone.co.uk

Dorset

The Knoll House   01929 450 450
Studland Bay
www.knollhouse.co.uk
Gardens, pools, tennis, golf, health spa, playroom, children's restaurant, adventure playground.

Moonfleet Manor   01305 786 948
Moonfleet, Nr Weymouth
www.luxuryfamilyhotels.com
Play area, crèche, extensive leisure facilities including indoor pool.

Fairfields Hotel   01929 450 224
Swanage Road, Studland Bay
Small super-child-friendly hotel with a garden full of toys and great early suppers.

Sandbanks Hotel   01202 707 377
15 Banks Road, Sandbanks, Poole
Child-orientated hotel with direct access to the gorgeous sandy beach.

Essex

Swallow Churchgate Hotel   01279 420 246
Churchgate Street Village, Old Harlow
Comfortable hotel with indoor pool. Convenient for Stansted airport.

Gloucestershire

Calcot Manor   01666 890 391
Tetbury
www.calcotmanor.co.uk
Lovely Cotswold manor house with spa and pool. Additional beds and cots provided; play zone in a converted barn, children's videos, baby listening.

Hampshire

Watersplash Hotel   01590 622 344
The Rise, Brockenhurst

THE KNOLL HOUSE
Studland Bay

A peaceful oasis and wonderful atmosphere
where families matter
~
Easy access to three miles of golden beach
Outdoor pool (level deck), golf and tennis for all ages
Health Spa with plunge pool and sauna
~
Connecting rooms for families with children
Separate younger children's restaurant
Playroom and fabulous Adventure Playground
~
Open Easter - end October. Dogs also welcome

Studland Bay
Dorset
BH19 3AK
01929 · 450450
info@knollhouse.co.uk
www.knollhouse.co.uk

ONLY 2 HOURS FROM HEATHROW

Hertfordshire

The Grove   01923 807 807
Chandler's Cross
Fabulous designer hotel in stately home and grounds, with state-of-the-art spa, golf course, and Anouska's crèche and play area, which will occupy your children all day if required.

Inverness

Polmaily House Hotel   01456 450 343
Drumnadrochit, Loch Ness

Isle of Wight

The Clarendon Hotel and   01983 730 431
Wight Mouse Inn
Newport Road, Chale
Family-friendly hotel/inn on the picturesque south coast.

Priory Bay Hotel   01983 613 146
Eddington Road, St. Helens
www.priorybay.co.uk
Beautifully decorated, friendly country house hotel with private beach, outdoor pool, pretty grounds and tennis courts.

Lancashire

St Ives Hotel   01253 720 011
7 South Promenade, St Anne's on Sea
Family-owned hotel overlooking the beach, pier and promenade.

Leicestershire

Field Head Hotel   01530 245 454
Markfield Lane, Markfield

Northumberland

Granary Hotel   01665 710 872
Links Road, Amble

Ryecroft Hotel   01668 281 459
Ryecroft Way, Wooler

Perthshire

Gleneagles Hotel   0800 328 4010
Auchterarder
Playground, crèche.

Shropshire

Redfern Hotel   01299 270 395
Cleobury Mortimer

Suffolk

Ickworth Hotel   01284 735 350
Nr Bury St Edmonds
www.luxuryfamilyhotels.com
East wing of Ickworth House, within 1,800 acre National Trust estate. Indoor pool and nursery with spa and both adult and children areas (see ad above).

Warwickshire

Lea Marston Hotel   **01675 470 468**
Haunch Lane, Lea Marston

Wiltshire

Woolley Grange Hotel   **01225 864 705**
Woolley Green, Bradford on Avon
www.luxuryfamilyhotels.com
Play area, crèche, outdoor pool, bicycles (see ad left).

overseas travel

Holidays which the kids want do not necessarily match the holiday that their parents need. It all comes down to the type of childcare you want and can afford - from taking your own nanny, relying on childcare provided by a tour operator (crèche or kids' clubs) or simply baby listening. Babies do require their own passport to travel overseas. The companies we have selected below can offer advice (and special offers) throughout the year

Quo Vadis? Family Travel   **01279 639 600**
www.quovadistravel.co.uk
Luxury family holiday experts providing independent advice on the best holidays available, with tailor-made solutions and a hassle free booking service. They are all parents and have travelled extensively with first-hand knowledge of recommended worldwide destinations. Their new family holiday brochure is free and well worth consulting. This is a highly personal service with no fees.

Travelling with Children   **01684 594 831**
www.travellingwithchildren.co.uk
The one-stop online shop for all your family holiday and day-to-day travel gear.

camping

Canvas Holidays   **08709 022 022**
www.canvas.co.uk
An independent family camping holiday company providing self-drive camping and mobile home holidays in France and the rest of Europe.

Eurocamp   **0870 366 7558**
www.eurocamp.co.uk
Eurocamp is the market-leader in self-catering holidays to Europe. Holidays cater for families (including babies) on 167 superbly equipped holiday parcs in 9 European countries.

Keycamp Holidays   **0870 700 0123**
www.keycamp.co.uk
Fully equipped tents with 4 bedrooms or a luxury mobile home with shower and toilet. Camping sites are across France, Spain, Italy, Luxembourg, Austria, Switzerland and Holland.

homeswaps

Home Base Holidays   **020 8886 8752**
www.homebase-hols.com
International home holiday swaps.

family villages and resorts

CenterParcs   **0990 200 200**
www.centerparcs.com
20 holiday villages throughout Europe, including Longleat Forest in Wiltshire, Sherwood Forest in Notts, Oasis Whinfell in Cumbria and Elvedon Forest in Suffolk (see below).

Club Med   **020 7581 1161**
Kennedy House, 115 Hammersmith Road, W14
www.clubmed.com
All-inclusive holiday villages located all over the world. A number of them offer childcare facilities for babies and young children during the day with good family discount packages.

Sunsail   **023 9222 2300**
The Port House, Port Solent, PO6 4TH
www.sunsail.com
Family resorts in Antigua, Turkey and Greece. Many parents have recommended the Sunsail winter holiday in Antigua (but lament that taking a toddler on such a long-haul flight almost ruined it). Childcare additional.

family ski companies

Chilly Powder   020 7289 6958
www.chillypowder.com
The Chilly Powder chalet is situated in Morzine on the
French/Swiss border. Their in-house nanny can look after
babies (2mths+), with bottle-warming, sterilizer and baby-
listening service also available. A crèche in Morzine (1-4yrs)
provides all-day entertainment for toddlers and from 4yrs+ ski
school is provided by the Ecole de Ski.

Meriski   01285 648 518
www.meriski.co.uk
If you have your heart set on Méribel, then Meriski provides
either in-chalet nannies or crèche facilities (maximum of 8
places) from 9am-5pm Mon-Sat. Cots and highchairs are
provided in the chalets, as well as kids' meals cooked
separately by your chef. From 3yrs+ children can ski with Les
Petits Loups, a ski school run by Ecole de Ski Français,
accompanied by an English-speaking nanny.

Ski Beat   01243 780 405
Ski Beat offers holidays with childcare in 4 French resorts (La
Plagne, Les Arcs, La Tania and Val d'Isère). Crèches, nannies
and afternoon care. Care is provided between 8.45am-5pm
and includes lunch and facilities for sleeping as well as toys,
games and art & craft materials. If you are taking a whole
chalet you may want to hire a private chalet nanny.

Ski Esprit   01252 618 300
Holidays in France, Italy and Austria. Their Classic Childcare
option caters for children from 4mths-3yrs and the Spritelets
Ski School from 3yrs-5yrs (max 6 in a class). A Snow Club in
the afternoon keeps the non-skiing 3-5yr-olds well
entertained. The nannies are all English-speaking. Care is
available 6 days per week from 8.30am-5pm.

Ski Famille   01223 363 777
www.skifamille.com
Ski Famille doesn't charge extra for childcare. They provide
fully qualified nannies to your chalet where playrooms are
equipped with toys, games and arts/craft materials. When the
weather allows they encourage children to play outside. For
older children they ensure they are at ski school on time and
pick them up afterwards. Childcare is available between 9am-
4.30pm except on Saturday or Wednesday. They have
children's ski clothes for hire, sell nappies at cost and provide
baby bottles, sterilizers, highchairs, cots and bedding.

Ski Scott Dunn   020 8767 0202
Ski Scott Dunn provides private nannies, children's clubs and
the famous Scott Dunn Ski Schools to get even the youngest
snowbears off to a good start. Chalets are well equipped with
cots, highchairs, even Pampers, to enable you to travel
lightly. Children are also not expected to share their parents'
bedroom (for no additional cost).

"It is the personal touch which
is so important and has always
distinguished a Meriski holiday."

Understanding the needs of you and
your family is our speciality and the main
reason why so many of our guests return
year after year. Our alpine team in
Méribel are constantly on hand to help –
from making you a cup of tea to running
you to the shops with our complimentary
minibus shuttle service. Meriski even has
its own dedicated crèche in Méribel for
children of all ages.

Here's looking forward to welcoming you
to another great season in Méribel.

MERISKI
The Méribel Specialists

Call us now to reserve your brochure: 01285 648518
or visit: www.meriski.co.uk

good advice

And finally… our indispensable list of contacts and helplines, to help you navigate your way swiftly to the people, places and advice you need.

adoption

To adopt you need to be approved by the British authorities [at least 6mths]. The first step is to contact your local authority where a social worker will conduct a Home Study to assess your suitability to adopt. To adopt from overseas the government has to formalise the paperwork [6-9mths] and send the papers to the British Embassy in your chosen country

Adoption UK   0870 770 0450
www.adoptionuk.org.uk

After Adoption   0161 839 4930
www.afteradoption.org.uk

BAAF   020 7593 2000
www.baaf.org.uk
British Association for Adoption and Fostering. Information and advice for prospective parents; list of UK children looking for families [normally 5yrs+].

OASIS   0870 241 7069
www.adoptionoverseas.org.uk

Intercountry Adoption Centre   020 8449 2562
www.icacentre.org.uk
Advice and information and workshops for parents wanting to adopt from overseas.

Post-Adoption Centre   0870 777 2197
www.postadoptioncentre.org.uk
Daily advice line which offers advice, information and support to all affected by adoption.

Holli Rubin
Basuto Medical Centre,   020 7736 7557
29 Basuto Road, SW6
The Birth Company,   020 7725 0528
137 Harley Street, W1
www.Hollirubin.com
The decision to adopt a baby and the process can be very challenging - talking about it with a professional can be a powerful support during these times (see page 25).

councils

Your local council is an excellent source of information. Ask for the Children's Information Service department for enquiries about play centres, parks etc, the Early Years department for childcare and early education. Some produce little booklets about what's on offer for children in the borough, although they can sometimes be out of date. In the main we have provided the main switchboard numbers as the individual departments do get moved around during the year

Barnet CIS   0800 389 8312
www.barnet.gov.uk

Bromley CIS   020 8464 0276
www.bromley.gov.uk

Camden CIS   020 7278 4444
www.camden.gov.uk

City of Westminster CIS   **020 7641 7929**
www.westminster.gov.uk
(see ad right).

Corporation of London CIS   020 7332 1002
www.cityoflondon.gov.uk

Ealing CIS   020 8825 5588
www.ealing.gov.uk

Enfield CIS   020 8482 1066
www.enfield.gov.uk

Greenwich CIS   020 8921 6921
www.greenwich.gov.uk

Hackney Learning Trust   020 8820 7000
www.hackney.gov.uk

Hammersmith & Fulham CIS   020 8735 5868
www.lbhf.gov.uk

Haringey Childcare Information Service   **020 8801 1234**
www.haringey.gov.uk
(see ad right).

Hounslow CIS   020 8583 2000
www.hounslow.gov.uk

Islington CIS   020 7527 5959
www.islington.gov.uk

Kensington & Chelsea CIS   020 7361 3302
www.rbkc.gov.uk

Kingston upon Thames CIS   020 8547 6582
www.kingston.gov.uk

Lambeth CIS   0845 601 5317
www.lambeth.gov.uk

Lewisham CIS   0800 085 0606
www.lewisham.gov.uk

Merton CIS   020 8543 2222
www.merton.gov.uk

Newham CIS   020 8430 2000
www.newham.gov.uk

Richmond upon Thames CIS   020 8891 7554
www.richmond.gov.uk

Southwark CIS   020 7525 5000
www.southwark.gov.uk

Tower Hamlets CIS   020 7364 5000
www.towerhamlets.gov.uk

Waltham Forest CIS   020 8539 0864
www.lbwf.gov.uk

Wandsworth CIS   020 8871 6000
www.wandsworth.gov.uk

ex-pat advice

American Women's   **020 7589 8292**
Club of London
68 Old Brompton Road, London SW7 3LQ

Focus Information Services   **020 7937 0050**
13 Prince of Wales Terrace, London, W8 5PG

fatherhood

Families Need Fathers   **020 7613 5060**
134 Curtain Road, London, EC2A 3AR
www.fnf.org.uk

www.fathersdirect.com
The UK's national information centre for fatherhood.

naming ceremonies

If you want a secular naming ceremony, as opposed to a christening, then you have many options available to you. If you choose to focus the event on naming the child and making a public declaration of the commitment of parents and godparents then the following organisations will be able to guide you with a selection of formats (formal or informal)

Baby Naming Ceremonies   **020 7079 3580**
1 Gower Street, London, WC1E 6HD
www.humanism.org.uk
For a personal, unique and beautiful welcome for your child, the BHA, which has years of experience in preparing non-religious ceremonies, can help. Your child's naming ceremony can be an unforgettable public declaration of your commitment as parents and guide parents. The ceremonies are designed to be inclusive, so that families and friends can relate to what is said - whether or not they have religious beliefs.

paternity testing

Cellmark Diagnostics   **01235 528 000**
PO Box 265, Abingdon, Oxfordshire
www.cellmark.co.uk
5-day DNA test. Phone customer services for confidential

parenting classes & courses

These courses can help parents expand their knowledge and techniques for effective parenting, as well as know how to set limits, foster self-esteem and maintain a happy equilibrium in the home

The Parent Company   **020 7935 9635**
6 Jacob's Wells Mews, W1H 5PD
www.theparentcompany.co.uk
Evening seminars on discipline, self-esteem, sibling rivalry, raising boys/girls.

Parent Talk   **020 7450 9073**
www.parenttalk.co.uk
Parentalk is a charity launched in response to research which indicated that 1 in 3 parents feel like failures. They produce a range of booklets and parenting course pack aimed at helping parents to do an even better job. They also run parenting workshops at their London head office in SE1.

The New Learning Centre   **020 7794 0321**
211 Sumatra Road, NW6
www.tnlc.info
Regular parenting talks on issues such as building self-esteem, how to talk to your kids so they will listen etc.

money matters

In an area fraught with industry "speak" we asked Josephine Blythe, who is a mother of two and a Partner of St. James's Place Partnership, to outline some of the things that we all should think about when it comes to finance.

"Having a baby can be the most exciting time in any woman's life and there is no doubt that it can also be the most worrying time for many reasons, not least of which is the financial impact it may have on your household.

Firstly there is the issue of loss of the mother's income while she is on maternity leave and how this may impact the monthly household budget.

There may be **maternity benefits** paid by an employer to claim, or you may be entitled to some maternity benefits from the state. And, once your child is born you are entitled to **Child Benefit**.

There is also the new **Child Trust Fund** initiative whereby the Government will make a contribution of £250 for any child born after 31st August 2002. The website www.childtrustfund.gov.uk has a good amount of information and a list of CTF funds.

Once you have dependents you have to think more seriously about what would happen if the income of the household were to stop if the major "breadwinner" were to die prematurely or become too ill to work. A careful review of your **life assurance**, critical illness cover and income protection policies is vital. As is writing a formal **Will**, to make certain that money passes into the right hands on your death.

You may want to look at moving to a bigger house to accommodate your growing family and you may need to take advice on **mortgages**.

You may be keen to build up capital for your child's future for, perhaps, **school fee planning**, stakeholder pensions for children or there may be gifts of money from grandparents which you want to invest. There are a raft of different products available offering very tax efficient ways of investing.

And what about if you have finished work to bring up your child, what do you do with the **pension scheme** left behind at your employer and equally, how are you going to provide for your own old age if you no longer earn an income?

Whatever your goals and aspirations for your new family, it will be your financial position which will allow those goals to be fulfilled. As a mother, I strongly urge all parents to have a thorough and regular review of their financial affairs.

financial services

Foreign & Colonial   **0800 136 420**
Management Ltd
Exchange House, Primrose Street, EC2A 2NY
www.fandc.com/sfc
An experienced provider of savings plans for children from F&C. First in investment trusts (see ad opposite).

St. James's Place
Partnership   **01635 582 424**
www.sjp.co.uk
St. James's Place Partnership specialise in providing wealth management advice in the areas of investments, pensions and family income protection. (see ad pg 207).

helplines

Action for ME   **01749 670 799**
Pregnancy Network
www.afme.org.uk

Action for Sick Children   **020 8542 4848**
www.actionforsickchildren.org

Action on Pre-Eclampsia   **020 8427 4217**
www.apec.org.uk

THE ST. JAMES'S PLACE PARTNERSHIP

Our Personal Approach to Wealth Management
Stands out from the Crowd

As a mother, I understand how daunting it can be to plan your children's long term financial security. We all want our families to be protected against unforeseen events and we want to invest for their future.

I specialise in providing a personal service to help you plan your family's financial security.

Whether it be school fee planning, investments for your children, life assurance, pension planning or anything else to do with your money, I am offering a free, no obligation financial review to all Baby Directory readers.

Why not call, email or write to me for an informal chat about your own wealth management needs.

To ensure your wealth is growing and your family is protected, long into the future, call Josephine Blythe on 01635 582424 or email at: Josephine.blythe@sjpp.co.uk

ST. JAMES'S PLACE
PARTNERSHIP

FINANCIAL ADVICE YOU CAN TRUST

Past performance is not a guide to future performance

SJP2022-VR1 (09/05)
FH213

Anaphylaxis Campaign www.anaphylaxis.org.uk	01252 542 029
Anti-Bullying Campaign	020 7378 1446
Assoc for Improvements in Maternity Services www.aims.org.uk	020 8390 9534
Association for Postnatal Illness www.apni.org	020 7386 0868
Baby Milk Action www.babymilkaction.org	01223 464 420
Bedwetting Education Advisory Line www.bedwetting.co.uk	0800 085 8189
Birth Crisis Network	01865 300 266
Birth Defects Foundation	08700 707 020
British Allergy Foundation www.allergyfoundation.com	020 8303 8583
British Association for Early Childhood Education www.early-education.org.uk	020 7539 5400
British Dyslexia Association www.bda-dyslexia.org.uk	0118 966 8271
British Epilepsy Association www.epilepsy.org.uk	0113 210 8800
British Institute for Brain Injured Children www.bibic.org.uk	01278 684 060
British Institute for Learning Disabilities www.bild.org.uk	01562 723 010
British Stammering Association www.stammering.org	020 8983 1003
Caesarian Support Network	01624 661 269
Cerebral Palsy Helpline (SCOPE) www.scope.org.uk	0808 800 3333
Child Bereavement Trust www.childbereavement.org.uk	01494 446 648
Child Death Helpline	0800 282 986
ChildLine www.childline.org.uk	0800 1111
Children's Information Service www.childcarelink.gov.uk	0800 960 296
Cleft Lip And Palate Association (CLAPA) www.clapa.com	020 7431 0033

Coeliac UK 01494 437 278 www.coeliac.co.uk	
Contact-A-Family www.cafamily.org.uk	020 7383 3555
Cot Death Society www.cotdeathsociety.org.uk	0845 601 0234
Council for Disabled Children www.ncb.org.uk	020 7843 6000
Cruse Bereavement Care www.crusebereavementcare.org.uk	0870 167 1677
Cystic Fibrosis Trust www.cftrust.org.uk	020 8464 7211
Daycare Trust www.daycaretrust.org.uk	020 7840 3350
Diabetes UK (ex-British Diabetes Association) www.diabetes.org.uk	020 7323 1531
Disability Alliance www.disabilityalliance.org	020 7247 8763
Down's Heart Group www.childrens-heart-fed.org.uk/downs.htm	01525 220 379
Down's Syndrome Association www.dsa.uk.com	020 8682 4001
Dyspraxia Foundation www.dyspraxiafoundation.org.uk	01462 454 986
Enuresis Resource & Information Centre (ERIC) www.eric.org.uk	0117 960 3060
Foundation for the Study of Infant Deaths www.sids.org.uk/fsid	020 7233 2090
Fragile X Society www.fragilex.org.uk	01371 875 100
Group B Strep Support www.gbss.org.uk	01444 416 176
Herpes Viruses Association www.herpes.org.uk	0845 123 2305
Home Education Advisory Service www.heas.co.uk	01707 371 854
Home-Start UK www.home-start.co.uk	020 7388 6075
Hyperactive Children's Support Group www.hacsg.org.uk	01903 725 182

ISC: London & South East www.isis.org.uk/southeast	020 7798 1560	**Parentline Plus** www.parentlineplus.org.uk	0808 800 2222
Kidscape www.kidscape.org.uk	020 7730 3300	**Parents At Work** www.parentsatwork.org.uk	020 7628 2128
LOOK (National Federation of Families with Visually Impaired Children) www.look-uk.org	0121 428 5038	**Parents for Inclusion** www.parentsforinclusion.org	020 7735 7735

ISC: London & South East 020 7798 1560
www.isis.org.uk/southeast

Kidscape 020 7730 3300
www.kidscape.org.uk

LOOK (National Federation 0121 428 5038
of Families with Visually Impaired Children)
www.look-uk.org

Meet A Mum Association (MAMA) 01761 433 598
www.mama.co.uk

Meningitis Research 08088 003 344
www.meningitis.org

Meningitis Trust 0845 600 0800
www.meningitis-trust.org.uk

Miscarriage Association 01924 200 799
www.miscarriageassociation.org.uk

Multiple Births Foundation 020 8383 3519
www.multiplebirths.org.uk

National Advice Centre for 0845 604 0414
Children with Reading Difficulties

National Asthma Campaign 020 7226 2260
www.asthma.org.uk

National Autistic Society 020 7833 2299
www.nas.org.uk

National Childbirth Trust 0870 444 8707
www.nctpregnancyandbabycare.com

National Council for 0800 185 026
One-Parent Families
www.oneparentfamilies.org.uk

National Deaf 020 7250 0123
Children's Society
www.ndcs.org.uk

National Eczema Society 020 7388 4097
www.eczema.org

National Endometriosis Society 020 7222 2781
www.endo.org.uk

National Family Mediation 020 7383 5993
www.nfm.u-net.com

National NEWPIN 020 7358 5900
www.newpin.org.uk

NHS Direct 0845 4647
www.nhsdirect.nhs.uk

NSPCC Child Protection 0800 800 500
www.nspcc.org.uk

Parentline Plus 0808 800 2222
www.parentlineplus.org.uk

Parents At Work 020 7628 2128
www.parentsatwork.org.uk

Parents for Inclusion 020 7735 7735
www.parentsforinclusion.org

Positively Women 020 7713 0222
Relate: 020 8367 7712
National Marriage Guidance
www.relate.org.uk

RNIB 020 7391 2245
www.rnib.org.uk

Sexual Abuse 020 8950 7855
SCOPE 020 7619 7100
www.scope.org.uk/

Serene 020 7404 5011
(incorporating Cry-sis)

Sexual Health & 0800 567 123
National Health Helpline
Stillbirth And Neonatal 020 7436 7940
Death Society (SANDS)
www.uk-sands.org

TAMBA 0870 770 3305
www.tamba.org.uk

The SHE Trust 01522 519 992
(Simply Holistic Endometriosis)
www.shetrust.org.uk

Women's Domestic 0161 839 8574
Violence Helpline
www.wdvh.org.uk

Women's Health 020 7251 6580
www.womenshealthlondon.org.uk

Gingerbread 0800 018 4318
www.gingerbread.org.uk
Leading support group for single parents.

Kids No Object 01243 543 685
Lymington, Farwell Avenue, Eastgate, Chichester,
West Sussex

Single Parent Travel Club 0870 241 621
www.sptc.org.uk

useful tradesmen

ARCHITECTS
Simon Miller (RIBA) 020 8201 9875
This architect's mantra is "The good new is you've had a
baby. The bad news is you've got no space"!

George Powers Associates 020 7498 5927
The Studio, 9a Emu Road, SW8 3PS

CLEANERS

As soon as your first child arrives you will realise that you cannot possibly attain the previous levels of tidiness and cleanliness in your home. These agencies are well aware of your requirements and have reputable services providing staff of a high quality and efficiency. I don't think you can ever have too many helping hands in this department, and if you've DIY-ed most of your life, then this is the time to let go…

A Bit of Help   020 7476 0020
Help with cleaning, ironing services, party helpers and nannies on call.

Mrs Browns   020 7736 0080
Staff Agency Ltd
149 Wandsworth Bridge Road, SW6
Providing help in your home, with the children or in the care of elderly relatives. Good reputation for being adaptable and providing kind carers.

Simply Domestics   020 8444 4304
www.simplydomestics.com
Providing childcare and clearning.

CLUTTER CLEARERS

Whatever you feel about someone telling you how to put things away, I think pregnancy is the time in your life where your natural nesting instinct should be exploited so that you get things well organised for a busy few months ahead. Or maybe you've got 4 children already and no one can agree on what should go where…

No More Clutter   07974 076 675
www.nomoreclutter.co.uk

Clear Space   020 7233 3138

Simply-Sorted   020 8769 7276

HOUSE AND GARDEN
Polly the Flower Lady   07880 882 645
Fresh, cut flowers every Wednesday (Streatham & Balham).

Richard the Handyman   020 8672 3555
Get Richard in for ¹/₂ a day for plumbing, electrical, carpentry, locks, pointing and plaster patching.

0800 Handyman   0800 426 3962
Hang blinks, fix leaky taps, assemble furniture, install a shower, lights, tiling and painting.

D.Maguire Electrical Services   020 7502 0507
Faulty wire? Ring Maguire! NAPIT registered electrician with 22 years experience - 14 as chief electrician at Madame Tussauds.   Covers mainly Central, North, East and South East postcodes (recommended by the editor)!

Floor Trade Direct   01256 880 253
home service offering big savings on all types of carpet, wood stone, laminate and vinyl.

Austins Painters   020 8671 4221
Interior and exterior redecoration.

Window Cleaning: SJ Bridgeman   020 7404 5011
High recommended for be reliable and trustworthy.

Pet Nanny   020 8875 0341
www.petnanny.co.uk
For those going on holiday and worrying about what to do with cats and dogs, call Serena and she will arrange for one of her carers either to visit your cat on a daily basis, or care for your dog in their home.

Video Magic   020 7585 1139
www.videomagic.co.uk
Set your videos to music and transfer it to CD, DVD or VHS.

Working Opportunities

Camerson Coaching   07932 033 975
www.scameroncoaching.com
Your baby is going to change everything - maybe what you want to do work wise. Plan your transition back into the workplace or find new career options by working with a professionally trained life coach and working mum. Call for a half-price intro offer and build confidence, motivation, focus and achieve results quickly.

Scribble pad

READERS

If you think there is a service or product we should know about and include in the next edition, drop us a line, or an e-mail: **editor@babydirectory.com**

☐ This is a new product, service or facility.

☐ Oops! You've missed this.

☐ Change of address, new branch, etc.

☐ Please send me a media pack.

Name of product, service or location ....

Address ....

....

Postcode .... Tel No ....

E-mail address .... www ....

Contact name and tel no (if different from above)

....

We would very much appreciate your comments about errors or omissions, please let us know. **You will receive a free copy of next year's book for your efforts.**

Page ....

Feedback...

....

....

Your own name, address, 'phone number, e-mail address (all optional)

....

....

Many thanks for taking the time to fill in this form

Please send completed form(s) to:

The Baby Directory, 7 Brockwell Park Row, London SW2 2YH
Tel: 020 8678 9000   Fax: 020 8671 1919   E-mail: editor@babydirectory.com

220 order form

To order by telephone call: **020 8678 9000**
or order via our secure website at **www.babydirectory.com**
or send this order form with your cheque to:
The Baby Directory, 7 Brockwell Park Row, London SW2 2YH

Title	Price	Qty	Postage	Total
The London Baby Directory (All London postcodes)	£8.99		£1.50	
The East Baby Directory (Essex, Cambridgeshire, Suffolk & Norfolk)	£5.99		£1.00	
The Central Baby Directory (Oxfordshire, Berks, Bucks, Northants, Beds & Herts)	£5.99		£1.00	
The South East Baby Directory (Surrey & S. Middlesex, Hampshire, Sussex & Kent)	£5.99		£1.00	
The South West Baby Directory (Somerset, Dorset, Wiltshire, Gloucestershire, Devon & Cornwall)	£5.99		£1.00	
The West Midlands Baby Directory (Herefordshire, Shropshire, Staffordshire, Warwickshire, W Midlands, Worc.)	£5.99		£1.00	
			Total Order Value	

Please print clearly
Name . . . .

Address . . . .

. . . .

. . . . Postcode . . . .

Tel . . . . E-mail address . . . .

METHOD OF PAYMENT (please tick appropriate box)

Cheque/Postal Order ☐   Credit Card ☐

Please make cheques payable to **The Baby Directory Limited**

Card Number ☐☐☐☐ ☐☐☐☐ ☐☐☐☐ ☐☐☐☐ ☐☐☐☐

Issue No ☐☐   Expiry Date ☐☐☐☐   Valid from ☐☐☐☐   Security code ☐☐☐

Signature . . . .

How did you hear about the Directory?. . . . . Leaflet Code ☐☐

If you would like to receive our monthly e-newsletter please tick here ☐

The Baby Directory is an invaluable reference guide for mothers-to-be
The Times

Forget about wading through the local paper for mother and baby contacts - The Baby Directory has done it for you
Pregnancy & Birth

Indispensable and essential
Practical Parenting

A mine of useful information
The NCT

"The Baby Directory is an invaluable reference guide for mothers to be"

The Times

The London Baby Directory at £8.99

All London postcodes

The South East Baby Directory at £5.99

Surrey & South Middlesex, Hampshire, Sussex, and Kent

The Central Baby Directory at £5.99

Herts & N Middlesex, Northamptonshire, Buckinghamshire, Berkshire, Bedfordshire, Oxfordshire

The East Baby Directory at £5.99

Norfolk, Suffolk, Cambridgeshire, Essex

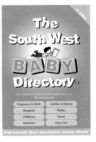

The South West Baby Directory at £5.99

Somerset, Dorset, Wiltshire, Gloucestershire, Devon & Cornwall

The West Midlands Baby Directory at £5.99

Worcestershire, West Midlands, Staffordshire, Shropshire, Warwickshire, Herefordshire

The East Midlands Baby Directory at £5.99

Leicestershire, Rutland, Nottinghamshire, Lincolnshire, Derbyshire

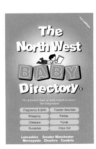

The North West Baby Directory at £5.99

Lancashire, Greater Manchester, Merseyside, Cheshire, Cumbria

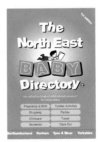

The North East Baby Directory at £5.99

Northumberland, Durham, Tyne & Wear, Yorkshire

The Scotland Baby Directory at £5.99

Scotland, Northern Ireland, The Islands

central london congestion zone

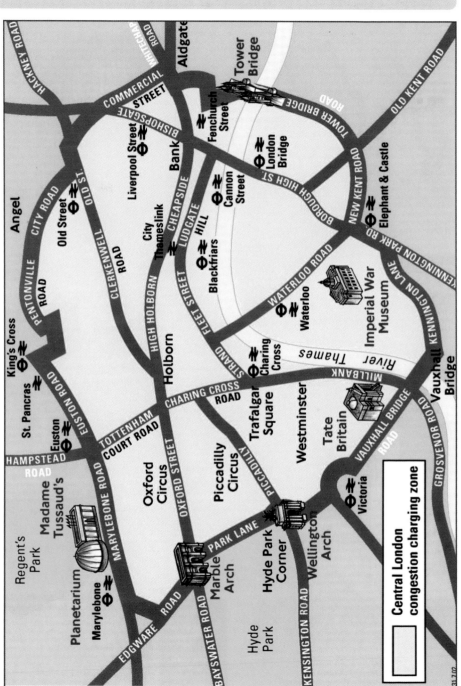

Central London congestion charging zone

congestion charge payment line   0845 900 1234
www.cclondon.com